The Richmond Bread Riot

Women at War

by

Douglas O. Tice Jr.

WWW.OAKLEAPRESS.COM

The Richmond Bread Riot: Women at War © 2021 by Douglas O. Tice Jr. All rights reserved. No part of this book may be used or reproduced in any manner whatsoever without written permission except in the case of brief quotations embodied in critical articles and reviews. For information visit:

www.oakleapress.com

DEDICATION

This book is dedicated to my wife, Martha Murdoch Tice, my son, Douglas Tice III, and my daughter, Jane Tice Powell.

Richmond's Oregon Hill taken from the south bank of the James River soon after the War by Mathew Brady [1822-1896] or Alexander Gardner [1821-1882]. The Tredegar Iron Works can be seen in the foregorund at the bottom of the hill. The Virginia State Penitentirary is in the upper right corner. This print was supplied by the American Civil War Museum in Richmond.

CONTENTS

Foreword & Acknowledgements 7
Introduction 9
Chapter 1: Rioting for Food 11
   Food Riots In The Confederacy
Chapter 2: Richmond's Woman's Riot 23
   Bread or Blood
Chapter 3: Reaction and Aftermath 39
   Rioters in The Newspapers
   The Bread Riot — Conclusions
Chapter 4: The Bread Riot Joins the Lost Cause 63
   The Jefferson Davis Interview by An Unnamed
      Special Correspondent
   Still Later Newspaper Articles
Chapter 5: Jefferson Davis and The Bread Riot 66
   Bread Riot History According To Jefferson Davis
Chapter 6: Mary Jackson, Huckster and Riot 73
Chapter 7: Other Tales of the Bread Riot 82
   A Fictional Firsthand Account
   Blood or Bread — Riot Injury
   Was There Bread at The Bread Riot?
APPENDIX A - The Public Guard, Virginia's "Standing Army" ... 93
APPENDIX B - Minutes of the Richmond City Council 95
APPENDIX C - Richmond Newspaper Articles, 1863-64 99
APPENDIX D - City of Richmond Hustings Court
   Minute Books, No. 28 & 29 183
APPENDIX E - Richmond Newspaper Articles,
   1888-89 & Later 192
ENDNOTES 228
Addendum 254
About the Author 255

Belvidere Hill Baptist Church in the Oregon Hill neighborhood, where the women gathered to plan their march on the stores. Sketch by Mrs Perry L. Mitchell.

Foreword & Acknowledgements

I have long been drawn to the study of history, and since moving to Richmond in the 1960s, the American Civil War has been of particular interest. This book represents the culmination of a 50-year journey in that regard, involving several hundred hours of research and documentation. It is, I believe, the most comprehensive and accurate historical accounting of the events surrounding the Richmond Bread Riot, which took place on April 2, 1863, midway through the War. I was drawn to this episode due to its human-interest aspect. In a broad sense, it marks the beginning of the women's suffrage movement in the South, in that similar protests occurred in other regions of the Confederacy at about the same time.

The manuscript of this book was essentially completed about ten years ago, but I was unable to find a publisher at that time. Recently, my son urged me to take up the work again and see it to completion, and I have done so with his assistance and with that of Stephen Hawley Martin, Publisher of The Oaklea Press.

A great deal has happened in the intervening years with respect to the study of Civil War history and the attitudes toward that conflict. This is particularly apparent when one considers the advent of Black Lives Matter, the destruction of the Confederate monuments in Richmond and elsewhere in the South, and the threatened erasure of all Confederate names from streets and public buildings. I acknowledge the justice inherent in those events and recognize that they were long overdue.

With respect to what my research has revealed, however, the women who participated in the Richmond Bread Riot did not include African-Americans. Rather, the disturbance was instigated primarily by white women of the laboring class, many of whom had sons, husbands, and loved ones away at war. They were assisted by men who joined in the disturbance after it was already in progress. Nevertheless, I believe it is important to at least acknowledge the current turmoil, and what took place in Richmond during the summer of 2020, because it is reminiscent of the Richmond Bread Riot that took place so long ago.

I would like to acknowledge my family, particularly my wife, Martha, and son, Doug, for their help and support in seeing this project to completion, and to Stephen Hawley Martin of The Oaklea Press, who pulled together all the pieces to produce this volume.

Introduction

The Richmond Bread Riot took place midway during the Civil War, on Easter Thursday, April 2, 1863. A loosely organized band of women violently confronted the town's merchants and helped themselves to large amounts of food and other goods. While the numbers are elusive, hundreds participated, and not just women. Downtown streets were crowded with observers, many sympathetic and cheering, and some who rose to defend besieged storekeepers. During a period of two hours or less, stores were sacked over a wide area. Underscoring the difference between that era and our own, the mayor of Richmond, governor of Virginia and president of the Confederacy each went into the streets where they personally attempted to restore order.

Richmond's colorful riot has been surrounded by controversy and misconception — not surprising given an abundance of confusing and conflicting eyewitness accounts. A fundamental misunderstanding of the event has continued to our own time, as is demonstrated by numerous modern historical accounts that continue to rely on a distorted and misleading tale related many years after the war by former President Jefferson Davis.

The Bread Riot described in this book differs significantly from Davis-centered traditional accounts. The narrative is based upon a wide range of resource materials, some of which has been little used by historians. Much of the more important material is included in the appendices, including contemporary Richmond City Council minutes, court records and newspaper accounts of the day, and a large number of eyewitness accounts published by a Richmond newspaper in 1889 and 1890; Jefferson Davis's own version was originally published in one of these articles. While the 1863 newspaper accounts have frequently been used by historians, the court records and later newspapers have not.

The material contained in the appendices, particularly the newspaper articles, presents lively and entertaining descriptions of a colorful episode of Civil War and Richmond history. These accounts are

The Richmond Bread Riot

valuable evidence of the riot because they come from persons or agencies directly involved and otherwise depict circumstances of the time. For example, the contemporary accounts from the *Richmond Examiner* describe court hearings and trials, with details furnished by rioters and others; court witnesses included both the governor and mayor. Moreover, as we have very little information on the women involved in other Southern food riots that occurred during this period, the Richmond accounts are doubly important for the insights they may provide on the circumstances of women rioters elsewhere.

It is not surprising that the resource materials for the Richmond disturbance contain differing and conflicting versions. Part of the confusion stems from the fact that the bread riot was not a continuous melee; rather it was a number of confrontations between different mob groups, storekeepers, and the authorities. It is unlikely that any one individual witnessed the whole affair. Yet, the accounts reveal a reasonably complete description of events. Inevitably some uncertainty remains, but the materials in this volume provide a basis for a more accurate and detailed description than traditionally given. Not to be overlooked is the close look provided in the Confederate capital of a group of ordinary citizens, forgotten people of the war, along with their national, state and local governments and even the free press during this most stressful period of our nation's history.

CHAPTER 1: Rioting for Food

Our Sovereign Lord the King chargeth and commandeth all persons being assembled immediately to disperse themselves, and peaceably to depart to their habitations.

— From the English Riot Act of 1714

In the history of western civilization, mob violence in all its forms has played a substantial role. Peasants rebelled during the middle ages over services exacted by serfdom, and as the feudal system began to disintegrate they demanded equality. The English Peasant Revolt of 1381 demonstrated "that the peasant had grasped the conception of complete personal liberty, that he held it degrading to perform forced labour, and that he considered freedom to be his right."[1] A basic and early form of popular protest was the food riot, which proliferated in England and France during the 18th and early 19th centuries.[2] New Yorkers rioted in 1837 over the high cost of flour.

The classic European food riot arose out of the anger of ordinary citizens who believed they were being deprived by profiteers of their "right" to purchase food, usually grain or flour, at fair or traditional prices and commensurate with wage levels. Frequently, these disturbances were instigated by women. The riot ensuing when a mob confronted a grain holder did not always involve looting and stealing; it was not unusual for the men and women through threats of bodily harm to succeed in acquiring necessities at affordable prices. The food riot largely disappeared by the second half of the 19th century, apparently due to technological improvements in grain production and distribution.

Food Riots In The Confederacy

The Confederate Capital, Richmond, had its food revolt, more famously known as the Bread Riot. This widely reported event on April 2, 1863, was the South's largest civilian disturbance of the Civil

The Richmond Bread Riot

War. But Richmond was not alone, as a rash of similar but smaller scale incidents took place throughout the Confederate states in the spring of 1863 and sporadically as late as 1865. These disturbances, as was often the case with European riots, were instigated and carried out by women, though often with male assistance. No doubt, this is attributable to one of the causes of the riots, the fact that the male breadwinners were away at war. The sketchy details of these incidents provided primarily in newspaper accounts are sufficient to reveal the women's common goal of overcoming wartime shortages of food and other necessities. They also reveal increasing dissatisfaction of civilians on the home front.

The reasons for Southern food shortages during the war are complex and in many respects related to reasons for the ultimate failure of the Confederacy itself. The South was initially unprepared for war in many ways, certainly with respect to feeding all of its citizens. Even prior to secession the area did not produce sufficient food crops for its own consumption. Southern agriculture was concentrated on cash crops of cotton, corn, sugar, rice, tobacco, and wheat, and many of these products were grown for export to the North and to Europe. Rather, the states joining the Confederacy had found it less costly to import large quantities of their food supply from the North.[3] Food imports included meat, grains of all sorts, dairy products, and potatoes.[4] The South's food production in 1861, the largest ever, was only about half of that needed for the region. With the loss of Northern food sources, it became urgent for the Confederacy to persuade its farmers to change from traditional non-food crop production, particularly cotton, to essential food products. These efforts were led by governmental and community leaders, including newspaper editors. Restrictions on crops that could be grown were imposed by law in some states.[5] Notwithstanding resulting improvements in food production, the Southern states were never able to produce and supply foodstuffs in quantities fully adequate to feed both their civilian and military populations. The problems were most severe in the larger towns and cities, largely because of the complete dependency of population centers on the delivery of food products.

The Richmond Bread Riot

At the outset, the seceding states lost the resources of the border states that remained with the Union, a factor exacerbated when the South lost full use of the Mississippi River in the summer of 1863.[6] Early on, military operations caused losses of livestock and disrupted the growing of crops. As the war continued, more and more croplands were subjected to enemy occupation. Farm production was also adversely affected by the loss of labor to the military.

Food supply and distribution were severely hampered by the Confederacy's inadequate and undependable transportation system. This was particularly true with respect to the delivery of food to the home front, whose needs were secondary to the military. The South's railroads were undependable to begin with, and they became prime targets for Union capture and destruction. The Union blockade largely prevented any meaningful importation of iron necessary to build railway parts and equipment.[7] A historian of the economics of the blockade has written that "not a single new rail was manufactured in the Confederacy during the war."[8] Because factories and foundries were turned to the production of tools of war, worn out rolling stock and railway equipment as well as wagons and implements of all types became virtually irreplaceable.

By 1863 the Union blockade of the Confederate coast line had become increasingly effective in its original goal of starving the rebellious states; of particular concern was the failure of blockade runners to bring to Southern ports appreciable amounts of necessary commodities for the civilian home front. Shipping companies that ran the blockade were in business for profit. Recent studies of the blockade's economic effect have demonstrated that it was more profitable for the ships' owners to bring in luxury items, and so they did.[9] Confederate policies toward blockade running actually exacerbated the problem. Although the South's inability to import necessities was critical, the larger impact of the blockade may have been its decimation of the Confederacy's rail transportation system and the severe restrictions it imposed on inland water transportation. The modern view is that the blockade played a large part in ultimate Confederate defeat. A Confederate naval officer stated, not too many years after the war, that the blockade "shut the Confederacy out from the world, deprived it of supplies, weakened its military and naval strength."[10]

Perhaps most critical of all factors affecting the availability of food on the home front was the Confederate policy of impressment — the forced purchase by the commissary and quartermaster departments of an endless variety of foodstuffs, provisions, clothing, animals, equipment and tools of all sorts, even slaves for forced labor. Impressment began during the first year of the war after voluntary citizenry contributions proved inadequate. It was based on necessity rather than legal right and proceeded on the theory that the army would go without food and supplies otherwise. The manner that the Confederacy's policies were implemented led to food shortages on the home front and provoked great controversy throughout the South. People bitterly complained about the government's schedule of prices paid to citizens for impressed goods, which in the spring of 1863 reflected about half of market price. The difference between market value and the lesser prices paid has been described as a "highly discriminatory tax . . . ."[11] Impressment caused significant civilian food shortages for two reasons: Food was taken away by the "pressmen," and the low prices induced producers to hide surpluses and reduce production.

Impressment also led to another economic evil of the day, speculation, which was the major complaint of ordinary citizens. The detested "speculators" purchased goods often at higher than government prices and brought them to market at even higher prices that many could not afford.[12]

Not until March 1863 did impressment have the authority of Confederate law. Previously, it had been carried out under directives and price schedules issued by the war department. Under the new legislation, prices were to be set by commissioners appointed for each state and price disputes were to be resolved by a system of arbitration. Commissary General Colonel Lucius Northrop's department had primary responsibility for impressment of food items and other provisions. Northrop, who was personally blamed for many of the home front supply problems, was extremely unpopular. Diarist Mary Chestnut described him as "the most cussed and vilified man in the Confederacy."[13] According to Northrop's biographer, Jerrold

The Richmond Bread Riot

Northrop Moore, when the new schedules of prices were prepared in 1863, "it had been decided to fix the schedule-prices well below market values to try to put a brake on inflation." The schedules were "hated" and when implemented, "set up a sustained bellow of rage."[14] The effect of the new price schedules was the opposite of that intended, leading to even more shortages and higher inflation. The impressment law would be twice amended before the war ended, but its problems were never to be resolved, which historians have largely attributed to Northrop's incompetence. Undoubtedly, impressment was a contributing factor to Confederate defeat.[15]

Another key factor leading to the food riots was the increasing destitution of Southern families. Recent studies have chronicled the devastating impact of the Civil War on the Confederate home front.[16] By 1863, the patriotic fervor that had supported secession and armed resistance to the "Yankee invasion" had largely disappeared. For the women of poor families left behind when their husbands and sons marched off to war, devotion to the Cause, to the extent it had ever existed, had given way to the despair of hunger for themselves and their children. Under the deprived conditions in which these families were forced to live, the idea of Confederate victory became meaningless.

These families could expect little outside assistance. Traditionally, public relief for Southern poor had been provided on a local level, by private groups or municipalities. Although the Civil War brought increased efforts from these sources, the ability of localities to provide public aid to their needy citizens was soon overwhelmed by the increasing needs of families whose primary care-givers were serving the Confederacy. State governments recognized the needs of such families and enacted legislation to provide aid. All of the states of the southeast, the Deep South, and Texas passed relief measures, beginning with South Carolina in 1861. Assistance took various forms, primarily direct cash payments or distributions of food and other supplies. Of the Southern states, North Carolina appropriated the most relief funds, a total of $26,000,000.

State provision of welfare relief to the poor was a radical notion at the time. Even more unprecedented would be similar action by the Confederate government. In March 1862, congress appropriated five million dollars to be distributed for purposes of relief to the states in proportion to the number of soldiers they provided.[17]

Unfortunately, the welfare assistance provided by the Confederacy and the Southern states was far from adequate, providing no more than "a bare subsistence."[18] Thus, the shortages of food and other necessities had led to inflation and speculation so severe that by 1863 many families were unable to purchase goods even when they were available. This was the state of things when Southern women decided to take matters into their own hands.

In the Spring of 1863, newspapers in the South expressed increasing concern over the dwindling food supplies, rampant inflation and high prices, speculation in food and necessities and, most particularly, the impressment policies of the Confederate commissary department. In March, the *Lynchburg Republican*, in the apparent belief that citizens were indulging themselves, noted the growing scarcity and high prices of food and suggested a remedy: "[O]ur people must live on less! They must quit eating so much and such variety, and they must quit it at once."[19] Editorial attitudes toward the rioters would differ. For example, the *Richmond Examiner* was initially sympathetic when the women of Salisbury confronted that town's merchants. Yet the paper roundly condemned those undertaking similar actions on its own doorstep. Many editors agreed, while others remained more or less sympathetic toward the women. Indeed, some communities reacted with compassion, recognizing the hardships imposed on the poor by the war.

A preview of events to come was witnessed in New Orleans on August 1, 1861. Three hundred irate women marched to the mayor's office in protest of the city's failure, two days previously, to approve an appropriation that would have provided monthly financial relief to families of Confederate soldiers. The gathering ended peacefully after the mayor promised assistance to the women, as was soon provided by the establishment of a free market to be supported by the city and private sources.[20]

Southern women began forcefully to challenge supply problems in 1862. In April, soldiers' wives attempted to take bacon from a merchant near Cleveland, Tennessee. In June, soldiers' wives demanded cotton from a supply depot in rural Bartow County, Georgia, and when refused they broke open bales and helped themselves. There were two other incidents in Georgia in November: a "party of ladies" raided a store in Cartersville, and in Dalton women demanded "salt or blood" from a state depot. In December, twenty women in Greenville, Alabama, forced a railroad agent "to divide a large sack of salt."[21]

The year 1863 would see the most serious outbreaks of the war. In February, a group of female "regulators" raided a government depot in Bladenboro, North Carolina, and carried away sacks of corn and rice. Five of the women were later sentenced to five months in jail.[22] There were three incidents on Wednesday, March 18. On that day in Atlanta, a group of fifteen or twenty local women, claiming to be wives and daughters of soldiers, visited grocery stores on Whitehall Street. Their leader, a "tall female with determination in her eye" was armed with a navy revolver. According to a local newspaper, the women were "well dressed—wearing golden earbobs and breastpins." They had money and did not plead poverty or pressing need. However, they refused to pay the grocery prices asked by the merchants. In one store, after being informed that the price of bacon was $1.10 per pound, they seized bacon valued at $200.00 at the point of a revolver. The women took other provisions, vegetables, meal, "&c.,&c.;" they paid "whatever prices they thought proper." An Atlanta newspaper was sympathetic to needy women, then and later, and compared the taking of groceries to recent government impressments; the article noted that the women were "tolerated . . . owing to [the storekeepers'] patriotism." The gathering was dispersed by the police.

An Atlanta official, Marshal Williford, asked the women to return on the next day, stating that he would attempt to "relieve . . . necessities" of those who were "really worthy and deserving." A few days later Williford reported that in response to his offer, 233 women, relations of men in the war, had registered. The sum of $1,132.50 was collected from citizen contributions and divided among the women.

The Richmond Bread Riot

Williford had also learned that none on the list were the "seizers" of the previous Wednesday. The tall female leader of the women, who had seized the goods, was the wife of a shoe-maker "receiving very high wages . . . and in comfortable circumstances."[23]

Salisbury, North Carolina, was the site of the second incident on March 18. A group of fifty to seventy-five women, mostly soldiers' wives, descended on several of the town's merchants. An observer facetiously described the event as "one of the gayest and liveliest scenes of the age." Armed with axes and hatchets and followed by a "numerous train of curious female observers," the women were intent on purchasing flour at the government impressment price. They first approached the railroad depot but were turned away. The women next approached the store of Michael Brown, whom they believed to be a speculator in flour. Brown initially refused to yield to the women's demands, but after they attacked his front door with hatchets, he agreed to give them ten barrels of flour at no charge. The women demanded and received three more barrels of flour at another store. They then accosted a reputed speculator in salt. Denying he was a speculator, the man gave the women a bag of salt and a twenty-dollar Confederate note. The proprietor of another store gave them a barrel of molasses. Finally, the women returned to the railroad depot, where they forced their way in and seized ten barrels of flour. The next morning, the women met again and succeeded in the difficult process of dividing their spoils.[24]

A third disturbance on March 18 took place in Raleigh where about twenty soldiers' wives seized flour and grain from a government depot.[25]

Word of these outbreaks spread. Under the heading, "Another Female Raid," the *Daily Progress* of Raleigh reported that on March 30, 1863, approximately twenty women, mostly army wives, raided the corn crib of Dr. Goelet at Boon Hill in Johnson County, North Carolina. According to the owner, his crib held about forty barrels of flour that were part of his year's supply and not intended for resale. The results of the raid were not reported; however, the paper noted sympathetically, though the event was "greatly to be deprecated . . . people will not starve if they can help it."[26]

The Richmond Bread Riot

A mob in Petersburg, Virginia, attempted to have a bread riot on Wednesday, April 1, the day before the mob violence that erupted in Richmond. Petersburg city authorities were forewarned, and the apparently small group was quickly suppressed.[27]

On April 8, a group of twenty women attacked the front door of a storekeeper in Greensborough (now Greensboro), North Carolina. Although armed with axes, hatchets, pistols, bowie knives, and swords, the women offered little resistance when a magistrate ordered their arrest. They were taken to jail but soon released. On April 9, one of the women, an army wife with six children, wrote pathetically of the incident to Governor Vance. In her letter she reported that "a crowd of we Poor Women went to Greensborough yestarday for something to eat as we had not a mouthful meet nor bread in my house. . . ." The letter described the harsh circumstances under which the poor families were living. The gathering could hardly be called a riot as the women were placed "in gail in plase of giveing us aney thing to eat and I had to com hom without anything . . . ."[28]

A similar scene had taken place previously at nearby High Point. Also, during the same week as the affair in Greensborough, at nearby Durham's Depot, a gathering of women "hard cases" demonstrated to break open a warehouse and seize flour but were evidently put off by the authorities. An unsympathetic *Savannah Republican* portrayed those in both the Greensborough and Durham incidents as "the most degraded and worthless characters" and stated that "profligate, unprincipled men . . . were hounding them on in each case."[29]

Columbus and Macon, Georgia, each had so-called calico raids in early April. On April 10, a group of about sixty-five women, armed and shouting curses, marched down Broad Street in Columbus and entered a store where they demanded cloth, "calico or bust by hokey." This foray was quickly dispersed when the town mayor ordered police to arrest every woman "who did not behave herself properly." One male bystander was sent to jail for expressing too much sympathy for the women. The Macon incident took place on April 3.[30]

The *Savannah Republican* on April 13 reported the Columbus raid, along with similar outbreaks in other Georgia towns, Augusta and the state capital, Milledgeville. The paper described them as "feeble outbreaks of females armed with pistols and bowie knives, headed by a few vagabonds . . . for the purpose of helping themselves to merchandize at what they considered fair prices . . . ." All were "promptly suppressed."[31]

In Alabama, near Lafayette, "fourteen women armed with 'guns, pistols, knives and tongues'" seized flour from a mill.[32]

Mobile, Alabama, far removed from the war zone, had initially suffered less from shortages than other Southern communities, and it also seems to have provided better for its needy families. The city managed to avert a food riot in the spring of 1863, when most of the Southern riots were taking place. However, inevitable shortages led it to suffer a bread riot on September 4, 1863, when hundreds of women armed with "hatchets, hammers, brooms, and axes" marched down Dauphine Street with banners proclaiming "Bread or Blood" and "Bread or Peace." They proceeded to ransack grocery stores. The Mobile riot was second in size only to that in Richmond, and as in Richmond, thousands of onlookers, many of them sympathetic, watched the women take food and clothing from merchants. When an army unit was dispatched to restore order, the soldiers refused to act against the women. As a result the matter was left to the civil authorities, whereupon the city's mayor addressed the throng and promised that their needs would be addressed if they would desist. This promise apparently satisfied the women for they disbanded, taking along the spoils of the day. The mayor made good on his promise and persuaded town citizens to provide assistance. A special relief committee alleviated the dire needs of Mobile's poor, and the city suffered no other similar outbreaks before the war's end.[33]

Also in September 1863, a group of women seized "badly needed" shoes from a store in Talladega, Alabama. The next month in Wilmington, a blockade runner was attacked and most of its cargo taken. In this incident, a home guard unit refused to fire on the mob.[34]

Sporadic outbreaks by Southern women continued into 1864 and 1865. In April 1864 a local home guard commander reported that in Burnsville, Yancey County, North Carolina, about 50 women had "assembled together . . . and marched in a body to a store-house . . . and pressed about sixty bushels of government wheat and carried it off."[35]

Savannah had a food riot on April 17, 1864, when women seized provisions from several stores "in order to appease their own hunger and that of their children." E.B. Long describes it as a "demonstration." Reaction was mixed. The *Savannah Republican* was sympathetic and called upon townspeople to come to the women's rescue. The paper published portions of a "card" written by one of the women asserting they must have food "by one way or the other." The judge of the police court released the women, at the same time denouncing them by stating their acts "were an outrage on all law and decency, and that when women become rioters, they cease to be women . . . ."[36]

In May 1864, a group of women, Confederate soldiers' wives and daughters, "respectfully petitioned" the commandant of Galveston Island for the opportunity to purchase flour at government prices, a privilege they had previously enjoyed. Upon being rebuffed, they made "boisterous and unbecoming demonstrations" at the commandant's residence and office. The women were arrested, then released. However, some of the ringleaders were taken again into custody and sent "with their children and chattels" to Houston.[37]

In January 1865 in the western North Carolina county of Yadkin, "a band of women, armed with axes" brought wagons to Jonesville in an attempt to "seize" corn. Unfortunately, their horses bolted and ran off with the wagons before they could load the corn. Later, these women or others met no resistance in a successful corn raid in Hamptonville.[38] Other civilian food demonstrations are mentioned in the footnote.[39]

"Bread or Blood!" — the rallying cry of the women who led the Richmond Bread Riot was not original to them.[40] In fact, the underlying causes of the Southern food riots were essentially similar to those in Europe: unfairly high food prices, perceived profiteering by merchants, and a group of citizens angered over their diminished abilities to care for their families.

Food shortages in the Confederacy had a serious impact on its military. Yet, I have found reports of only a couple of soldier food riots.[41] By and large, Confederate soldiers seem to have accepted their hardships and deprivations with some equanimity. The Southern women's riots tell a different story. Although these disturbances, including Richmond's, may have been minor events they reveal much about core problems in the Confederacy, and its capital, at a time in the war when military victory may still have seemed possible. As a distinguished historian has written, these outbreaks "were unmistakable signs of the Confederacy's disintegration, brought on not so much by hunger as by war weariness and resentment at high prices."[42]

Chapter 2: Richmond's Woman Riot
Spring 1863 - Richmond, Virginia

"These were verily days of horror."[43]

Prior to secession, Richmond had been a rather genteel community with a population of less than 40,000. By the mid-point of the war, however, the city's antebellum reputation for hospitality to strangers was being put to a severe test. With its numbers swollen by an influx of bureaucrats, military personnel, laborers, and refugees, the city's population in 1863 may have exceeded 100,000 persons. The stability of the community had been seriously undermined by a mass of people living under wartime conditions. Richmond had taken on a wide open quality; gambling and prostitution were flourishing, and crimes of violence had become commonplace. Unfortunately, the city's police force was too small to cope effectively with the widespread criminal activity.[44]

The winter of 1863 had been "long, bitter, [and] anxious," alternating severe cold with snow, sleet and rain. A snowfall on February 4 dropped the temperature to eight below zero, and the James River was frozen. Richmond's streets remained dark at night for much of the winter due to problems with the city gas supply. Just as spring was arriving, another heavy snow fell on March 19 and 20.[45] The city water works, which were hard pressed to supply the city's increased population, broke down at the end of March because it had been damaged by the melting snow.[46] This reduced most people to obtaining their supply from the muddy "Jeems" River or venturing to ancient wells.

In the Confederate capital, death was in the air, even though not from enemy bullets. The year began with an outbreak of small pox. Moreover, during the first three months of 1863, Richmond newspapers reported the following: a "murderess" executed at the foot of Poor House Hill, a young boy accidentally killed by members of the city battalion who were shooting at ducks on the canal basin, two

The Richmond Bread Riot

Yankee prisoners bound for exchange drowned upon the collapse of a bridge over the basin at Eighth Street, a soldier at Drewry's Bluff fatally injured in a snow ball fight, two Tredegar workers killed by the collapse of a snow-laden roof, and at least two Confederate army deserters executed at nearby Camp Lee. The worst of the local incidents took place on March 13 when an explosion in the Confederate States Laboratory on Brown's Island killed forty-five workers, mostly women, and injured many others. On March 20, as if Richmonders needed reminding there was a war on, they were given the opportunity to observe the remains of the "Gallant" Major John Pelham who had been mortally wounded at Kelly's Ford three days previously. Pelham's body, on its way to burial in Alabama, lay in state at the Virginia Capitol, where his face could be observed through a small window in the metal casket.[47]

For ordinary citizens on the home front the main concern in the Spring of 1863 was inflation and shortages of food and essential goods, which had driven prices skyward. Inflation struck the Confederacy from the outset, and by this time had reached alarming proportions, particularly in the cities. In January a Richmond newspaper published a schedule demonstrating that the weekly cost to feed a small family had risen from $6.55 in 1860 to $68.25 in 1863. Unfortunately, workers' wages had not kept pace.

Because of the excessive amount of Confederate currency in circulation, any shortage of goods was enough to send prices soaring. Reasons for the South's widespread food shortages have been discussed in the previous chapter. Immediate causes at this stage of the war were the general reduction in agricultural production resulting from military operations and Union occupation of farm lands, Confederate impressment of goods, the inefficient supply system that often failed to bring in available products, and the increasingly effective Union blockade of Southern ports.

Of particular significance for Richmond was the fact that the city competed directly with General Lee's army in securing food and other essential commodities. The government's method of impressment was denounced on all sides because the practice of paying a "market price" for products failed to account for the severe extent of current inflation. In March the war department's price schedule reflected about 50 percent of actual market value. Some rural counties, alarmed by the current impressment practices, were threatening to prohibit further exports of produce.

Despite the gloomy outlook on the home front, the people of Richmond and the Confederacy could still find room for hope in the ultimate success of their asserted independence. Their nation had existed for over two years and was still virtually intact in the face of the threats brought by the war. Militarily, things had gone well in Virginia, and there still seemed a possibility for success in the West. Because most Southerners probably did not yet realize the growing might of the North, it may have been conceivable to many that 1863 might be the last year of the war just as President Jefferson Davis had suggested in his January message to congress. Any such hope, however, had to compete with the increasing despair of civilians living in straitened circumstances on the home front. The illusion of Southern independence could continue only so long as citizens of the South were willing to support the war.

Bread or Blood

"Fasting in the midst of famine! May God save this people!"[48]

By late March 1863, the food situation in Richmond had become critical. There had already been a near panic earlier in the month when Confederate authorities ordered the seizure of all flour in mills and warehouses, a problem not yet resolved because the war department was ignoring a Richmond court order to desist. The late heavy snow of March 19 melted quickly, leaving roads in miserable condition. Consequently, the flow of food to Richmond came to a virtual standstill, and the food that could be found was being sold at "famine prices."[49]

As if to add insult to injury, Friday, March 27 was designated by President Davis as a day of fasting and prayer. On March 31, Colonel S. Bassett French, Virginia Governor John Letcher's military aide-de-camp, wrote to a friend in western Virginia requesting a supply of wheat; he said that wheat could not be obtained in Richmond, adding, "We are on the eve of starvation and unless the ways are opened up very shortly, we will all be laid low."[50]

While the conditions that led to the impending crisis were actually quite complex, to the average Richmonder, the problem was simple: It was the "extortioners" and "speculators," the merchants downtown who sold food and other goods at exorbitantly high prices. And it was those women who most desperately depended upon relatively uninflated wages for their existence who now felt compelled to take matters into their own hands. Already under severe stress due to the absence of husbands, fathers, and sons serving on distant battlefields, these women would have had justifiable fears for their own well being and that of their children. Under the circumstances, many, no doubt, felt that drastic steps were necessary because the government had removed their men and permitted such conditions to come about.

Mary Jackson, a middle-aged huckster in Richmond's second market, was the principal instigator for action. For some time she had been complaining of the high food prices to all who would listen, and late in March she promoted a meeting of women in the Richmond area to make plans to challenge the merchants. The meeting was to be held on the afternoon of April 1 in the Methodist church in Richmond's Oregon Hill neighborhood. When the women were turned away from that church, they moved over to the Belvidere Hill Baptist church in the same block. Oregon Hill, where Mary Jackson had previously lived, was a residential area of laboring families near the Tredegar Iron Works in southwest Richmond. The number of women who gathered in the small church was probably small; they came not only from Oregon Hill and other Richmond neighborhoods but also from outlying rural areas.

As the women met, it seems probable they were aware that in other areas of the South, groups of organized women had challenged merchants with demands that goods be sold to them at less than the prevailing prices. An account of the confrontation that had recently taken place in Salisbury, North Carolina, had been carried in the

The Richmond Bread Riot

Daily Richmond Examiner on March 27; according to the *Examiner*, the Salisbury merchants were successfully persuaded to sell at government prices by what was described as a "Woman Mob."[51]

At their church meeting the group led by Mary Jackson decided that early next morning they would meet in the second market and then go in a body to the state capitol to speak to Governor Letcher concerning the critical food and price situation. If the governor offered no satisfaction they planned to go to the merchants' stores and demand goods at government prices; if refused, they would take them by force. No doubt anticipating trouble in carrying out their plans, the women agreed to leave children at home, and some of them were to bring along weapons of a nature intended to persuade the merchants. Indicating that the women held little hope that the governor would offer any immediate aid, Mary Jackson instructed them that they were not to go along the streets like a "parcel of heathens;" they were to go quietly to the stores and make their demands. As further evidence of the women's planning, they arranged for transportation of seized goods in horse drawn wagons to be available in the downtown area.[52]

Virginia Governor John Letcher met a delegation of the women at the State Capitol and later addressed the mob in the Cary Street riot area.

The Richmond Bread Riot

The next day, Easter Thursday, April 2, 1863, was a "very fair" day as Spring weather had finally arrived.[53] Richmond's second market was located at Sixth and Marshall Streets in a large tin roofed building that included a vegetable, meat and fish market along with a police station.[54] Mary Jackson was there early. She was seen carrying a bowie knife and an unloaded six-barrel pistol. As she went about informing those who had missed yesterday's meeting of what was planned, Jackson boldly announced the group's intentions to two police officers. Accosting Officer William Griffin, she threatened him that he had better stay out of the streets as the women intended to shoot down every man who did not aid them in taking goods. Today, Jackson warned Griffin, she "would have bread or blood!" Both policemen warned her to behave, but neither took any action to prevent the gathering at the capitol.

Shortly after 8:00 a.m. the women, many of whom carried weapons, were on their way from the market to Virginia's capitol square, some four blocks away. Capitol square is a public park and setting for Virginia's capitol, although in 1863 it was would not have been as well maintained as the modern square. The original structure, which was designed by Thomas Jefferson and completed in the late 1700's, overlooks the James River, about a half mile to the south. At the bottom of the hill on Bank Street was the Confederate treasury and district court. President Davis's offices were located here on the third floor, and if he had looked out a window that morning, he might have seen the gathering of determined women. The capitol in 1863 looked much as it had since completion. The original structure was substantially modified by the addition of wings in the early 1900's.[55]

It is estimated that as many as two or three hundred women gathered at the capitol, where they were joined by unknown numbers of "half grown" boys. A short distance from the entrance to the capitol grounds is the governor's mansion, the residence of Virginia governors since 1814. John Letcher, the first of Virginia's two Civil War governors, had taken office on January 1, 1860. He was a fifty-year old former congressman from Lexington in western Virginia. Like many Virginians, he had opposed secession until President Lincoln

The Richmond Bread Riot

Virginia State Capitol Square where the women assembled on Thursday, April 2, 1863.

called for troops following the attack on Fort Sumpter. After Virginia joined the Confederacy, Letcher, who admired Jefferson Davis and believed in his leadership, became an energetic and staunch supporter of the Southern cause. In 1863, inflation was one of his state's most serious problems, and Letcher had "publicly condemned 'speculators' and 'extortioners.'"[56] Letcher was at breakfast as the women gathered in the square on the morning of April 2, and they sent a delegation over to call on him at the mansion. There, they first met the governor's aide, Colonel French, who asked them what they wanted. Speaking for the women, another of their leaders, Mary Johnson, who was later described as a determined woman of about 60, told French that the women "wanted bread, and bread they would have or die." Colonel French told them they were not proceeding in the right way, but he apparently passed on their request because soon afterwards the governor himself spoke to a group of women outside

The Richmond Bread Riot

the capitol. Governor Letcher expressed sympathy but offered no solution to the women's needs and told them that any forced attempt to take goods would be "over the point of the bayonet." One postwar account states that the women reacted to the governor's remarks with a "deaf ear," laughing "derisively."[57]

Having gained no satisfaction from the governor, the women and boys departed en masse from the square sometime before 9:00 a.m. and proceeded south in the direction of the mercantile area near the river and canal basin. As they proceeded, their ranks were increased by an apparently large number of males. The presence of the men was to add a perhaps unplanned element to the coming disturbance, as some of them would need little encouragement to join the women's cause. Many males would not engage in the riot but were sympathetic to the women, giving verbal encouragement, and some physically restrained others from interfering with the women.

As some of the crowd came down Ninth Street past the Confederate war department, clerk John B. Jones stepped out to watch them pass. In his diary, Jones stated that he asked where the women were going, and a "seemingly emaciated" young woman replied that they were going to find something to eat. Jones expressed hope for their success, noting they were heading in the right direction. He wrote that the crowd maintained silence and good order as it moved toward its destination; although other accounts differ on this, silence and good order would have been in compliance with Mary Jackson's instructions.[58]

The women's destination and the primary scene of the Bread Riot was the area of Main and Cary Streets, bounded on the west by Twelfth Street and Seventeenth Street on the east. This area, which includes Shockoe Slip, contained a variety of merchants' shops, commission houses, and trading establishments. Some of the stores contained government supplies, and the rioters would take goods belonging to the Confederate commissary.

The disgruntled women made their way down to Cary Street, just a few blocks from the capitol. Although they may have started out in silence, by the time the women reached their destination, they had become a "noisy and turbulent" mob. And despite Mary Jackson's forthright earlier warning to the police officers, when the women arrived at their final destination, there was no one in authority to hinder them. It was thus initially left to the store-keepers to defend themselves.

A group of women led by the sixty-year old Mary Johnson, who had earlier demanded bread at the capitol, approached the grocery firm of Pollard & Walker on Cary Street between Twelfth and Thirteenth Streets. The time was about 9:00 a.m.[59] Although the women held a "brief parley" with the proprietors, there is no historical record that the women then or later gave the merchants an opportunity to sell products at government prices. Now that the mob's intentions were obvious, all merchants who had not already done so closed and barred their doors. At this point what began on Cary Street has been known ever since as "The Richmond Bread Riot."

The main body of mob participants split into smaller groups and in short order attacked in the same block Pollard & Walker's grocery, Tyler & Son, a commission house for food and other articles, which included government supplies, and the shoe and hat store of John Hicks. With male assistance the women charged barricaded doors with hatchets and axes, shattering windows and battering in doors.

Mary Johnson led the attack on Pollard & Walker and was first to enter. She was assisted by one, Virgil Jones, who later claimed he had joined the women only after they entered Cary Street. A crowd of some seventy to eighty persons rushed in and looted the store, ignoring a proprietor's pleas to desist. Similarly, the other stores were quickly entered and stripped. According to one eyewitness, Hicks' shoe store was "thoroughly eviscerated" in about 10 minutes, after which "a large part of the crowd literally stood in the shoes of the proprietor." Looters included a Confederate soldier who left Hicks with six or seven pairs of shoes which he was taking for "his mess." Goods taken included not only food but also a large variety of dry goods, mostly necessities, such as material and clothing. The losses suffered by Tyler & Son were later calculated to be $6,467 and those of Hicks, $13,530.[60]

Other merchants were more fortunate, their stores being so stoutly defended as to deny access to the disorganized mob. Disor-

The Richmond Bread Riot

ganized they may have been, but the women left an impression of a formidable force. A druggist who observed the mob from his shop at Fifteenth and Main Streets later described the mob as "frantic and fearful.... You might as well have attempted to stop a whirlwind as to have stopped that mob of enraged and yelling women."[61]

Undoubtedly, most of the rioters would not be arrested, so that an enduring problem for historians of the Bread Riot is the estimation of the number of women and men who actively participated. Secondarily there is the question of the number of onlookers. These figures cannot be established with any precision. Many differing, some excessive, estimates have been given. As related, there may have been two or three hundred women gathered earlier in capitol square. It is likely that by the time they began breaking into the stores, their numbers had been increased. My conclusion is that there were probably no more than five hundred rioters, most of them women. The estimate is based on the limited number of stores actually attacked and the number of people arrested. The rioters were greatly outnumbered by the onlookers, of whom there were likely thousands.[62]

Seeing the women leave capitol square, Governor Letcher sent for Richmond Mayor Joseph Mayo to go to the scene and read the riot act, a time-honored procedure for ordering the dispersal of an unlawful assembly. The sixty-seven-year-old Mayo had been mayor of Richmond since 1853. As mayor, he was also a city magistrate, and the governor's message interrupted his morning session of mayor's court.

Governor Letcher also sent his aide Colonel French to summon the Public Guard, a light infantry company of state militia that served locally, primarily to guard state property such as the capitol. Then the governor himself with several aides headed toward the locale of the mob as did other state and city officials. Someone also sent for the local Catholic bishop, John McGill, who would later attempt to reason with the women.

After the initial stores had been sacked on Cary Street, some of the rioters had moved up one block to Main Street where at least three other merchants were attacked, including the shoe store of James Knotts (Knote, Knot) and the dry goods store next door of I.

Marcuse. Marcuse would testify that he gave goods, including socks, to the women in hopes of appeasing them; nevertheless, one side of his store was "entirely stripped."[63] E.B. Spence, a clothier whose shop was located at Thirteenth and Main Streets, attempted to address the crowd from a window of his store. Apparently his plea was ignored, and he was pulled or knocked, unharmed, from the window.[64] Other Main Street stores in this vicinity that may have been come under siege were Page's Shoe Store and the dry goods shop of Jacob Ezekial.[65] Although Jefferson Davis and John B. Jones were to claim that the women took jewelry in the riot, their assertions find no support in the contemporary newspaper reports of stores involved or in the list of recaptured goods that would appear in the *Examiner* on April 6. Michael B. Chesson has located a jewelry store, Mitchell and Tyler, that stood in 1863 in the Main Street riot area.[66] However, it is more likely that any jewelry taken in the riot came from one of the other stores mentioned, probably that of I. Marcuse.

Possibly around the time these stores were being broken into, Minerva Meredith, a tall middle-aged woman, was observed leading a group of women down Main Street past Knott's shoe store. According to later testimony of a witness who knew Meredith, she was holding up a pistol and "inciting the women to violence." Somewhat later, these same women surrounded a wagon load of beef being driven to the city hospital. They seized the wagon, drove it away, and apparently the beef was never recovered. The steward of the city hospital had been driving the wagon. He had known Minerva Meredith for years and could have been sympathetic to the women. Richmond city council later approved payment for the loss.[67]

William P. Munford, a prominent Richmonder and president of the Young Men's Christian Association, is reported to have spoken to the rioters in two locations during the morning. According to one account, he spoke at Twelfth and Cary Streets, a location indicating it would have occurred early in the riot. Munford, with no apparent impact on the mob, stated he had come from the governor's mansion and relayed a message from the governor that "he would see to it that there should be no suffering among the people . . . but that it was his

The Richmond Bread Riot

duty to see that the laws should be observed, and at all hazards he would put a stop to the proceedings if they commenced to pilfer."[68] This statement rings true because it is similar to the earlier statement of Governor Letcher at the capitol. Another account has Munford in the vicinity of the first market telling the rioters that food would be provided if they would desist. This location suggests it took place near the end of the rioting.[69] Munford would be good to his word because the Y.M.C.A. later distributed food from its location on Bank Street.[70]

At about the time the mob moved to Main Street, some responsible men in the crowd began to make efforts to quell the riot by helping the merchants resist the looters. Also at this time, the police finally arrived and began to make some arrests. At Knotts's shoe store, several men led by John B. Baldwin, a Confederate congressman from Staunton, Virginia, attempted to hem the rioters in the store, and some of the men took items from the women and threw them back into the store.

Richmond First Market, located at 17th and Main Streets, where the mob was confronted by the Public Guard.

The Richmond Bread Riot

Mayor Mayo's arrival on the tumultuous scene and his reading of the riot act at several locations appear to have had no effect on the mob confronting him.[71] As the governor and other officials arrived in the area between Thirteenth and Fourteenth Streets on Cary and Main, they no doubt found the streets jammed with scores of people. Most were merely observers, but it is likely that the governor now saw in full swing the plundering of stores by hundreds of men and women.

After a while, Governor Letcher, standing on a cart, was able to gain the attention of some part of the crowd; this was probably near Fifteenth and Main Streets. He then made a short speech to those present. At first he expressed sympathy for people's needs, but then he forcefully told them that mobs would not be allowed and demanded that the crowd disperse in five minutes or else he would order the public guard to fire on them. Some accounts state that the guard unit was present when Letcher made this speech. Other versions state that the military had not yet arrived, and the governor told the mob the soldiers were on the way. In either event, within a few minutes following Letcher's talk the crowd scattered from the area where he had spoken. Some accounts of the riot incorrectly mark this as the end of the Bread Riot.

While the governor's firm action dispersed a crowd in one location, the disturbance was not yet over as the original mob had become fragmented, and the riot broke out anew or was continuing down in the vicinity of the first city market at Seventeenth Street between Main and Franklin. This is area today known as Shockoe Bottom. Here, a group led by a male rioter and, amazingly, sixty-year old Mary Johnson broke open the door and sacked the dry goods store and dwelling of Minna Sweitzer (Schweitzer, Schwitzer) on Franklin Street.[72] Encouraging this attack was the women's leader Mary Jackson. John Baldwin and other men led by him had also come to this location and attempted to protect the storekeepers in the area.[73] A newspaper would later report that Mary Duke, a soldier's wife and mother of four children, pointed a navy revolver at the defenders. These events probably took place just prior to the arrival of the public guard at the first market.

After being summoned by the governor, about twenty armed members of the public guard had assembled in capitol square under the command of its elderly acting captain, Edward S. Gay. From all that had taken place since the women left the capitol, it seems that it took the unit at least an hour to reach the scene of the rioting after it began. According to most accounts, the unit was on foot; it first came to Capitol Square and then proceeded down to Main Street. These men may have stopped in the vicinity of Main at Fifteenth Street and supported Governor Letcher in his threatening speech. The unit continued eastwardly down Main to Seventeenth Street, where it turned left and went up one block north to Franklin. No doubt these soldiers, probably with fixed bayonets, drove before them any remainders of an unruly mob on Main Street. By this time, however, most of what was left of the crowd seems to have congregated near the old market in the vicinity of Sweitzer's store. The arrival of the public guard here, at between 10:00 and 11:00 a.m., was enough to send any trouble makers scurrying and appears to have effectively ended the plundering of stores in downtown Richmond.

Many of those still remaining in the streets now left the first market area, and moved back westward toward capitol square and the Confederate treasury department. On either Franklin Street or possibly Main around Governor (Thirteenth) Street the apparently sizeable remnants of the crowd were met by Confederate President Jefferson Davis, who had been alerted to the disturbance and, probably on horseback, came down from his office just up Bank Street. Also at this gathering were Captain Gay with his public guard unit and probably Mayor Mayo. It is doubtful whether the governor was present. Captain Gay is said to have pleaded with the crowd to go home and spare him the pain of firing on his own people. A Richmond resident wrote after the war that the captain was upset because some of the rioters were wives, sisters and daughters of men in the public guard.[74]

President Davis stood on a dray, and immediately gaining the attention of the crowd, he made a brief talk to them as had Governor Letcher previously. While it is reasonably certain that most of the persons before him had been bystanders or onlookers to the riot and possibly some empty-handed rioters, the president, in his own account given many years later, seems to have assumed he was addressing the looters of stores.

One observer later said that President Davis gave an eloquent speech. Initially expressing sympathy for the hardships of the people of Richmond, he then told them they had started out for bread and wound up in a pilfering expedition. He indicated their needs could be met in a proper way but that their conduct would actually deter farmers from bringing food to the city. In closing his remarks the president emphasized the seriousness of what had happened this morning and ordered the crowd to depart or else they would be fired upon by the public guard. As Davis finished his talk, the crowd silently began breaking up, and soon the street was clear.

With this dispersal of the crowd remaining in the downtown area, the Bread Riot essentially had come to an end. However, all of the women did not yet return to their homes. Mary Jackson, who was seen in the vicinity where President Davis made his appeal, was later arrested blocks away at First and Broad Streets. Carrying a bowie knife under her shawl, she was seized by police in a crowd of excited women just after they had attempted to break into a hardware store. As would later be shown, Mary Jackson apparently served strictly as a leader of the women and made no personal attempt to take any goods during the riot. A number of other women and men were also arrested during the riot and later.[75]

The timing of the morning's events must remain imprecise. The conclusion that the public guard arrived at the old market between 10:00 and 11:00 a.m. is based upon court testimony that the first store, Pollard & Walker, was broken into at about 9:00 a.m. and upon an estimate that the riot was over by around 11:00 a.m. However, this estimate is difficult to reconcile with the statement of Colonel French in later years that it took the guard unit just twenty-three minutes to reach the capitol grounds after the alarm was sounded. Although the time that the public guard was summoned is unknown, it presumably was called out when the women left the square before 9:00 a.m. However, if the unit gathered so quickly it should not have taken it over an hour to reach the old market area.

The Richmond Bread Riot

Compared with civil disturbances of our own day, Richmond's Bread Riot was a small affair. It probably lasted two hours or less, the various sources name as many as ten stores invaded, and there seems to have been little or no personal injury.[76] Nevertheless, the event was to be of great concern to the authorities in Richmond. It remained to be seen what steps would be taken to prevent a recurrence of the violence and to control the potential damage to morale in the South and loss of prestige in the North. Additionally, perhaps some relief might be provided to those in need.

Chapter 3: Reaction and Aftermath
A Disgraceful Riot

"Men's hats are not bread...."

Even before the Bread Riot mob was dispersed, the Y.M.C.A. began distributing food to the needy. Three barrels of rice along with meat and bread were distributed on the day of the riot, with distribution continuing the following day. Also, on the next day, a smaller group of women gathered in the streets demanding food. However, the situation was easily handled by the city battalion, another local military unit which had been activated to prevent another disturbance. In fact, the effective measures now taken by authorities prevented further violent outbreaks in Richmond during the remainder of the war, even though economic conditions would become much worse.

After seeing the mob disperse, President Davis returned to his office in a state of excitement. He was no doubt aware that such incidents, particularly here in the Confederate capital, could well have serious consequences. The riot was an obvious embarrassment to the government, and Davis was concerned lest it be construed abroad as more serious than he believed it was. Consequently, that same day the secretary of war sent a message to the local telegraph office requesting that nothing "relative to the unfortunate disturbance" be sent over the wire. Similar requests were made to the Richmond newspapers.[77]

At 5 p.m. on the day of the riot, Richmond City Council held a called meeting at city hall, just across the street from the Virginia capital square. The first order of business was to send requests for Governor Letcher and Mayor Mayo to attend, which they did. The minutes of this meeting reveal the council's urgent sense of alarm and outrage at the "disgraceful riot . . . instigated by devilish and selfish motives." The council members' belief was that the riot was

Richmond City Hall, across the street from the State Capitol, location of Mayor's Court and Circuit Court.

The Richmond Bread Riot

not caused by needy persons inasmuch as the city's poor had been amply provided for.[78] Mayor Mayo perhaps best expressed this viewpoint in his court the next morning as he strongly rebuked a hapless woman arrested as a rioter who claimed to be poor:

> *There is no reason why there should have been any suffering among the poor of this city; more money has been appropriated than has been applied for. It should be, and is well understood, that the riot yesterday was not for bread. Boots are not bread, brooms are not bread, men's hats are not bread, and I have never heard of anybody's eating them. Take your seat!*

Rioters in The Newspapers

"The true account of a so-called riot."

The *Daily Richmond Examiner*, whose editor held no love for Jefferson Davis, ignored the government's request to suppress the story and on the following Saturday published the first of many accounts of the court proceedings against the arrested rioters, along with an editorial condemning the incident. In its editorial, the *Examiner* suggested that in the event of future riots, participants should be shot on the spot.[79] The *Richmond Whig* in an editorial on Monday, April 6, ridiculed the government's request for newspapers to keep quiet about riot, stating that the Confederate authorities who made the suggestion were "deficient in intellect" if they believed a "female riot could occur in Richmond ... and not be known outside of the city limits ...."[80]

In April 1863 Richmond could boast five daily newspapers, which comprised the center of the Confederate news industry and exerted considerable influence over the Southern press elsewhere.[81] By this time in the war, Confederate leaders were coming under increasing criticism in Southern newspapers. Probably the most outspoken and abusive of all was the *Richmond Examiner*, which had begun to turn against President Davis as early as the fall of 1861.

The Richmond Bread Riot

The *Examiner* frequently attacked both the Confederate administration and the congress and was "downright scurrilous" in its blasts at the president.[82]

A very popular newspaper published in both daily and weekly editions, the *Examiner* was described by one journalist as an "enterprising sheet, [which] always has the news, is fond of the sensational, pitches into everybody and everything, and is altogether one of the most readable and attractive newspapers in the South."[83]

The *Examiner* was owned and edited by John Moncure Daniel, a "misanthrope, a cynic, and a somewhat unstable individual, who was easily provoked into controversy." The well-known Southern writer Edward A. Pollard was associate editor, and he shared Daniel's hostility toward Jefferson Davis.[84]

With the *Examiner's* intensely critical policy against the Confederate administration, it is not surprising that its editors chose to ignore the War Department's request to suppress news of the "unfortunate disturbance" of Thursday morning. On Friday, April 3, the paper broke the news of the riot in a brief statement of persons arrested, and its Saturday edition carried a full story of the rioter proceedings held Friday in Richmond mayor's court. On Saturday the paper also carried a biting editorial which left no doubt about the *Examiner* editors' views on the riot. The following is an excerpt:

> *The reader will find in the report of evidence in the Police Court, the true account of a so-called riot in the streets of Richmond. A handful of prostitutes, professional thieves, Irish and Yankee hags, gallows-birds from all lands but our own, congregated in Richmond, with a woman huckster at their head, who buys veal at the toll gate for a hundred and sells the same for two hundred and fifty in the morning market, undertook the other day to put into private practice the principles of the Commissary Department. Swearing that they would have goods "at Government prices" they broke open half a dozen shoe stores, hat stores, and tobacco houses, and robbed them of everything but bread, which was just the thing*

The Richmond Bread Riot

they wanted least. Under the demagogue's delusion that they might be "poor people," "starving people," and the like, an institution of charity made a distribution of rice and flour to all who would ask for it. Considering the circumstances, it was a vile, cowardly, and pernicious act; but the manner in which it was received exhibits the character of this mob. Miscreants were seen to dash the rice and flour into the muddy street, where the traces still remain, with the remark that "if that was what they were going to give, they might go to h–l." It is greatly to be regretted that this most villainous affair was not punished on the spot. Instead of shooting every wretch engaged at once, the authorities contented themselves with the ordinary arrest, and hence the appearance of the matter in the police report of the morning.

For several weeks after the riot, the *Examiner* carried accounts of the proceedings and trials of the rioters. Modern readers will see a big difference between the reporting of news in 1863 and today. Contrary to the usually straight-forward and seemingly unbiased news reports of our modern press, the *Richmond Examiner* reporters, who are never identified, gave free rein to their own views and prejudices. Perhaps most noticeable today are the many racial, ethnic and sexist slurs in both news accounts and editorials. Of course, this personal approach to the news was not unique to the *Examiner*.[85]

The *Examiner* customarily gave prominent coverage to all court proceedings held in Richmond. These accounts were carried under the heading, "The Courts," usually on page one. In fact, apart from the editorial noted above, the paper's story of the bread riot is told almost exclusively through its courts column. Given the nature of the news media in our own day, it is difficult to understand why the paper did not give more direct news of the riot, especially since the *Examiner's* offices on Governor Street (or Thirteenth) below Franklin were within approximately two blocks of the major rioting.[86]

The *Examiner* initially reported the names of forty women and twenty-four men arrested from the riot. The *Richmond Sentinel* named two additional rioters arrested, one male and one female.[87]

The Richmond Bread Riot

The court proceedings began with the accused rioters taken before the mayor's court, which in the bread riot cases served as a court of preliminary examination. The presiding magistrate of the mayor's court heard evidence against accused rioters and either dismissed charges or sent them for further examination and possible trial for felony in Richmond's Hustings Court or for misdemeanor before the circuit court. Actually, very few felony trials came out of the riot.

The *Examiner* covered both the mayor's court preliminary trials and the trials before the Hustings and circuit courts. Nearly all the reported rioter cases were completed by early fall of 1863. Unfortunately, for reasons not clear the newspaper stories do not present a complete record of what happened to every person originally named as arrested. In many of these cases it is likely that the charges simply were never prosecuted. Also, because there were rioters who gave false names some persons may have later been put on trial under different names. It is the possible name differences that make it difficult to determine precisely how many persons were arrested.

Although the *Examiner* was the first newspaper to break the news of the Bread Riot and carry accounts of the trials, other Richmond papers soon began to report on these proceedings. I have found, however, that the *Examiner* accounts are usually much more complete than those of the other papers. The principal question about these accounts is whether the *Examiner* reporters gave accurate reports. On the basis of all available evidence the paper's riot articles seem to be quite reliable.

In fact, the extensive *Examiner* court accounts, being based upon sworn statements of both participants and witnesses recorded soon after the event, should be considered the best and most reliable evidence of the story of the riot. Moreover, while these accounts do not in themselves contain a complete Bread Riot history, they do furnish a guide against which all other riot evidence may be measured.

Full transcripts of the most informative 1863 and 1864 newspaper articles relating to the riot from the *Richmond Examiner* and other Richmond newspapers are in Appendix C.

The Richmond Bread Riot

Rioters in Court

> *The court room presented an appearance never approached in strangeness... The male rioters, 15 or 20 young men of the veriest rowdy class, occupied the prisoner's boxes... The female prisoners, 30, perhaps,.. more of whom were clad in furs and silk than calico, were ranged round the court room, sitting on barrels of flour, piles of bacon, and piles of dry goods. The goods recaptured from the rioters filled the balance of the space... not occupied by policemen and lawyers, a flock of the latter being gathered like vultures by the scent of the prey....*[88]

It now remained for Richmond's courts to deal with several dozen arrested rioters. As related, three separate courts were to take part.

Most of the cases were to be prosecuted by Littleton Waller Tazewell, Richmond's commonwealth attorney since 1858. Born in Richmond in 1817, his father was a first cousin of Virginia Governor Waller Tazewell. Littleton Tazewell attended the College of William and Mary in 1836 and later practiced law in Mecklenburg County, Virginia, where as a whig he was also elected to the Virginia Senate. He ran for Congress in 1855, was defeated and subsequently returned to Richmond to practice law. In the summer of 1865 he was defeated in his bid for reelection as commonwealth attorney, but when his opponent, Marmaduke Johnson, declined to accept the position, Tazewell was elected. However, he died on November 30, 1865, just a few days after the election. According to Mr. Tazewell's obituary in the *Daily Richmond Whig*, "the State had neither an abler nor more faithful prosecutor." [89]

Little biographical information is available on the rioters' lawyers named in the newspaper articles. The best known was George Wythe Randolph, a grandson of Thomas Jefferson, who served briefly as Confederate secretary of war in 1862; in 1863 he was elected to Richmond city council and to the Virginia senate.[90]

The Richmond Bread Riot

MAYOR'S COURT

Richmond's mayor's court was a police court, and all rioters appeared here initially for preliminary hearings. Such proceedings were comparable to hearings on probable cause even though the testimony of witnesses seems to have been as extensive as it would have been in a full trial. In 1863, mayor's court was presided over usually by Mayor Joseph Mayo and on occasion by Hustings Court recorder James K. Caskie.[91] Court was held daily except Sunday in the first floor northeast room of Richmond city hall across the street from the state capitol.

Hearings for the rioters began on Friday, April 3. Mayor Mayo, entering court that morning, looked upon a courtroom crowded with accused rioters, lawyers, and policemen; the rest of the space was filed by the prosecution's tangible evidence — piles and piles of goods recovered from the mob. Richmond newspapers have left a colorful description of Mayo's courtroom during 1863. "Of all the inconvenient, hot close, unsuited places for the conducting of public business, we know of none which begins to compare with the Mayor's Court room." The judge was "too closely cooped behind his 'oyster box' to hear with comfort the matters before him." The room itself was a "little pen". Accused were "packed together in a narrow compass, scarce large enough for a chicken coop."

Ventilation was also a problem — the lawyers "were jammed together like bearings in a barrel pulling and blowing for want of air, while the large space in rear of the bar is occupied by idlers . . . , their feverish breaths filling the room with fumes of onions and bad whiskey."[92]

According to the *Examiner*, there were fifteen to twenty male and "perhaps" thirty female rioters in court during the first days of the proceedings. To this must be added the physical evidence of the riot, a great quantity of goods "recaptured" from the mob, which filled the balance of the courtroom space.

Mayor Mayo, "Old Joe," had had a harrowing experience with the mob on Thursday morning, and the irritation he expressed toward rioters appearing before him during Friday's court session is understandable. A knowledgeable magistrate, Mayo was the author of the standard text of the day for the guidance of magistrates and court officials.

Joseph Carrington Mayo was born in Powhatan County, Virginia, in 1795 and came to live in Richmond when young. He briefly studied medicine in Philadelphia in 1814 but returned to Richmond where he studied law and was licensed to practice in 1820. He became commonwealth attorney in 1822, a position he held until 1852. He served in the Virginia house of delegates from 1846-50 and also served on city council for 13 years. Mayo was Richmond's mayor from 1853 until removed by Federal authority in 1865 and was again elected mayor in 1866, serving until 1868.

He retired to New Kent County, Virginia, in 1868 where he served as commonwealth attorney until his death on August 8, 1872.[93]

Mayo's occasional irritable temperament revealed in newspaper articles is a side of him not found in law or history books. In one amusing and revealing courts column, the *Examiner* noted that the mayor, who was "crabbed and cross" that morning, issued a severe rebuke to a newspaper reporter for misquoting one of the mayor's "trivial cases." The account goes on to note that courtroom conditions made it absurd to think that a reporter could catch every remark by the mayor, "especially as he mumbles them so." Another article humorously refers to the mayor as "his royal rotundity." [94]

The difficulty of hearing anyone speaking in the courtroom must be kept in mind. In the early riot articles the *Examiner* reporter obviously had trouble understanding names given by those brought before the judge.

The mayor's court hearings went on for several weeks. From the newspaper accounts, fairly extensive evidence was presented as to each person brought to court. After hearing evidence in a case, the mayor then decided whether the accused rioter should be tried in the city's circuit Court for misdemeanor or tried in Hustings Court for felony. The accused was then sent on to the appropriate trial court.

CIRCUIT COURT

Most of the rioters were tried, if at all, on misdemeanor charges before Judge John A. Meredith in the City of Richmond Circuit Court located in the state courthouse on the grounds of the Virginia capitol. A grand jury returned indictments against 19 persons "charged with participating in the" riot. Trials of these and others were held in circuit court.

Many of Richmond's circuit court records were destroyed along with the state courthouse during the evacuation fire of April 3, 1865, and no contemporary records of the rioters in this court have been found.

Under Virginia law, the misdemeanor rioters were tried before a jury. If an accused was found guilty, the jury could impose a fine, with the judge imposing any jail sentence. The judge could also set aside a guilty verdict. Although many charges in the rioter cases had been brought under the general accusation of participating in the riot, it appears most of the accused were tried not for the crime of riot but for stealing goods or receiving stolen goods. Court dismissals of the charges or acquittals by the jury usually resulted from the inability of the prosecutor to establish that goods in possession of an accused were booty of the riot.

The *Examiner* trial accounts often summarized the evidence in a particular case. An example of what may have been a typical prosecution for engaging in the riot was the case of Margaret A. Pomphrey, a resident of New Kent County, east of Richmond. The commonwealth alleged that the accused went into Pollard & Walker's store and took a quantity of bacon. Mr. Pollard testified that he knew Mrs. Pomphrey very well, that during the riot he saw her going out of his store with two pieces of bacon, and he said to her, "is it possible that you too are robbing me?" The accused did not deny taking bacon. Her defense was that she was walking by the store and observed women taking goods and thought that they were distributing free food just as the Y.M.C.A. had been doing. According to her testimony, she went in and took bacon but did not hear Mr. Pollard remonstrate her.

Pomphrey's lawyer argued that she had only accidentally been involved in the riot, that she had passed the store, saw bacon being distributed, "and, thinking it a free barbecue, proceeded to help herself. . . ." It was doubtful she had heard Mr. Pollard because of the "noise and tumult." The jury obviously did not believe this fanciful argument and promptly returned a guilty verdict. Her sentence was light. The jury imposed a fifty-dollar fine, and Judge Meredith sentenced her to thirty days in city jail. The *Examiner's* article on this particular trial is notable for giving a fairly complete summary of the lawyers' arguments in a riot case.

Another revealing trial was that of John E. Lowry, a fifty- year-old man who operated a shoe shop and hotel in his residence on Cary Street near Fourteenth. He was charged with engaging in the riot. The evidence was that another rioter, Eliza Jane (Lucy Jane) Palmeter, who resided in Lowry's residence, brought two shoulders of bacon stolen from Pollard & Walker to the house. When police came to search for the bacon, Lowry took them to the second floor, where the bacon was found in a box containing female wearing apparel. Lowry acknowledged the bacon had been brought there by Palmeter. His defense was that he was not home when the bacon was left and did not know of it until later. There was no evidence that Lowry was present during the rioting. The commonwealth argued that Lowry knew the character of Palmeter and that the riot was taking place, and he must have known the bacon was stolen during the riot. After trial the jury convicted Lowry and imposed a fine of one hundred dollars. Two days later, Judge Meredith granted the motion of Lowry's lawyer to set aside the verdict. The judge found that there was no proof the bacon was taken during the riot but that the accused might have been prosecuted for receiving stolen goods. The court granted Lowry a new trial, but after the commonwealth declined further prosecution he was discharged.[95]

The girl who brought the bacon to Lowry's "hotel," Eliza Jane Palmeter, was 14. Described by the *Examiner* as a "notorious thief and street walker," she had been arrested on April 2 in a wagon loaded with flour, bacon, hats, and shoes. Although the newspaper indicates she was sent on for trial in the circuit court, the paper carried no further report of her case.[96] Palmeter is the only arrested rioter identified by the paper as a prostitute. Her residence at Lowry's might suggest the true nature of his establishment.

The Richmond Bread Riot

Minerva Meredith, the pistol-carrying leader of a group of women who made off with a wagon load of beef bound for the city hospital, was called up before the mayor on April 4. The *Examiner* described her as "full six feet high, rawboned and muscular, and about forty years of age." Witnesses against her expressed some confusion as to whether they saw Minerva on the morning of the riot or whether they might have seen her sister. Minerva forthrightly replied in court that she was the one they saw, and she was the one with the pistol. She was sent on to trial in the circuit court where she was found guilty, fined one-hundred dollars and sentenced to six months in jail.[97]

As noted previously, the *Examiner* did not reveal the disposition of all of the rioter cases. With respect to the circuit court trials, the newspaper's accounts reveal that eleven women and two men were convicted of misdemeanor. Most of those convicted received rather lenient treatment from the court. Several of the rioters were reported as acquitted, but in many instances, the result of trial or whether there was a trial never appears in the newspaper.

HUSTINGS COURT

Wartime records of Richmond Hustings Court, which the court's clerk kept in his home, have been preserved.[98] This court was located in Richmond city hall, and the few felony trials of rioters were held here before Judge William H. Lyons.[99]

The Hustings Court of Richmond had undergone many changes since its establishment in 1782. Although for many years it performed legislative, judicial, and executive functions for the city, by the 1860's the court's duties were mostly judicial. In its original form, the court was comprised of the mayor, recorder and aldermen who had limited criminal jurisdiction and exercised the authority of justices of the peace. However, in 1860 the Virginia general assembly for the first time authorized a judge of the Richmond Hustings Court. With its judge on the bench, the court was given felony jurisdiction over offenses committed within the city. Judge Lyons was the first judge of the court.[100]

The Richmond Bread Riot

Even after 1860, Hustings Court still maintained some of its original characteristics. During the Civil War the justices of the court, usually the recorder and aldermen (any four could act), met in monthly and quarterly sessions. Under the procedure of that day, when the mayor's court sent an accused on to Hustings for felony, another preliminary hearing was held before the panel of justices who heard evidence and determined whether the accused should stand trial before Judge Lyons. A record of the justices' proceedings was kept in the form of a minute book, and pertinent portions of the Hustings minutes that record the justices' consideration of the felony riot cases are set out in Appendix D.[101]

The Hustings Court minutes reveal the names of the nine persons who were originally charged with felony offenses arising from the bread riot. These minutes are essentially indictments and describe the charges in detail. For the most part, the individuals were charged with riotously and forcibly breaking into stores and stealing goods. Notably, Mary Jackson was charged with a felony for aiding and abetting the breaking in and destruction of Minna Sweitzer's dwelling on Franklin Street.

With one exception, the Hustings Court minutes do not reveal the dispositions of the felony cases. As with the misdemeanors, the only recorded outcomes of the Hustings trials are to be found in the *Richmond Examiner*. Fortunately, the paper provides an accounting of the results of all those charged with felony. Just one of the woman rioters was convicted of felony and sentenced to the penitentiary. She was sixty-year old Mary Johnson, who led the delegation of women who spoke with Governor Letcher. Johnson seems to have begun the riot when she took an ax to the front door of Pollard & Walker's grocery and later turned up at Minna Sweitzer's store near the old market. She was convicted of using a dangerous weapon in "stealing a large quantity of bacon" from Pollard and Walker and sentenced to five years in the penitentiary. However, the *Examiner* reports that Judge Lyons suspended imposition of the sentence to allow her to request clemency from the governor. Thereafter, nothing further of Johnson's case appears in the newspaper, and no record of a pardon request for her is to be found in the governor's papers for the period.

The Richmond Bread Riot

Three males were convicted of felony and sentenced to the penitentiary. Virgil Jones (alias George Jones, alias Orvell Jones) was a former member of the city battalion who had been dismissed from the unit three months prior to the riot for attempting to bribe a guard at the government lithography department to steal treasury notes. Jones had joined with Mary Johnson in breaking into Pollard and Walker and was convicted of using a dangerous weapon to steal bacon from the shop. Benjamin Slemper was convicted of stealing shoes and boots from James Knotts' store. Thomas Samani (Samanni) was convicted of breaking into the dwelling of Minna Sweitzer and stealing a large quantity of dry goods.

Another male accused, John Jones, was initially convicted of felony, but the Hustings Court set aside that verdict, and Jones was acquitted in a second trial. William J. Lusk, a Confederate soldier in the 17th Virginia Regiment was acquitted after a felony trial but was later convicted of misdemeanor in circuit court and sentenced to 12 months in jail. Lusk was pardoned by Governor Letcher on December 19, 1863, based on his military record. As discussed elsewhere, the felony charge against Mary Jackson was later withdrawn, and the ultimate disposition of any charges against her are not certain.

Frances Kelley (Kelly), charged with felony for stealing fifty pounds of bacon from Pollard & Walker, was tried in Hustings Court on March 1, 1864. At trial, she was described by the *Examiner* as "a tall, fine-looking, dark haired woman of forty, dressed in deep mourning . . . ." Kelley had been observed by a police officer in the company of Mary Jackson on the morning of the riot both in the second market and also later in capitol square. Her trial was delayed because she had left Richmond following her indictment; she was returned to Richmond by her bondsman. During her trial, Kelley's attorney in closing argument cited *Exodus* (Ch. 22, v.22) to the effect that "Ye shall not afflict any widow or fatherless child." Nevertheless, she was found guilty by the jury, which initially sentenced her to one year in the penitentiary. However, Kelley raised such a howl after the jury announced its verdict that Judge Lyons explained that because of the nominal value of the item stolen by Kelley "the jury might have punished her by confinement in the city jail." The jury thereupon retired and returned a new sentence that amounted to a conviction of misdemeanor, one month in city jail. This episode reveals a sympathetic court and might well have reflected the views of the Richmond community.[102]

The ninth rioter charged with felony was Sarah Champion, a thirty-five-year-old mother of three who lived in Rocketts. She was charged with assaulting store keeper James Knotts and stealing a quantity of candles and shoes. She was acquitted, according to the *Examiner*, because "there was no proof that she had been personally engaged in the riot, or was at any time near the scene of action."[103]

The Bread Riot — Conclusions

As an indication of the serious underlying economic problems then existing in the Confederacy, the Richmond Bread Riot stands out as a significant footnote to the history of the Civil War. Of course, it must be considered along with the many other Southern food riots. The best evidence we have about the women who brought on these disturbances are the 1863 articles from the *Richmond Examiner*.

RICHMOND'S ANGRY WOMEN

The denunciations of the Richmond rioters by city council, Mayor Mayo, and the newspaper editors have been noted. The *Examiner* in its April 4 editorial described them as "a handful of prostitutes, professional thieves, Irish and Yankee hags, gallows birds from all lands but our own . . . ." Such attacks were typical. The *Richmond Whig* on April 6 published its own editorial that not only condemned the women but also ridiculed the government for suggesting that no word of the riot be published. Following its editorial, the *Whig* supported its view by publishing a letter from an anonymous "looker on," whose "remarks . . . are very just and true as far as they go." The writer of the letter notes that a "fraction" of the women were "respectable" but suggests that most of them were of "the vice, the profligacy, the prostitution, the crime of the city . . . ." It is possible that this letter was actually additional editorializing by the *Whig*.

The Richmond Bread Riot

Any number of unflattering descriptions of the women can be found in contemporary writings. The following was attributed to a pro-Union Richmonder: "They looked like a flock of old buzzards, picked geese, and cranes; dressed in all sorts of old rigs . . . ."[104] Some of Richmond's middle class were aghast at the conduct of the women. Diarist Judith W. McGuire, who was not an eye-witness, allowed that "some of the women were really in want. . . . Others there were of the very worst class of women, and a great many who were not in want at all . . . ." She wrote that this was proven by women "supplying themselves with jewelry and other finery."[105] Sallie Brock Putnam, another diarist, provides a harsh second-hand account condemning the rioters and concluding: "It cannot be denied that *want of bread* was at this time too fatally true, but the sufferers for food were not to be found in this mob of vicious men and lawless viragoes who, [inhabited] quarters of the city where reigned riot and depravity . . . ."[106]

There is no question but that many, if not most, of the women rioters were of Richmond's lower economic classes. This and the idea that genteel and "proper" women did not pillage stores seems to account for much of the harsh reaction by newspaper editors and middle-class diarists. McGuire and Brock no doubt considered themselves among Richmond's better class, and their views of the women rioters reflect their ignorance of the struggles of the "worst class of" families after two years of war.

Modern studies of the Richmond outbreak have noted how the conduct of the mob in Richmond "horrified the Southern elite," reflecting "middle-class biases about the poor and gender-based prejudices against the female rioters."[107] These observations are undoubtedly correct, and today it is natural to feel sympathy for the sufferings of the women. Yet the contemporary reaction is understandable. Richmond had experienced an unprecedented and frighteningly violent uprising by hundreds, possibly thousands, of men and women. A war was on, and everyone was worried and tense. Who knew what mischief civilians might be capable of if they were not sternly suppressed and immediately discredited? The authorities were plainly eager to preserve peace on the home-front.

The Richmond Bread Riot

The transparently biased portrayals of the Richmond women simply do not stand up to the evidence recorded in the pages of *Richmond Examiner* during the Spring and Summer of 1863. The paper named at least forty women originally arrested. It seems a reasonable assumption that these women represented a fair sampling of those engaged in the riot.[108] In any event, the paper's descriptions of those arrested are the most complete information we have.

Of those arrested, the *Examiner* articles gave the residence locations of approximately sixteen women. These were predominantly within Richmond's working-class neighborhoods, a few being from outside the city. Contrary to the newspaper assertions, only one of the arrested women, Lucy or Eliza Palmeter, a fourteen-year-old, was revealed to be a prostitute ("a notorious thief and streetwalker").[109] Several of the women had husbands or sons in the Confederate military, and several were employed by the government or had husbands who were. Although one witness testified that she had been told by Mary Jackson that 300 women employed by Weisiger's, a government clothing establishment, would be involved in the riot, only one of the arrested women, Anne Enroughty, was identified with Weisiger's. The women rioters identified by the papers were both married and single, and their ages ranged from the teens to the sixties. Two married couples, both shopkeepers, were among the arrested, charged with receiving stolen goods that were found in their shops.

Michael Chesson's often-cited 1984 article in the *Virginia Magazine of History and Biography* provides a comprehensive look at the individual rioters and the merchants under attack. More recently, E. Susan Barber has written extensively of the women of Richmond during the Civil War; she gives a quite valuable description and analysis of the riot and the women.[110] Barber discovered two additional women rioters, who were not named in the newspaper accounts. They were Ann Donovan and Sarah Brooks, who worked in the Confederate ordnance laboratory on Brown's Island and were fired as a result of their participation.[111]

Additional insights are gained from the clemency petitions of several convicted rioters who sought pardons from Governor Letcher.

The Richmond Bread Riot

As noted, Minerva Meredith had been convicted of a misdemeanor and sentenced to a fine of $100 plus six months in jail. In her petition to the governor, Meredith admitted her guilt, stating that "without any foreknowledge of an intended riot she suddenly yielded to the excitement of the moment and was carried away by the surrounding circumstances." She described herself as "a poor illiterate woman - a grandmother now descending the hill of life - with impaired health [with] but little to hope or wish for outside of her humble home." The governor granted a pardon because of Meredith's poor health. It had been recommended by, among others, Mayor Mayo, Jacob Ezekial, a Main Street merchant in the riot area, and the governor's aide, Col. French.

Another petitioner, Mary (also known as Kate) Duke, had been convicted, fined $100, and sent to jail for six months. Her plea to the governor stated that her husband was in the Confederate army and that she had four children under age fifteen, all of them dependent on her for support. Three doctors who examined Duke recommended her release because she suffered from pulmonary disease, and her life would be endangered by continued confinement. Duke's clemency file is noteworthy for its inclusion of a touching letter to the governor from her fifteen year-old son pleading for his mother's release. Letcher approved a pardon for Duke.

However, Anna Bell (Anne Camp), a milliner on Broad Street, who had been fined $75 and sentenced to thirty days in jail, did not receive a favorable result. Her clemency petition states that she had three small children, two sons in the army, and a third son who had been discharged for ill health; her husband had died after serving twelve months in the army. Letcher declined to pardon Bell.

A fourth petitioner, Margaret A. Pomphrey, had received a light sentence of a $50 fine and thirty days in jail for stealing bacon from Pollard & Walker. She was perhaps the most well-off of the arrested rioters, owning "a farm and negroes" in New Kent County.[112] Pomphrey's clemency request states she had several young children living in New Kent and a son who had volunteered for the Confederate army at the beginning of the war. Although her petition was recom-

The Richmond Bread Riot

mended by the signatures of more than forty-five men, the available file does not indicate whether the governor pardoned Pomphrey.[113]

MALE RIOTERS

Less is known of the twenty-four male rioters identified by the *Examiner*. Only two of their residence locations were given, both in the downtown area. William Farrand and his wife operated a home grocery on Fourteenth Street next to Mayo's Bridge. John Lowry's place on Cary Street was used as a shoe shop and hotel. The Farrands were charged with receiving stolen property after goods taken during the riot were found in their home. The *Examiner* did not disclose the disposition of these charges. As mentioned previously, the charge against Lowery for engaging in the riot was dismissed after the prosecutor was unable to prove that bacon found in Lowery's home was taken during the riot.

Among the other men, two worked at the Confederate shoe shop; one was a huckster at the second market; four were members of Confederate military units; and three were present or former members of the city battalion who wore their uniforms in court. One of the males, Thomas Samani, was from a wealthy Richmond family, and the *Examiner* wrote that he was notorious for his involvement in forgery cases.

No source has identified any man as being involved in planning the riot. Rather, the circumstances suggest instead that the men impulsively joined to support the women only after the disturbance was underway.

STORES UNDER SIEGE

Various sources have named ten stores that may have come under attack during the riot. Some storekeepers in the riot area stoutly defended their shops and were able to hold the mob back. How particular stores were selected by the mob is unknown except as revealed by circumstance. It is well known that the women, along with many others, had railed against the merchant "extortioners" downtown, but this description may have included nearly all of the merchants. More telling, the women went directly from the capitol to two groceries on Cary Street where the riot began, and it is a reasonable assumption that these stores had been selected in advance. The initial store, Pollard & Walker, was robbed of bacon valued by the owners at $3,000.00. This supply must have acted as a magnet to the hungry women. Among the arrested, several were charged in connection with the bacon or other goods taken from this store. In fact, three of the rioters convicted for felony were charged with stealing bacon from Pollard & Walker. This includes the case of Frances Kelly, whose initial felony sentence was reduced to misdemeanor.

Michael Chesson has suggested that the rioters singled out Jewish merchants.[114] The newspapers of that day typically contained antisemitic statements, and such comments were not unusual during testimony taken at the rioters' court proceedings. For example, one witness mentioned the mob entering the "Jew store" (I. Marcuse) on Main Street.[115] Nevertheless, the evidence that Jewish merchants were targeted is circumstantial. In the second wave of attacks, the rioters left Cary Street and moved over to Main. Here, several of the stores entered by the rioters were operated by Jews, but just as many were not. The strongest indication that a Jewish store was targeted rests on the fact that after the mob abandoned its work on Main Street, perhaps after Governor Letcher's stern warning, they made for Minna Sweitzer's shop. She conducted business in her residence on Franklin Street several blocks away near the north end of the first market. It seems improbable that this unfortunate woman was randomly selected, a conclusion reinforced by the particular aggressiveness of the mob at her store.

DID THE WOMEN'S CIRCUMSTANCES JUSTIFY THEIR ACTIONS?

A difficult question to answer about the Bread Riot in the Confederate Capital is whether the women were in sufficiently dire circumstances as to justify their violent conduct? Alternatively, was their perception of unjust prices sufficiently accurate that history might exonerate them? The outbreak might be considered a continuation on a larger scale of the crime wave that had gripped the city for months.[116] However, it was more than this. The timing of the riot

The Richmond Bread Riot

is understandable. In March, there had already been several food riots in other Southern locations. As noted in Chapter 2, Richmond's riot may have been inspired by a group of women in Salisbury who were able to persuade merchants to sell goods at government prices. Moreover, Richmond's disturbance coincided with the near panic in the city that had resulted from the sudden food shortage in late March.[117]

There are no simple explanations for the complaints voiced by the city authorities and newspaper editors in the aftermath of the riot. In court on the day after the riot, Mayor Mayo angrily stated there was no reason for the poor to suffer because the city had already appropriated more relief funds than applied for. The *Richmond Whig* editorial of April 6 echoed Mayo's remarks, noting the absence of beggars in city streets and that "there have been fewer applications for charity than in any previous winter for many years." The *Examiner's* news reporter was to conclude that the women were not in such great need mainly because many of them retained attorneys, appeared well-dressed in court, and were able to put up bail.

However, the availability of government handouts seems an unlikely deterrent to long-simmering dissatisfaction of laboring families. The women were living in a country such as they had never known. In the midst of what they might perceive as an unending war, there was at least a belief that the government was doing nothing to relieve their suffering. In fact, the city, state and federal governments had proven themselves incapable of averting the inflation, shortages and speculation that seemed to be the root cause of all the trouble. Why, when public frustration had reached epic proportions, should the seriously disaffected resort to public charity (even if they had known it was available)?

Notwithstanding the official view, the suffering and deprivation of all classes of Richmond families at the time is well documented, and there were to be many expressions of sympathy for the women rioters. The fact that many of the women were well-dressed in court and represented by lawyers would seem to be of little consequence. Even after two years of war, a woman of any class might be expected to have at least one dressy outfit, and chances are that many of the lawyers' furnished their services at little or no charge.

The Richmond Bread Riot

That any of the women were actually near starvation may be doubted. Their venture on Easter Thursday was planned as a protest as much as anything, and they may have been sincere in hoping to *buy* goods at government impressment prices. Yet the fact that the situation quickly got out of hand could have been by design. Despite the seemingly innocent premise of their plan, later testimony before Mayor Mayo revealed the women were encouraged by their leaders to bring weapons with them as inducements to reluctant merchants. Importantly too, there was never any testimony that the women attempted to negotiate favorable prices with the storekeepers. Whatever their actual plan had been, it not surprising that the mob quickly resorted to violence and turned its attention to plundering whatever goods were available in the stores. The best record of the goods the women took, almost all food and other types of necessities, is the list recorded in the April 6 *Richmond Examiner*.

Any consideration of the cause and justification for the Richmond Bread Riot must take into account the large number of Southern food riots during the Spring of 1863. These incidents, described in Chapter 1, cannot be viewed in isolation. Rather it can be concluded that all Southern families faced fearful circumstances as the war headed into its third year. Their plight was due not only to shortages and high prices of all necessities but from the frustration of the drawn-out struggle, the loss of family members, and perhaps a general feeling that no assistance was likely to be provided by the powers that had brought about these conditions.

The Richmond riot was not in vain, however. Indeed, once the possibility of further outbreak was past, city council itself recognized the riot as evidence of genuine need. On April 4, two days after the riot, council passed a resolution providing for a committee to "report some plan for the relief of the meritorious poor." On April 13, council adopted a rather complex plan "for the relief of poor persons," including the establishment of a free market at the first and second city markets. (Any person who had engaged in a riot or unlawful assembly was not eligible.) The new measures the city undertook for relief of its poor might be considered the forerunners of a modern welfare system.[118] Richmond was to experience no similar disturbances for the remainder of the Civil War, even though conditions would become much worse before it was over. This may have been due in part to the new provisions for the needy as well as increased vigilance by the authorities. Perhaps also, Richmond's citizens of all classes realized there was little they could do in the face of the war's adversity and learned to live as best they could.

In summary, the Richmond women identified by the *Examiner* were with few exceptions of working-class families. A significant percentage of them had sons or husbands in the army. Their lives had been seriously disrupted and frustrated by conditions imposed on the home front by the two-year old war. Prospects for improvement seemed dim indeed, and it is little wonder that the women brought a formidable force to bear on those they believed responsible for their plight. It must have seemed they had nothing to lose, which is just about the way it turned out.

WHERE'S THE BREAD?

The tradition of calling Richmond's woman riot the Bread Riot began almost immediately afterwards and most likely took its name from the rioters' own words. Mary Johnson told Col. French at the capitol before the melee began on Thursday morning that the women "wanted bread, and bread they would have or die." Mary Jackson told a police officer that the women intended to have "bread or blood," a historical phrase that did not originate with her. In Richmond, as perhaps in other locations, bread stood strictly as a symbol for the women's hardships and for their goals. No bakeries were attacked, and although the besieged shops that carried food items may have stocked bread, the only food items listed in the April 6 *Richmond Examiner* were flour, bacon, sugar, and coffee. In fact, I have been unable to find any credible record of a rioter found in possession of a loaf of bread.[119]

While the riot did not live up to its name, it should not be considered a failure for that. It may not have been what the women had in mind, but Mary Jackson's Bread Riot succeeded in a larger sym-

The Richmond Bread Riot

bolic way by gaining the attention of the city authorities who made efforts to provide valuable assistance for those in need. The riot may have also been instrumental in relief measures adopted by both the state and Confederate governments.

Chapter 4: The Bread Riot Joins the Lost Cause

"Reminiscences of a Memorable Period of Our War History"[120]

Two years after the Bread Riot, the evacuation fire of April 3, 1865, destroyed virtually all of Richmond's Main and Cary Street mercantile area, including entire blocks of stores where the riot was most turbulent. For years afterwards the embarrassing woman mob was perhaps considered best forgotten along with many other aspects of the war. However, it was only natural that this colorful event would eventually be caught up in the South's post-war nostalgia wave we know as the Lost Cause.

On May 10, 1878, the *Richmond Daily Whig* noted that there was a danger of a newspaper war over the Bread Riot as several conflicting accounts of it had recently been published. The conflicts had to do, as they usually have since, with the question of whether President Davis or Governor Letcher should be given the "glory" of having ended the riot. According to the *Whig* the controversy had been initiated by the *New York Sun's* publication of an account of the riot by a Major Daniel. Apparently a newspaper war did not then materialize; at least, no contemporary follow-up articles were carried by the *Whig*.[121]

Ten years later, however, the Bread Riot war erupted in earnest after the *Richmond Dispatch* published then Virginia Senator John W. Daniel's story in its issue of December 16, 1888. Within the next several weeks two additional, lengthy articles appeared in the *Dispatch*. These were primarily a series of statements or letters to the paper from persons claiming to have witnessed the riot and relating their own versions of events on the morning of April 2, 1863.

The series of the first three *Dispatch* articles generated much heat over the Davis-Letcher controversy but in doing so also gave important information on many other aspects of the riot. As the largest collection of first-hand accounts, albeit many years after the fact, these newspaper articles and others published later are quite important to the riot's history. (All of the accounts discussed in this chapter will be found in Appendix E.)

Personal reminiscences expressed over thirty-five years after any event must be viewed with a great deal of skepticism. As might be expected, some of the later accounts are of dubious value. Even among those seemingly reliable, there are major discrepancies among the highly personal recollections, and this is a cause of confusion. Nevertheless, close comparison of the later accounts with the more consistent and reliable 1863-64 newspaper reports provides a key to reasonable resolutions of previously unanswered questions. Thus, these combined sources provide the probable course of the riot, the approximate locations and effect of the talks to the mob by both President Davis and Governor Letcher, and the part played by the public guard in ending the riot.

The Jefferson David Interview by an Unnamed Special Correspondent

After the interest shown in the Bread Riot by the initial *Dispatch* articles and the questions raised about the roles of Davis and Letcher, the paper decided to seek the former president's own account. Davis was then eighty years of age, living in retirement at his home, Beauvoir, on the Gulf of Mexico in Mississippi. On January 1, 1889, W.D. Chesterman, city editor of the *Richmond Dispatch*, wrote to Davis, sending him a copy probably of the paper's issue of December 30, 1888, and asking for his recollections of the "affair." Subsequently, in April, Davis was interviewed by a newspaperman at his home. The results of that interview were published by the *Dispatch* on April 28, 1889.[122]

There is something of a mystery about the Davis article because the *Dispatch* does not identify the interviewer except by the initials "WGW." Although definite identification has not been established, it is my belief that this "special correspondence" was written by William Griffin Waller, then managing editor of the *Richmond Times*. The *Times* and the *Dispatch* were competing daily newspapers in 1889. They later merged to create the present day *Richmond Times-Dispatch*.[123]

My conclusion that Waller conducted the Davis interview is based upon the following analysis. Assuming the likelihood that the interview was conducted by a Richmonder, I reviewed surnames in the contemporary Richmond city directories (1888, 1889), which revealed just a handful with the initial "WGW." From the occupations of these individuals, none other than Waller, a newspaper editor, appeared likely to have interviewed the former Confederate president or written a newspaper article. Also, Waller and William Dallas Chesterman of the *Dispatch* were both Confederate veterans. It is reasonable to conjecture they were acquainted and that both would have been interested in the recent riot accounts, which had created a controversy over Davis's appearance and speech during the riot. Of most significance, Waller was the widower of Jane Kempe Howell, younger sister of Mrs. Jefferson Davis, and he would therefore have had a natural entree to visit the Davis family. "WGW" mentions in the *Dispatch* article that one of the visitors to the Davis home at the time of the interview was Lizzie Waller, niece of Mrs. Davis. Lizzie was Waller's daughter. Finally, Waller's continuing contact with his late wife's family is indicated by his having sent a telegram of condolence to Mrs. Davis upon Jefferson Davis's death in December 1889.[124]

Still Later Newspaper Articles

On October 10 and 24, 1909, the *Richmond Times—Dispatch* carried additional stories on the Bread Riot. The latter article, although describing some questionable incidents, is valuable for presenting circumstances of Mary Jackson's arrest in a group of rioters attempting to break into a hardware store on Broad Street. This minor outbreak occurred apparently after President Davis made his appeal many blocks away.

Chapter 5: Jefferson Davis and the Bread Riot
The Former President of The Confederacy
Recollects The Bread Riot

". . . his society at once most entertaining and instructive."

Jefferson Davis was 80 years of age in April 1889, living in pleasant retirement at Beauvoir, his Mississippi gulf coast home. Although in apparent good health for his age, he had less than a year to live. Mr. Davis's later life was pleasant largely because of the admiration and respect accorded him as the former political leader of the short-lived Confederate States revolution. For many years, at least since General Robert E. Lee's death in 1870, Davis had undoubtedly been the first citizen of the South, the legendary ultimate symbol of the now burgeoning Lost Cause. He had outlived most of his critics and could be confident of his place in history.

Among the many visitors to Beauvoir that Spring of 1889 was a journalist who came to hear first-hand of the former president's experience in the wartime Richmond Bread Riot. The idea of such an interview had followed from the recent series of *Richmond Dispatch* newspaper articles of eyewitness accounts of the riot. Mr. Davis's own "recollections" were eagerly sought because many of these accounts had placed Davis at the scene of the riot and had raised questions about whether he had a part in ending the violence.

The resulting newspaper article published in *The Richmond Dispatch* on April 28, 1889, presents a fascinating portrait of Jefferson Davis in the last year of his life. The article notes that Davis was still erect in form and bright as ever, and the reporter was struck by the "ex-southern chieftain's" retentive memory and the fund of information "which he freely dispenses in the choicest language." The article concluded: "This and the varied career through which he has passed from the days of his early manhood to the present time added to his acknowledged pre-eminence as a fascinating conversationalist, are

The Richmond Bread Riot

what make his society at once most entertaining and instructive."

We can well imagine the charming and personable Davis sitting on the gallery at Beauvoir house regaling guests with colorful stories of his long and eventful life. His story of the time he ended the women's riot at Richmond with a mixture of persuasion and threats must have been an episode he particularly enjoyed. It was indeed a colorful tale he told.

On the morning of April 2, 1863, the president said he had received word in his office of a serious disturbance in the streets of Richmond, which the Mayor and Virginia Governor Letcher with his state forces were "entirely unable to repress." Davis went at once to the scene of the trouble and found a large crowd congregated at an intersection on Main Street. "They were headed by a tall, daring, Amazonian-looking woman, who had a white feather standing erect from her hat."

Davis noticed that, though the mob claimed to be starving, they had not confined themselves to food supplies but had also looted a jewelry store and clothing shops. From this observation he concluded that the mob wanted not bread "but plunder and wholesale robbery."

Shortly after he had arrived on the scene, Davis related, there appeared a military company composed of armorers and artisans employed by Confederate Chief of Ordnance, General Josiah Gorgas. The unit was under the command of a grim and resolute old captain, a native of Richmond.

President Davis then mounted a dray that was blocking the street and addressed the "formidable crowd of both sexes." He reminded them that although they claimed to be suffering from lack of bread, they had taken jewelry and finery instead. Dramatically, he emptied his pockets of money and threw it to the mob. Then he took out his watch and told the crowd to disperse within five minutes or else he would order the military to fire on them. Before the time expired, the riot was over "and the famous misnamed bread riot was at an end."

Closing the interview, the unnamed newspaper correspondent noted his view of what he had heard: "This is a succinct and truthful account of this trouble which created so much excitement at the time and of the part which ex-President Davis bore therein."[125]

The Richmond Bread Riot

Bread Riot History According To Jefferson Davis

Few historians have successfully related the story of the Richmond Bread Riot, and this can be largely credited to Jefferson Davis's own recalling of the event as published by the *Richmond Dispatch*. His version was used by Varina Davis in her 1890 biography, *Jefferson Davis, Ex-President of the Confederate States of America*. Although her book sets out the Bread Riot portion of the *Dispatch* article within quotation marks, she cites no source. Evidently, few historical writers have been aware of the original publication source.

But aspects of Davis's story are hardly reliable. His statement that "the Mayor and Governor Letcher with the State forces under his command were entirely unable to repress" the disturbance is troublesome. The former president's account implies that he came on the scene at the height of the riot and stopped the looting, and he also gives himself full credit for sending the mob home. Most historians and Davis biographers have taken him at his word. Perhaps quite naturally, writers of Southern history have relied heavily upon the personal experiences of the president of the Confederacy. Accepting Davis's account completely, most major Civil War histories of the past fifty years that include an account of the Richmond Bread Riot have portrayed Davis as the major actor in ending the riot and dispersing the mob. Notable exceptions are the accounts of Michael B. Chesson and Davis biographer, William J. Cooper, Jr., who states that Davis "greatly exaggerates" his bread riot role.[126]

Beginning at least as early as 1878 when the *Richmond Whig* reported the publication of Major (later Senator) John W. Daniel's account of the riot, there was a controversy over whether President Davis or Governor Letcher was responsible for ending the riot. So far as many historians have been concerned, this controversy was conclusively decided by Jefferson Davis.

However, as the material in this book makes clear, the eighty-year-old Davis's version of his predominant role in ending the riot was a less-than-correct reminiscence, and it did a disservice to Governor Letcher, albeit perhaps unintentionally. On this point the record should be set straight.

The Richmond Bread Riot

The essence of the controversy is whether President Davis or Governor Letcher addressed the rioters and persuaded them to end their unlawful acts and return to their homes. Unquestionably, during the morning of the riot both Davis and Letcher did speak to sizable crowds, and in each instance those particular crowds quickly dissolved. However, as we have previously seen, these gatherings took place at different times, and the people addressed were not exactly the same.

To review, the women had left the Virginia capitol grounds sometime before 9:00 a.m. After they left, Governor Letcher did two things. He sent word to Richmond Mayor Joseph Mayo to read the riot act to the mob, and he ordered the summoning of the public guard. For the latter a signal bell located on the capitol grounds was rung, and in addition the governor's aide-de-camp, Colonel S. Bassett French, went in person to the guard barracks located on south Fourth Street, about three-quarters of a mile from the capitol. Colonel French wrote to Governor Letcher in 1878 that it took just twenty-three minutes from the sound of the bell until the public guard members reached the western gates of the capitol.[127]

In the meantime, the women had reached their destination, and rioting was in progress. The first stores attacked were on Cary Street, near Thirteenth, and the women seemingly encountered no resistance except that put up by the store keepers. Next, the mob went up to Main Street probably between Thirteenth and Fifteenth Streets and broke into stores there. Here, for the first time, some citizens attempted to put down the disturbance. Although some individuals were arrested, the rioting continued.

Finally, Governor Letcher reached the riot scene on Main Street, near 15th. He may have been accompanied by the public guard but probably was not. When the governor arrived, Mayor Mayo was there, standing in a cart reading the riot act. Later witnesses were practically unanimous in saying that the mayor's efforts had no effect on the disturbance. The governor then replaced the mayor in the cart and gained the attention of the crowd.

The Richmond Bread Riot

Because of the events that had preceded his arrival, it is almost certain that Governor Letcher here confronted both rioters and onlookers when he spoke. Whether the governor's talk actually interrupted the looting of any stores is unclear but would seem doubtful.

Years later, Letcher and other observers stated that after making a brief talk the governor took out his watch and gave the crowd five minutes to leave the scene or else be fired upon. His threats were effective, and it appears that there was no further disturbance on Main Street.[128]

The riot had not yet ended, however. Later, or perhaps even while the governor was still speaking, portions of the mob moved down to the first market area at Seventeenth Street and attacked Minna Sweitzer's store on East Franklin Street.

The evidence suggests that after Letcher's address to the crowd, the public guard moved east down Main Street toward the first market. It is possible but not certain that the military unit arrived in time to break up the disturbance at Sweitzer's store. It does appear, however, that as it moved down Main Street the guard effectively dispersed any remaining rioters and prevented further attempts on stores in the downtown area.

Following these events there was still a large crowd in the riot area; the accounts strongly suggest they were primarily onlookers, who walked ahead of the public guard up Franklin Street in the direction of the custom house and the president's office. Then, and only then, did Davis appear on the scene. The precise location where Davis met this crowd is in conflict, but it can be reasonably fixed in the vicinity of Governor (Thirteenth) and Franklin Streets, just over two blocks from the president's office on Bank Street between Tenth and Eleventh. The rioters had earlier passed down Main Street just south of this location where at Thirteenth Street E.B. Spence had been pulled from the window of his store. Significantly, there are no reports of rioting in the vicinity of Franklin Street at the time Davis appeared.

It was probably here at around 11:00 a.m. that Davis, standing in a wagon, delivered his famous Bread Riot speech. The looting of stores had ended, Captain Gay and the public guard were on hand, and Davis, much disturbed by what had happened, no doubt followed

The Richmond Bread Riot

his political instincts. In his newspaper interview, the elderly Davis described the military company present as a Confederate unit composed of employees of General Josiah Gorgas, chief of ordinance.

When Jefferson Davis's later recounting of his experience in the Bread Riot is compared with the 1863 sources and the accounts of the many other eyewitnesses published in the 1888 and 1889 *Richmond Dispatch* articles, notable discrepancies appear. It can be accepted that Davis accurately recalled addressing the crowd, which resulted in clearing the streets. (His statement that he threw his pocket change at the mob is not supported by the account of any other observer.) However, the balance of his version seems less plausible than many of the others. For example, it is most unlikely, as Davis implies, that before he made his speech he went down among the crowd and witnessed the breaking in of stores. Further, when he describes the women's leader as a "tall, daring, Amazonian-looking woman, who had a white feather" in her hat, he is almost certainly embellishing his tale.[129] Davis is the only observer who mentions a woman with a feather in her hat.

In fact, it seems that Davis fashioned his version at least in part from other published sources. Interestingly, even thirty-six years after the event the former president stood by the wartime government view that the women did not need bread "but that they were bent on nothing but plunder and wholesale robbery" and that they had taken jewelry and finery instead of food. This statement is belied by the *Richmond Examiner's* description of the goods, much of it food and necessities, seized by authorities and brought into court on the first day of hearings before Mayor Mayo.

Even more obviously inaccurate was Davis's suggestion that a Confederate military unit was on the scene. One of the few irrefutable facts about the Bread Riot is that the public guard, a unit of state militia under the control of the governor of Virginia, was the only organized military unit to reach the streets of downtown Richmond while the riot was in progress.

In his 1878 letter to Governor Letcher, Colonel French argued that President Davis could not have been the person to give an order to the public guard since it was a state military unit. While possibly

The Richmond Bread Riot

true concerning the law, given the nature of the emergency facing the authorities, French's legalistic reasoning is unpersuasive. It can hardly be doubted that the guard would have obeyed direct orders of the President of the Confederacy.

The fundamental fault with the Davis version concerns his apparent perspective of the incident. If he recalled confronting a crowd of rioters, he was probably sincere in assuming that his threatening speech was primarily responsible for ending the riot. But the people to whom he spoke were hardly a band of rioters and in fact were mostly onlookers. This conclusion is supported not only by an analysis of the many accounts but, more emphatically, by an editorial that appeared in the *Richmond Whig*, on the following Monday, April 6. Commenting, critically, on the fact that it would have been impossible to comply with President Davis's request to suppress news of the "great 'bread' riot," the Whig's editor noted in passing, " . . the eloquent harangue of the President in a furniture wagon to a crowd of innocent men, squares away from the scent of female burglarism in broad daylight . . . ."

In conclusion, the Davis-Letcher controversy is specious, resting on false assumptions. Actually, the rioting was ended by the show of force from an armed militia unit and not by the spoken words of either individual. The governor should be given credit for promptly calling on the public guard to restore the peace.

The Richmond Bread Riot reveals both President Davis and Governor Letcher as courageous leaders. Each, independently, seized his opportunity for forceful action to stem a serious civil disturbance that, as we now know, reflected on the stability not only of Richmond, Virginia, but of the Confederate nation. Their actions demonstrated their recognition of the necessity for preserving the will of the Southern people to continue their struggle for independence.

Not the least important historical aspect of the riot is that it allows us to witness the Confederate president demonstrating his mettle publicly and under extreme pressure. He acquitted himself quite well, even if less dramatically than he later portrayed.

Chapter 6: Mary Jackson, Huckster and Rioter

> "I was washing in my yard, and Mrs. Jackson came by and told me that the women were going to hold a meeting to arrange about demanding goods from the merchants at Government prices...."[130]

Mary Jackson was a woman of undoubted leadership ability. Her actions in inciting the women led directly to the Bread Riot and thereby left a revealing and indelible impression of mid-war Richmond and the Confederacy. Moreover, once the immediate crisis caused by the women was over, the city fathers put aside their indignation and soon adopted important relief provisions for the poor. While Jackson has often been noted as the women's leader, her role in the long-term effects of the riot has not been recognized.

Although she gained notoriety through the 1863 newspaper articles, Mary Jackson's personal life remained in obscurity. Richmonders of her day seem to have taken but little notice of her. Possibly this was partly because of her laboring class background and the embarrassment she brought to the once genteel capital of Virginia. It must be assumed that she also brought great embarrassment to her family, which may have made great effort to protect her and their privacy.

Even so, a close study of Jackson's riot activities as revealed primarily by the *Daily Richmond Examiner*, combined with other previously undeveloped evidence can produce at least a glimpse of this notable woman.

Often referred to by the *Examiner* as a huckster (a hawker or peddler who sells goods on the street), Mary Jackson operated from a stall in Richmond's second market, located at Sixth and Marshall Streets. The initial *Examiner* mayor's court article on April 4, 1863, described her as "a good specimen of a forty year old Amazon, with the eye of the Devil." The newspaper noted also that two weeks previously Jackson had purchased two veals outside the city for $100 which on the same day were offered for sale at $250.

The Richmond Bread Riot

The *Richmond Whig* in its disdainful editorial of April 6 described the women's leader as a virago, and made the improbable statement that she "is known to have made a fortune by market-gardening . . . ."

At her first court appearance Mrs. Jackson's husband, unsuccessfully seeking her release on bail, told Mayor Mayo that he owned $7,000 worth of real estate.[131] A Richmond police officer testified that Mrs. Jackson accosted him on the morning of the riot and told him to keep out of the street that day as the women intended to shoot every man who did not assist them. To another officer Jackson vowed "bread or blood" and extended her threats to the mayor.

At the time of her arrest, which took place after President Davis had made his appeal to a crowd near the riot area, Jackson was in a group of excited women who had attempted forcibly to enter a hardware store on Broad Street.[132] She was armed with a bowie knife; other witnesses had seen her during the morning carrying a pistol.

The later famous rebel war clerk, John B. Jones (Mr. Joynes), testified in court that he knew Mary Jackson from her frequent applications at the Confederate War Department for a discharge of her son from the army. She had told him of a meeting of three hundred women at the Baptist church in Oregon Hill to organize a plan to demand bread at government prices. According to Jones, Jackson said the mayor had been informed of the movement and had threatened to break it up but was told that "if he attempted it he would get a ball put through him." From the bench, Mayor Mayo promptly though vaguely denied having heard of the women's plans.[133]

Following her initial hearing in mayor's court, Jackson was sent on to stand for a felony trial before the Hustings Court. The principal charge against her seems to have been that she incited the attack on Minna Sweitzer's store on Franklin Street. This fact is verified by the Hustings Court minutes for April 15. On April 23, Jackson went before hustings Judge William H. Lyons on another request for bail. In the account of this hearing, the *Examiner* described her as "an athletic woman of forty, with straight, strong features, and a vixenish eye. She was dressed in a silk dress, plaid shawl, nun's bonnet, with a long cape and black kid gloves." The reporter noted that no charges had been made against Jackson for taking anything during the riot.

The Richmond Bread Riot

At this bail hearing, Robert Redford, a fellow huckster in the second market and a sympathetic witness, testified he had known Mrs. Jackson seven years, that she lived on a small farm beyond the new fair grounds, that the road to her house was dangerous and many robberies had been committed on it. He said Jackson had a knife which she used to cut the bacon she sometimes brought to the market. On the morning of the riot, Jackson brought nothing to the market to sell, and Redford saw her leave the market around eight a.m. He next saw her in a crowd of women around 11:00 a.m. on Franklin Street near the custom house.[134]

Jacob L. Woodson, another friendly witness, testified that he saw Mrs. Jackson on the morning of the riot just as the women were leaving capitol square on their way to the stores. The crowd of women were 200 yards ahead of Mary Jackson, and he said to her, "I thought Jackson always led his Army, and your Army's ahead of you;" Her reply: she "was sick of the business had enough of it."

The testimony of Martha Jamison, another rioter, at the bail hearing is the best source concerning Jackson's role in organizing the women to make their demands on the Richmond merchants. Jamison was present at the church meeting on April 1. Addressing the women from the pulpit, Mary Jackson told them she didn't want them to go along the street like a "parcel of heathens" but to go quietly to the stores and make their demands. If the merchants did not consent the women were to break into the stores and take the goods. Jackson had said that 300 women who worked at the Government clothing establishment, Weisiger's, would be involved. Also, she had sent word to the women in nearby Hanover County that they must come to participate in the "proceedings". She threatened that the women who did not participate were to be "mobbed."

Leonard Chamberlayne, a second market grocer, testified that when he heard Jackson exhort the women in the market he attempted to persuade some of them to abandon their plans. However, Jackson, in a threatening manner, demanded that he stay out of it, which he apparently did.

According to the *Examiner*, after hearing the evidence, Judge Lyons denied bail for Mary Jackson, "not thinking the suspicion of her guilt light, and not believing that her health would be endangered by confinement."[135]

The next *Examiner* mention of Mary Jackson is on August 18, 1863, when it is reported that on the previous day she had been surrendered into court by John N. Davis and Alice Perdue, Mary's mother, who had previously posted her bail. New bail was then given by Charles W. Allen, who was Mary's brother in law.[136] Thus, perhaps unknown to the *Examiner*, sometime after bail was denied in April, Mary Jackson had been released from jail.

The last found newspaper mention of Mary Jackson was in the *Examiner* edition of October 12, 1863. It is there reported that the charge of felony could not be made against her, and she had been sent on to circuit court to be tried for misdemeanor before Judge Meredith. The reporter suggested the probability that if she were not eventually acquitted altogether, she would receive only nominal punishment.

The fact that the Richmond newspapers did not report the disposition of Mary Jackson's criminal charges suggests the likelihood that they were dismissed, although it is possible is that she reached some kind of plea agreement with the prosecutor. In either event, the conclusion to her case evidently failed to gain the attention of the newspapers, a surprising omission after all the riot coverage in the *Examiner*.

Another unfortunate shortcoming of the newspaper articles is the virtual absence of information connecting Mary Jackson personally with other women she may have led in the riot. From the circumstances, one might assume that she was acquainted with most of the women who gathered at the church on Thursday afternoon as well as many of the others who joined the women on Thursday morning. There are a few tantalizing clues of possible connections. The account of Mary Duke, a convicted rioter who was pardoned by Governor Letcher, is related in Chapter 3. Duke's pardon papers included a letter from her son, Andrew Perdue. Perdue was Mary Jackson's maiden name. A connection between Duke and Jackson may also be inferred from the fact that they were both charged with leading the attack on the store and home of Minna Schweitzer on Franklin Street.

The Richmond Bread Riot

Another Duke-Perdue connection is found in a mayor's court account of the *Richmond Daily Dispatch* of May 1, 1862. Several women, who had been brought before the mayor on the preceding day, had been involved in a "feminine rumpus" in "the Valley." This was presumably Shockoe Valley, a working class neighborhood that extended along Shockoe Creek (near Sixteenth Street) northward from the James River. The area, today known as Shockoe Bottom, also included the first market and many business shops. The newspaper account relates that "Miss Katy Duke, proprietress of a general commodity shop," had some time previously been the victim of a raid by the provost guard, which seized a barrel of spirits. Miss Duke, apparently believing Minerva Meredith was behind this mischief, caused the rumpus; she was supported by others, including a couple of boys, Andrew Perdue and Johnny Camp. The *Dispatch* implies that these boys were notorious miscreants in the valley. Minerva Meredith, who would be one of the prominent rioters the following year, had brought charges against her tormentors, and they all appeared before the mayor. In court, Meredith's "good character" was supported by police officers. The mayor required the offenders to give security of $100 to keep the peace for twelve months. A court witness to the altercation was "Mrs. Camp, Milliner."[137] Ann Camp, a milliner on Broad Street, was to be convicted for her Bread Riot activities. "Little" Johnny Camp, a possible relative, was mentioned in the *Richmond Examiner* article of April 4, 1863, as having sold shoes to a rioter.

The foregoing article supports a possible connection between Mary Jackson and Mary Duke, and even Minerva Meredith. The 1866 Richmond directory lists a Mary Duke operating a "fancy goods" shop in her home on Twenty-second Street, also in Shockoe Bottom.[138] Another tenuous connection is revealed in a *Richmond Dispatch* article of June 18, 1861. Minerva Meredith's name was mentioned in connection with another incident. A slave, who was charged with using "insolent, provoking and incendiary language" in Meredith's presence, was brought before the mayor. The incident took place when Meredith went into the shop of Walter Duke on Broad Street.

The Richmond Bread Riot

Admittedly, these newspaper articles provide no more than hints of possible associations. More concrete evidence concerning Mary Jackson and her family is found in records of the City of Richmond and surrounding counties. She was born Mary Perdue probably around 1822 and was married to Elisha Jackson, a painter, in 1848. Mary's mother was Alice Goode Perdue; inconsistent records reveal that her father was either Bartholomew, Bartlet or Irby Perdue. According to the 1850 Richmond census, the Jackson family consisted of Elisha, age 27, Mary 28, Francis, 6, and James A., 1. Mary had at least two additional children after 1850. It is possible that either Mary or Elisha had been married previously because if the census information is correct, the child Francis would have been four years old during the year of their marriage.[139]

It will be recalled that the Baptist church where Jackson spoke to women on the day before the Bread Riot was located in Oregon Hill, the working-class neighborhood in southwest Richmond.[140] The Jacksons had lived in this neighborhood in 1856. Real estate records reveal that in 1858, a residential property was purchased for Mary Jackson's lifetime use. It was located on Elmwood (now West Main) Street in Sydney, a town or neighborhood adjoining Oregon Hill and then just outside Richmond city limits. The deed to this property actually conveyed title to Robert R. Howison, an attorney, as trustee for Mary.[141]

The Jackson family apparently lived in Sydney from 1858 until 1860, when that property was sold, and Mary's trustee received for her benefit a deed to a seven-acre farm property located two miles from Richmond on Deep Run Turnpike (now West Broad Street). The deed of conveyance specified that Mary was to have a life interest in the property, which would pass to her children upon her death, free of any claim of her husband. The Jackson farm is shown on the map of the City of Richmond and outlying areas that was prepared by the U.S. Army Corps of Engineers after the war.[142] It was located in the vicinity of present-day Roseneath Street.

With respect to Mary Jackson's business at the second market, a significant entry is found in the Richmond City Council minutes for

The Richmond Bread Riot

March 26, 1863, just one week before she precipitated the Bread Riot. The minutes relate that Elisha Jackson had petitioned council for relief from a confiscation under the city's ordinance governing operation of the markets; the petition was rejected.[143]

Henrico County records show that Mary Jackson died on December 12, 1866, survived by three children, James Andrew Jackson, Samuel Jackson and Esther D. Jackson. Her cause of death is shown as "child birth." In the year 1868 a court proceeding was brought to sell the interests of her minor children in the seven acre Henrico farm property.[144] An advertisement of sale contained in the partition suit file shows that the land contained a farm dwelling and a peach orchard. This property was finally sold under court authority by a deed dated March 8, 1877.[145]

The foregoing summary of the evidence on her life and activities, provides a sketchy but revealing portrait of Mary Jackson. In April 1863 Jackson was approximately 41 years age. She was a large woman who appeared to be healthy and robust (an "Amazon", "athletic"). No doubt she was used to hard farm work. The Jacksons were churchgoers, probably Baptist or Methodist.

Although little of Mrs. Jackson's personal characteristics may be drawn with certainty, most assuredly in April 1863 she was extremely angry and contemptuous of the civil authorities of Virginia's capital city.

There has been a general assumption that Jackson was motivated to incite the women solely because of the scarcity of food and high prices, the principal factors on which the riot is blamed. But we can see that she may have had other more compelling motivations. The Jacksons were apparently embroiled in controversy with city authorities over the confiscation of goods from their second market booth. Moreover, perhaps the strongest motivation of all for a mother, she had been frustrated in frequent attempts to obtain a discharge from the army of her 19-year-old son Francis.[146]

That Mary Jackson may have acted largely because of her desire for retribution against the authorities gains support from the fact that she made no apparent effort to take anything for herself or family in the plundering of the stores. Throughout the disturbance she merely continued in her fanatical leadership role. This might have been because Jackson had no real need to steal goods. Her husband presumably was able to work. The family owned its own farm and had a market business. Finally, as did many of the arrested women, Jackson appeared in Court well dressed.

The evidence about Mary Jackson raises questions which can never be satisfactorily explained but which suggest interesting possibilities. For example, why were the real estate purchases in 1858 and 1860 placed in trust for Mary rather than deeded directly to her? From all the circumstances surrounding these transactions, a plausible inference may be drawn that these properties were purchased for Mary by her mother, Alice Perdue, and if so, the trust arrangement may have been merely a way to conserve the property for Mary's children, Mrs. Perdue's grandchildren. Also there might have been some disharmony between Mary Jackson and her husband Elisha.

Another possibility is that Mary suffered from some physical or mental impairment, which made a trust arrangement desirable. Her behavior, to the extent we can observe it in 1863, must raise at least a question about her mental stability, even discounting the newspaper reporter's description of her "eye of the Devil" and "vixenish eye."

Perhaps the most perplexing question about Mary Jackson concerns the disposition of the charges against her and why the final action in her case was never revealed by the newspapers. As stated, I believe it likely Mary's case was dismissed by the prosecution. This may have been for the legal reason suggested by the *Examiner* reporter that a case could not be made against Jackson because she had not stolen anything. However, this explanation is difficult to accept. Given the overwhelming evidence of her actions, she surely could have been convicted of some misdemeanor charge related to inciting or engaging in a riot.

A more plausible explanation is that Jackson received sufficient support from influential persons to persuade the authorities to quietly drop her case after the furor over the riot had passed. And Mary was not without influential friends.

The Richmond Bread Riot

Her mother, Mary G. Perdue, and brother-in-law, Charles W. Allen, a prominent builder, may well have been helpful to her. And at least three lawyers were looking after Jackson's interests. Eaton Nance appeared with her in court in the riot case; John N. Davis posted bail for her upon her initial release from jail; and Robert R. Howison was trustee for her in both the 1858 and 1860 trust deeds. All three of these lawyers were prominent members of the Richmond Bar. While there is no other evidence of their activities in Jacksons's behalf, it may certainly be inferred that they did what they could to protect her against from criminal prosecution.

Even with such scant information being available about Mary Jackson in spite of her notoriety, one senses the desperation of her family and friends to protect her private life from public view and ultimately from history. After the initial furor over the riot had passed, Jackson's representatives seem to have been successful in having the authorities discontinue her prosecution. This may reinforce the admittedly speculative notion that Mary suffered from some physical or mental infirmity. The existence of such a condition could have justified the state's dropping of the case. Jackson's death just three years later lends some support to this possibility.

Chapter 7: Other Tales of the Bread Riot

"We are Starving. As soon as enough of us get together we are going to the bakeries and each of us will take a loaf of bread."

— Mrs. Roger A. Pryor,
Reminiscences of Peace and War (1904), p. 238

Many incidents have been depicted in Bread Riot lore that I have either not used in the narrative story or merely mentioned in passing. Some of these depictions are fictional or at least of questionable reliability. Others may have taken place away from the major disturbance and cannot be placed in the context of the riot as I have described it. Nevertheless, there are several recorded incidents that deserve further comment.

A Fictional Firsthand Account

The riot account of Mrs. Roger A. Pryor (Sara Agnes Rice Pryor), which includes the quote above, has been given prominence by historians.[147] It is undue prominence, comparable though on a lesser scale to the prominence given Jefferson Davis's version of the riot.

Roger and Agnes Pryor are an interesting study. Prior to the Civil War, Roger was a lawyer, a distinguished journalist and a member of Congress. In 1863, as a brigadier general in the Confederate army, he became dissatisfied with his command assignments, resigned from the army and immediately enlisted as a private in the cavalry. Shortly after the war, the Pryors moved to New York City, where they lived the rest of their lives. In New York, Mr. Pryor had a distinguished career as a lawyer and later as a judge.[148]

Sara Pryor's book, *Reminiscences of Peace and War*, was apparently written in the early 1900s. She recalled the Pryor family's lives from the 1850's until just after the end of the Civil War. (A second volume was published in 1909.) Although Virginia natives, the Pryors never lived for any extended time in Richmond. And according to *Reminiscences*, Sara spent most of the war years in various locations away from Richmond, often staying near her husband wherever he was serving in the field. At the time of the Bread Riot, she was in southside Virginia.[149]

At page 237 of *Reminiscences*, Sara Pryor includes what some historians have taken to be a factual encounter on the morning of the Bread Riot between the author's friend, "Agnes," and one of the disaffected women. Presented under the guise of a letter to the author dated April 4, 1863, Agnes describes her conversation "yesterday" in Virginia's capitol square with "a pale, emaciated girl, not more than eighteen . . . ." Agnes' description of the girl and the ensuing conversation between the two is sympathetic to the needs and motives of the women. As the women departed on their foray, Agnes observes the crowd, "more than a thousand women and children . . . until it reached the dignity of a mob—a bread riot." The balance of the Agnes letter is a brief and sympathetic summary of the riot itself, though it does not purport to be an eye-witness description. In the concluding paragraph, Agnes states that *"not one word* has been said in the newspapers about it."

My conclusion is that the letter from Agnes describing the scene in capitol square is fictional. Indeed, I would argue that all of the letters from Agnes (Sara Pryor's middle name) are fictional literary devices that allow *Reminiscences* to tell a more rounded story of the war. There are eight Agnes letters in the book, all purportedly written from Richmond. Agnes also appears in other places in the book in conversation with Sara. Sara states at one point that she would like to give Agnes's full name but will not do so because the lady "is now living, and, being a respectable lady of the old school, is averse from seeing her name in print."[150]

Sara Pryor's *Reminiscences* is a charming and classic volume of Civil War literature. As recorded history, however, it must be examined very carefully. In the first place there are minor factual discrepancies in Pryor's capitol square letter. The letter is dated April 4, 1863, and states that the scene took place "yesterday." The Bread Riot took place on April 2, not April 3. The letter also incorrectly states that nothing about the riot had been reported in the Richmond

The Richmond Bread Riot

newspapers. In fact, a short article reporting the names of arrested rioters appeared in the *Richmond Examiner* of April 3, and the April 4 issue contained a lengthy editorial deploring the riot and the first of the lengthy court articles.

More important than these inaccuracies, the conversation between Agnes and a "pale, emaciated girl," and the statements attributed to "a fat old black Mammy" who "waddled up the walk" are simply too fanciful. Not only is the episode improbable, but its sympathetic tone is unlike that of most 1863 diarists, many of whom expressed indignation at the women's actions.

However, one prominent war-time source that would have been available to Sara Pryor at the time she was writing her book and which was sympathetic to the women was the diary of war clerk John B. Jones, published in 1866. Jones frequently complained of the high prices in Richmond, and the women would naturally have had his sympathies. A comparison of the Pryor *Reminiscences* with Jones's diary entry for April 2, 1863, strongly suggests that Sara Pryor drew upon his diary when she fashioned her riot story.

Jones describes the women leaving capitol square and passing by the war department on their way down to Cary Street. He "asked a pale boy where they were going. A young woman, seemingly emaciated, but yet with a smile, answered that they were going to find something to eat." Jones wished them success, noting "that they were going in the right direction to find plenty in the hands of the extortioners." Jones goes on to summarize what happened during the riot though not from an eye-witness perspective. Sara Pryor's summary of the riot itself is plainly derived from Jones' account.

The Pryors' Civil War experiences have recently been described by John C. Waugh in *Surviving The Confederacy—Rebellion, Ruin and Recovery—Roger and Sara Pryor During the Civil War*. While the Pryors' story is a worthy one and long overdue, the author relies uncritically on Sara Pryor's *Reminiscences* and accepts "Agnes" as a historical person and her letters as factual accounts. I believe he is mistaken. "Agnes" is Sara Pryor, and her Bread Riot tale should be regarded as Lost-Cause literature and not primary resource material.[151]

The Richmond Bread Riot

Other Fictions: Yankee Influence and Spies

In its lengthy editorial published two days after the riot, the editors of the *Richmond Examiner*, in condemning the riot, noted that there had been similar episodes elsewhere and suggested that the instigators were the same in all, "emissaries of the Federal Government" who traveled by train from one city to the next. Referring to recent intimations in the Northern press of a "wonderful secret machinery . . . to overthrow the South," these outbreaks were "what they [the Northern newspapers] meant."[152]

The *New York Herald* published its "refugee" story of the Richmond riot a week later. This correspondent, in what seems to be a direct response to the *Examiner* editorial, reports that Richmond officials were attempting "to mislead the public" concerning the loyalty of Richmond citizens. The "refugee" concludes: "The fact of [the rioters'] destitution and their respectability was too palpable, and the authorities are forced to admit . . . that starvation alone incited the movement."[153]

Time has failed to produce any evidence of the *Richmond Examiner's* notion that roving "Federal emissaries" had any influence on the uprising in Richmond. A more serious question is whether Yankee spies already in Richmond were involved either in the planning, carrying out, or aftermath of the Bread Riot. There is no reliable evidence for any of these suppositions.

To be sure, at least one claim has been made for the influence of Richmond's spy network in the event. The late Robert W. Waitt, a long-time Richmond resident and knowledgeable local historian, claimed that a member of his family, Thomas McNiven, had headed a wartime spy ring that was active in the Bread Riot. McNiven's wartime activities were transcribed by Waitt many years after they had been related to him by McNivan's daughter. Historians who have examined these recorded recollections have found them unreliable. Waitt's transcript does not reveal spy activities in the riot except to state that the riot was organized with the help of "a lot of American dollars. . . ."[154]

The Richmond Bread Riot

Unfortunately, the diary kept by Richmond's most famous Yankee spy, Elizabeth Van Lew, is incomplete for 1863 and does not mention the Bread Riot.[155]

Compared with the available evidence surrounding the Richmond area women who met and planned the riot, who went to the state capitol to meet the governor, and who led the mob to the sacking of stores, it is hardly credible that spies made any significant contribution to the event.

Because many of the arrested women though claiming poverty were represented by lawyers, outside money at this later stage cannot be ruled out. But this is doubtful. What would be the point? It was to the benefit of the North to keep the Richmond populace in a state of poverty and unrest. As suggested previously, it is more probable that Richmond lawyers had sympathy for the women and represented them in the riot trials for little or no charge.

Blood or Bread — Riot Injury

In Chapter 3, I wrote that there appears to have been little or no personal injury suffered in the riot. No reports of injury were mentioned in either the Richmond newspaper court accounts of 1863 or the articles of 1888-1889. However, other sources have noted three random incidents of injury.

The most graphic and detailed of these accounts is found in a letter dated April 3, 1863, from a Confederate soldier, Hal Tutwiler, to his sister in North Carolina. The complete letter is in the footnote.[156] Tutwiler reports that "[w]e have had a dreadful riot here on yesterday . . .;" while at work he "heard a most tremendous cheering . . ." and when he went to investigate "found that a large number of women had broken into two or three large grocery establishments, & were helping themselves . . . to everything eatable they could find." From his letter it is not clear whether Tutwiler actually witnessed the rioting or other events described in his letter or is merely reporting what he had heard.

However, toward the end of the letter after he has mentioned events of the following day, April 3, Tutwiler is quite clear in stating

The Richmond Bread Riot

that he saw a shop keeper cut off the fingers of a woman who put her arm in a window to steal something. However, he describes the riot taking place over two days, and he does not specify whether this incident happened on April 2 or April 3. There are no reports of stores being broken into on April 3. In fact, the rioters were in court before Mayor Mayo on that day.

Another suggestion of injury was included in Richmonder Ernest Taylor Walthall's post-war family history and memoir published in 1908. In describing the looting of stores in the vicinity of Twelfth and Cary Streets, he mentions obscurely and almost in passing, "There was a hatchet in someone's hands," and blood flowed from a Mr. Tyler.[157] Conceivably, this could be the same incident related by Tutwiler.

Finally, on April 23, 1863, the *Richmond Examiner* published an article from the *New York Herald* containing an account of an injury as included in a first hand report on the Bread Riot by "a refugee from Richmond." The refugee stated a surprisingly accurate summary of events surrounding the plundering of stores by "a body of females, numbering about three hundred" on the morning of April 2. After noting that some individuals had attempted unsuccessfully "to resist the women," the refugee says that a "man who struck a female was wounded in the shoulder by a shot from a revolver . . . ."[158]

Other than the incident involving the storekeeper Tyler, it is difficult to find a place for these uncorroborated injury reports in a narrative of the Bread Riot. They were all serious enough to have been mentioned in the 1863 Richmond newspaper articles or in the later articles. Tutwiler's letter is certainly specific as to the incident he described. However, his credibility is undermined by his describing the riot as taking place over two days. Moreover, given the large number of persons jammed into the streets and around the stores, I find it difficult to accept that it was personally observed by him or, unless it was the same as the Tyler incident, that it took place during the rioting on the morning of April 2. Even more unlikely is the "refugee's" account of the man being shot by a revolver. It is the only account I have found that there was gunfire during the riot. Surely, this sort of violence would have been prominently mentioned by others on the scene.[159]

Activities of the Fire Brigade

A Richmond diarist wrote that at the suggestion of Governor Letcher the city fire engines were called out and sprayed the mob with fire hoses. However, this incident is not mentioned in other accounts; if it took place at all, it was must have been away from the main scenes of the rioting.[160]

Sympathetic Confederate Surgeon Encounters Governor Letcher

During the riot, after Governor Letcher gave his talk to a segment of the mob, which had the effect of dispersing the crowd in the vicinity of Fifteenth and Main Streets, a Confederate surgeon from Florida, Dr. Thomas M. Palmer, refused to depart even though personally confronted by the Governor. Dr. Palmer, described by the *Examiner* as a "middle aged, portly man," told the Governor that "there was a power behind the throne mightier than the throne." When Letcher asked who the power was, Palmer replied, "the people."

Just after this exchange, Mayor Mayo came up, and he also ordered Palmer to disperse. When Palmer still refused, Mayo said, "I hold in my hands the laws of Virginia, and in their name, I order you to depart." At this point some citizens arrested Palmer but then released him. That evening, Palmer was arrested for participating in the riot based on an affidavit of the Governor.   Both Letcher and Mayo later testified against Palmer in mayor's court. They claimed that Palmer used language "calculated to encourage the rioters" and failed to depart the scene when so ordered by the governor. Dr. Palmer had support, however. He had been a member of the Florida secession convention, and his loyalty to the Southern cause was vouched for by the Confederate secretary of the navy and members of congress.[161] Later, upon Palmer's arraignment in Richmond circuit court, his lawyer urged the judge to quash the indictment, which was done after the prosecution entered a *nolle pros*.[162]

The Richmond Bread Riot

Was There Bread At The Bread Riot?

It was noted in Chapter 4 that no credible account had been found of bread taken during the riot. Bread is certainly not mentioned in either the list of recovered goods described in the April 6 *Richmond Examiner* court article or in any of the articles that followed. However, several riot accounts mention bread.

Richmond lore has it that someone threw a loaf of bread at Jefferson Davis while he was addressing the crowd near his office. Actually, such an incident was reported in *The Richmond Dispatch* of January 20, 1889, in an article summarizing the previously published accounts of the riot. According to the article, "an intelligent citizen" who was present "remembers" that during the President's speech, "a woman threw a loaf of bread at Mr. Davis, and Mr. Davis in the quietest manner possible and with signal eloquence used the incident to argue that bread could not possibly be so very scarce here, else it would not be parted with upon such small provocation."[163]

While the story is probably apocryphal (it was not mentioned by Davis in his own account), it had a symbolism that over time could only add to the perception that it was Davis's speech that brought the Bread Riot to a close.

Two sources have been found that mention bread as a subject of the women's plunder. The *New York Herald's* report by a "refugee," mentioned previously, states simply that the women "commenced helping themselves to bread, flour, meat, articles of clothing & c."

A more descriptive and interesting firsthand account that includes bread was published in the *Washington Post* of March 4, 1888. The article is taken from a manuscript of reminiscences by "Aunt Mag Loughborough," a wartime Richmond resident.[164] Her recorded experiences of the Bread Riot include incidents not found in any other eye-witness account. Aunt Mag reports that she was employed in an office of the Confederate treasury department located on Richmond's Broad Street, where she and "a number of ladies were occupied in numbering and signing coupon bonds . . . ." They had heard rumors of "a body of disorderly women and boys . . . assembled on the capitol square clamoring for bread." The next morning, she heard cries

The Richmond Bread Riot

of "Bread, bread, give us bread." "A motley crowd of women and boys" came out of a side street and seemed to be intent on entering her workplace. She was able to enter the building ahead of the mob. The doors were closed and barred against forced entry, which "foiled" the mob's demands to obtain government currency.

The crowd, according to Aunt Mag, then turned its attention to "more accessible plunder." They quickly sacked a milliner's shop and a shoe store. Then came a bakery: "they next proceeded to break in a bakery and appease their famished stomachs by emptying the flour into the streets and trampling the bread beneath their feet."

However, the crowd was soon interrupted by soldiers sent by the governor. Upon arrival the troops fired blank cartridges, which "amused" the mob, "causing a laugh and jeers." The soldiers were able to break up the crowd only by charging them with fixed bayonets.

Aunt Mag Loughborough's reminiscences of the rioting on Broad Street are out of the mainstream of other eye-witness versions. It will be recalled that after the riot had been broken up in the downtown area by the arrival of the public guard, a new disturbance took place on Broad Street. This was where riot instigator and leader Mary Jackson was arrested.

A credible eye-witness description of the Broad Street incident that fits within other accounts was carried in the *Richmond Times-Dispatch* of October 24, 1909. (Appendix E.) This account by Thos. R. Evans, who in 1863 was an eight or nine year old school boy, names a bakery that was located on Broad Street and specifically states that the mob passed it by for an unsuccessful attack on a hardware store. Evans says the soldiers arrested Mary Jackson in this area. However, neither Evans nor any other witness mentions the soldiers firing blank cartridges or that the mob attempted to break into an office of the Confederate Treasury Department and steal currency. The latter incident, without corroboration, seems particularly improbable.

To summarize all the sources, bread may have symbolically inspired the riot, but it was not a serious objective of the woman mob.

APPENDICES

Appendix A: The Public Guard, "Virginia's Standing Army" 93

Appendix B: Minutes of Richmond City Council 95

Appendix C: Richmond Newspaper Articles of 1863-1864 99

Appendix D: City of Richmond Hustings Court Minutes 183

Appendix E: Richmond Newspaper Articles, 1888-1889 & later ... 192

Richmond women pass a Union Soldier on their way to get government rations during the occupation following the War, as sketched by Alfred Rudolph Waud [1828-1891].

Appendix A: The Public Guard, "Virginia's Standing Army"

The public guard, also known as the state guard, had been established by act of assembly in 1801. The light infantry unit's primary mission was to protect state property in Richmond, and it was not considered part of any state militia.

Prior to the Civil War, the guard had been housed in the Virginia state armory located at the south end of Sixth Street near the river. In 1861 the armory was converted to a manufactory and ordnance depot, and the public guard barracks were moved across the canal to a row of brick houses next to Pratt's Castle on Fourth Street at Gamble's Hill. An article in the *Daily Richmond Examiner* of November 7, 1863, described the unit's barracks as "a miserable shanty." They were located nearly three- quarters of a mile from the west gate of the state capitol. Edward Scott Gay (1795-1874) was acting commander of the public guard at the time of the Bread Riot. There is some confusion over his rank at this time, as some accounts refer to him as lieutenant and others as captain. The allotted officers of the unit were a captain and two lieutenants. Charles Dimmock was the regular captain, having served in that capacity since 1844. However, Dimmock had been on detached service as Virginia's colonel of ordnance since 1861. During his absence Lieutenant Gay served as acting commander. Because Gay was acting captain of the guard at the time of the riot, it is appropriate to refer to him by that title. Heber Ker, the other lieutenant of the unit, was also present at the Bread Riot. Years after the war, a Richmond resident wrote that among those participating in the bread riot were wives, sisters and daughters of men in the public guard; for this reason Captain Gay was nervous when he ordered the crowd to disperse. He told the crowd that if they did not leave, he would order the firing of "two balls and a buckshot" at them, whereas the men's weapons were actually loaded with a ball and two buckshot.

The Richmond Bread Riot

Captain Gay was appointed lieutenant in 1841 and promoted to permanent captain following Dimmock's death in October 1863.

America's volunteer militia companies flourished during the 1850s, and the glory of the public guard was at its height during this time. One hundred men strong, it was referred to in those days as Virginia's "standing army." It is said that Richmond boys irreverently referred to the unit as the "blind pigs," derived from the letters, "P.G." worn on members' hats: "And a pig without an eye is a blind pig."

The public guard was abolished in 1869 by Virginia's provisional reconstruction governor. The closest modern equivalent to this unit is the Virginia state capitol police, which today stands watch over the state capitol grounds.[165]

Appendix B: Minutes of Richmond City Council

Thursday April 2, 1863

At a called meeting of the Council of the City of Richmond held on the second day of April 1863.

Present: David J. Saunders, Esquire, President, Messrs. Scott, Crutchfield, Griffin, Epps, Denoon, Stokes, Hill, Richardson, Wynne, Glazebrook, and Burr.

On motion of Mr. Hill, the reading of the proceedings of the last meeting was dispensed with.

The President stated to the Council that he had convened the meeting for the purpose of taking some action in reference to the disgraceful riot which had taken place in the City this day.

Mr. Hill moved that His Excellency the Governor of Virginia and the Mayor of the City be waited on and invited to attend the Council and unite with it in its proceedings on this occasion. The motion being carried, Messrs. Hill and Wynne, who were appointed a committee for that purpose, retired, and soon after returned with the Governor and Mayor, who were introduced to, and took seats with the Council.

Mr. Scott moved that Mr. Richard F. Walker, member elect of the new Council, who was in the room, be invited to a seat with the Council and aid in its deliberations. The motion was carried, and Mr. Walker took a seat with the Council.

Mr. Hill then offered the following preamble and resolutions, to wit:

WHEREAS a disgraceful riot has occurred this day in our favored and quiet City, ostensibly for want of provisions, but in reality instigated by devilish and selfish motives; and

WHEREAS the Council of the City of Richmond have heretofore appropriated liberally for the support of the poor, and the citizens generally have freely contributed to their necessities on all occasions when applied to;

WHEREAS no recent applications have been made by the poor to the Council or to the citizens; Therefore

Resolved: First that the said mob or riot was uncalled for and did not come from those who are really needy, but from base and unworthy women instigated by worthless men who are a disgrace to the City and the community.

Resolved: Second, that the Committee of Police, with the Mayor of the City, be authorized to make all necessary arrangements to suppress all such riots by civil or military power, and that said committee make such regulations as they may deem expedient.

Resolved: Third, that the Council do tender their thanks and gratitude to President Davis, Governor Letcher, Mayor Mayo, and Honorable John B. Baldwin, for their timely and appropriate addresses and exertions during the continuance of this disgraceful affair, and by which the Council believe it was more speedily quieted.

Resolved: Fourth, that the thanks of the Council be presented to Captain [Edward S.] Gay and his officers and men for their timely aid in restoring order.

Resolved: Fifth, that the Mayor be instructed to arrest and bring before the proper tribunal all persons engaged in this mob or riot and all aiders, advisers, or abettors, thereof, so that they may be punished for this heinous offence.

Resolved: Sixth, that the Committee of Police, with the advice of the Mayor, be authorized to increase the police force to one hundred men or more, and that the Mayor be authorized to arm them if he deems it expedient.

Resolved: Seventh, that the honor, dignity, and safety of the City shall be preserved at all hazards, and that no expense shall he spared to obtain the same.

Resolved: Eighth, that the sum of one thousand dollars he placed at the disposal of the Mayor, under the advice and direction of the Committee of Police, to carry out these resolutions.

Present: Mr. Haskins.

Mr. Glazebrook moved that the Governor and Mayor be requested to address the Council upon the subject of the resolutions before the vote be taken upon them. The motion was carried and those gentlemen proceeded, accordingly, to address the Council, both of them approving the resolutions.

Mr. Burr moved that the resolutions be voted on separately. The motion being carried, the resolutions were read, seriatim, and severally adopted: the Thirteenth Rule being suspended before the vote upon the Eighth Resolution was taken.

The preamble was then adopted.

Mr. Burr offered the following which was adopted:

Resolved, That the people of the surrounding country may be assured that all provisions sent by them to this City, if seized by a mob will be paid for by the City, and that every power possessed by the authorities will be exercised to the utmost limit to prevent any repetition of the riot which has broken in upon the hitherto uninterrupted order and quiet of this City.

Mr. Scott offered the following, which was adopted:

Resolved, That the Committee on Police be instructed to enquire into the expediency of reporting an ordinance to require all persons, who have not been residents of the City for twelve months, to give bond and security in such penalty as the committee may think proper, that they will be of good behavior during their residence in the City.

A communication was received from Henry Myers, Superintendent of the City Hospital, announcing the seizure and confiscation by the rioters of today, of 310 pounds of beef purchased by him for the use of the hospital, which on motion of Mr. Glazebrook, was referred to the Committee on Hospitals.

Mr. Wynne offered the following which was adopted:

Resolved, That the Mayor be authorized to offer a reward of fifty dollars a piece for the conviction of any individual who was engaged in the riot which took place today; and that the Auditor is hereby authorized to pay all orders drawn by his honor, in favor of the parties who make the arrests.

Mr. Scott offered the following which was adopted:

Resolved, That the Committee on the City Jail be authorized to secure some suitable place for the confinement of prisoners, should

The Richmond Bread Riot

the City Jail be insufficient for their reception. The Council then adjourned.

– David J. Saunders, President[166]

Appendix C: Richmond Newspaper Articles of 1863-1864

Daily Richmond Examiner:
March 27, 1863
April 3, 4, 6, 7, 8, 9, 11, 13, 16, 20, 21, 23, 24, 27, 28, 29, 1863
May 2, 4, 6, 7, 8, 9, 11, 13, 15, 28, 30, 1863
June 4, 5, 17, 18, 22, 23, 24, 1863
August 18, 1863.October 12, 1863
November 21, 1863
February 11, 1864
March 1, 1864

Richmond Whig:
April 6, 1863

Daily Richmond Enquirer:
October 10, 1863

Richmond Dispatch:
November 14, 16, 1863

The Richmond Bread Riot

DAILY RICHMOND EXAMINER- Friday, March 27, 1863

The "Woman Mob" at Salisbury, North Carolina - A "Raid" on the Speculators - A gentleman very kindly called on us some days ago, and gave us an account of the "woman mob" at Salisbury, of which he was an eye-witness, but for want of room we have not been able to make use of the facts so courteously furnished us. The story is thus told by the Banner, published at Salisbury, where the affair occurred:

Between forty and fifty soldiers' wives, followed by a numerous train of curious female observers, made an attack on several of our business men, last Wednesday, whom they regarded as speculators in the necessaries of life, for the purpose, as we are informed, of demanding an abatement in prices, or forcibly taking possession of the goods they required. The first house visited was Mr. M. Brown's. They demanded he should sell them flour at $19.50 per barrel. This he declined to do, alleging that his flour had cost him more than twice that sum. They then said they were determined to have the flour, and would take it, unless he would sell it to them at the price Government was paying for it, and accordingly went to work with hatchets on his store room door. After some time spent in vain efforts to open the door, a parley was had, and Mr. Brown agreed to give them, free of charge, ten barrels, if that would satisfy them. They accepted the offer, the flour was rolled out and hauled off.

They visited a number of other stores where the same scene ensued, most of the parties pacifying them by some good-humored remark, and by presenting them, in many instances, with supplies free of charge. Finally they visited the North Carolina depot in search of flour supposed to belong to Mr. Weil, and other parties believed to be speculators in this and other provision articles. They found, and took forcible possession of ten barrels flour belonging to some one in Charlotte. This completed the day's work. The next morning was spent in settling the question of division-delicate, and as it proved, a difficult question. There was some disputing, flashing of eyes, and some angry words. It was, however, accomplished, whether satisfactory to all or no, we cannot say.

The affair was aimed as a blow at the speculators, who have run up provisions to famine prices, and instigated, in part, by pinching want. The Banner says:

These proceedings were also caused, in part, by pinching want. It is said there are many families in this town and vicinity who have not tasted meat for weeks, and sometimes months together. Of course they have had no butter, molasses or sugar. Many of them have no gardens and consequently no vegetables of their own raising; and the scarcity and high price of potatoes, peas, beans, &c, render it extremely difficult if at all possible for them to obtain these articles. What, then, have they to support life? Bread and water!

The Banner again justly remarks:

Avaricious hoarders of grain and other provisions for high prices must open their eyes to the danger of their selfish and covetous practices. It is impossible for the poor to endure the hardships and privations these two classes have imposed upon them. They cannot, they will not, and it is the part of wisdom to recognize the truth and provide against the danger which threatens the good order and well being of the country. Speculators must stop their operations or they will ruin themselves and every one else.

DAILY RICHMOND EXAMINER - Friday, April 3, 1863

THE COURTS

MAYOR'S COURT - PRESENT RECORDER [James K.] CASKIE - Thursday, April 2, 1863.

The following named parties, arrested in unlawfully and riotously breaking into the stores of merchants, and feloniously stealing various articles of merchandise, were brought into court by policemen and citizens, and committed to jail for examination to-day: Frank Walliss [also, Wallip, Wohleb], Benjamin Stamper [Slemper], Mary Woodward, Mary Waster [Wasley], Mar. [Mary] Butler, Sarah

Coghill [alias Martha Taliaferro], Martha Burnett [Barnett], Sally [Sarah] Mitchell, Lawrence Martin, Alexander Jenkins [Jennings], Morgan Burns, Henry Cook, Alexander H. Murray and John Jones.

CITY INTELLIGENCE

Aid For The Poor. - We are authorized to state that the Young Men's Christian Association are perfecting arrangements at their Army Depot, Bank Street, to furnish the poor, and especially the wives who have husbands and sons in the field, with all needful supplies of the necessaries of life in such quantities as may be procured by the contributions of the benevolent citizens of the community. Yesterday three barrels of rice, and much meat and bread was distributed to such of the poor who applied.

We learn further that of twenty-five thousand dollars appropriated a year ago, we believe, by the City Council of Richmond, five thousand dollars of the amount remains undistributed. The most liberal movements, we are assured, are on foot to relieve the wants of the really deserving poor of the community, and none need suffer if they but make their wants known.

***DAILY RICHMOND EXAMINER* - Saturday Morning, April 4, 1863**

[Editorial]

The reader will find in the report of evidence in the Police Court, the true account of a so-called riot in the streets of Richmond. A handful of prostitutes, professional thieves, Irish and Yankee hags, gallows-birds from all lands but our own, congregated in Richmond, with a woman huckster at their head, who buys veal at the toll gate for a hundred and sells the same for two hundred and fifty in the morning market, undertook the other day to put into private practice the principles of the Commissary Department. Swearing that they would have goods "at Government prices" they broke open half a dozen shoe stores, hat stores, and tobacco houses, and robbed them

The Richmond Bread Riot

of everything but bread, which was just the thing they wanted least. Under the demagogue's delusion that they might be "poor people," "starving people," and the like, an institution of charity made a distribution of rice and flour to all who would ask for it. Considering the circumstances, it was a vile, cowardly, and pernicious act; but the manner in which it was received exhibits the character of this mob. Miscreants were seen to dash the rice and flour into the muddy street, where the traces still remain, with the remark that "if that was what they were going to give, they might go to h——l." It is greatly to be regretted that this most villainous affair was not punished on the spot. Instead of shooting every wretch engaged at once, the authorities contented themselves with the ordinary arrest, and hence the appearance of the matter in the police report of the morning.

If it were the only thing of this sort which has appeared in Southern cities, it would not be worth attention. But as the reader has already seen from our columns, some two weeks ago there was one in Atlanta, immediately followed by one in Mobile; which was succeeded by another in Saulsbury [Salisbury]; then in Petersburg; and the very next day by this in Richmond. Now if these were unconcerted, tumultuous movements, caused by popular suffering, they would not, could not, have this regular gradation of time from one city to another in the line of travel from South to North. It is impossible to doubt that the concealed instigators in each case were the same. Having done the work in one city, they took the cars to the next. That they are emissaries of the Federal Government, it is equally difficult to doubt. For sometime past the Northern press has teemed with intimations of some wonderful secret machinery which was at work to overthrow the South. This is what they meant. No doubt the next arrival of Northern newspapers will be filled with lies about these thief-saturnalia which will shame MUNCHAUSEN. As three hundred Yankee prisoners went off by flag of truce on yesterday, the whole story, with all the additions which malice and invention can supply, has already got as far as Old Point. No doubt either, that they be will represented as "bread riots!" Bread riots! while this and every other city of the South has always had large appropriations for the poor uncalled for; when labour is so scarce that everything in

The Richmond Bread Riot

human shape that is willing to work can make from two to four dollars in the day; when seamstresses refuse two dollars and a half with board, because the said board does not include tea and butter! Plunder, theft, burglary and robbery, were the motives of these gangs; foreigners and Yankees the organizers of them.

One thing is certain, that if any exhibition of the sort occurs again, it must be put down in such a manner that it will never be repeated. There would never have been but one if the ammagistrates and citizens of the town in which they occurred had done their duty. A most contemptible notion, that such disturbance is a shame, which must be hidden - (as well try to hide the sun!) - led them to coax and wheedle the audacious miscreants engaged in it. That course ensured their recurrence. It always does so. When an individual permits himself to be black-mailed by a scoundrel, he is always bled again and again till he is exhausted; so too, a community which permits itself to be bullied by its criminal population, must expect to find it bolder every day until it rules all. We know that a street rabble, of which a cowardly king was afraid, once got such possession of Paris that it produced an anarchy of blood and horror which lasted two years: lasted till the mob met a Corsican lieutenant who was not afraid of it or aught; when it vanished in a whiff of powdersmoke and never was heard of again. - Times of revolution and war are always fertile in this species of crime, and unless checked properly it becomes exceedingly dangerous to the public cause. There is only one way to check it properly. The opportunity to do so should not be avoided, or approached reluctantly, but eagerly sought and pursued to its very utmost extent of availability.

It is useless to dwell on this truth. For citizens who have arms in their hands and yet permit their money and property to be ravished from them by cowardly burglars and thieves, because they are incited to come in a gang of fifty in broad daylight, instead of by twos or threes at midnight, we have no sympathy. If the officers of the law, with the ample force and power in their hands, have not enough decision and energy to do more than arrest highway robbers and disperse a mob of idlers at their heels, whose presence there deserved immediate death quite as well, no words or arguments can furnish them with the pluck they lack.

THE COURTS

MAYOR'S COURT - April 3d, 1863. - The following named parties were charged with engaging in a riot on Thursday, and encouraging and inciting others to engage in the said riot.

Frank Wallip [Walliss, Wohleb], Benjamin Slemper, Mary Woodward, Mary Waster [Wasley], Mary Butler, Sarah Coghil [Coghill, alias Martha Taliaferro], Martha Burnett, Sally Mitchell, Lawrence Martin, Alexander Jenkins [Jennings], Morgan Burns, Henry Cook, Alexander H. Murray, John Jones, W. [William] J. Lusk, James Hampton, Ann Briggs, Thomas Samani, C. Lannegan, Elizabeth [Kate] Ammons, Lucy Jane Palmeter, John D. [E.] Lowry [Lowery], Margaret Denning, William Farrand, Francis [Sarah] Farrand, John Hopkins, Susan [Frances] Kelly, Mary Jacobs, Martha Fergusson [alias Martha Jamison], Jennett Williams, Mildred Imry [Melinda Emory], Martha Smith, Francis Brown, Anna Bell [Anne Camp?], Andrew J. Hawkins, Peter Blake, Sarah Champion, Mary Jackson, huckster.

The case of William Farrand and wife was first taken up.

Mr. John D. Harvey testified that on Thursday, he saw three boys go into Farrand's house shortly after the riot began; two of the boys had a pot of butter each, and the third boy had six or eight pair of women's shoes; after the riot was over he and Mr. Isaac Walker and officer Perrin went to [Farrand's] house and found the shoes but could not find the butter.

Cross examined by [A. Judson] Crane—There was a riot yesterday. Mrs. Farrand denied that any boys had brought any shoes or butter there, but after the shoes were found she acknowledged the boys had brought the shoes there.

Officer [John D.] Perrin testified that after Mr. Harvey found the shoes he found two other pairs and a quantity of dry goods under Mrs. Farrand's bed; this boy, John Hopkins, was there and had in his possession a new pair of pants and this hat, which has been identified by Mr.[John T.] Hicks as a hat that had been taken from him during the riot.

Mr. Isaac R. Walker corroborated the testimony of the previous witness, and added that he had found a package of money marked "$1,050" in a band box; Mr. Farrand claimed the money; Farrand was drunk; only knew where the shoes and other goods came from from the fact that, on the way to the cage, someone ran out of Mr. Knote's [James Knotts'] and said, "there are the shoes taken from us this morning"; Farrand keeps a grocery, sugar, cakes, &c.; there were nine pair of shoes, some men's, some women's.

Mr. Charles H. Wynne went with Mr. Harvey and others to Farrand's; Mrs. Farrand protested that no goods had been brought there; to Farrand's credit, be it said, he was decidedly drunk; when the shoes were found, Farrand said a Miss Hinchman brought the shoes there; Mrs. F. said a boy had brought the shoes there; just as she said that this boy, John Hopkins, came in, and Mrs. Farrand said, "there is the boy that brought the shoes here"; the boy had a new pair of pants on his arm, which he said he had bought from little Johnny Camp; as the goods of all sorts were about to be removed from the house, a man named Roane, an employee at the Government shops came in and claimed the goods as his; Farrand lives in the last house on Fourteenth street, next to Mayo's bridge.

The prisoners were sent on to the Hustings Court.

The case of Anna Bell was next taken up.

The prisoner was dressed in a handsome suit of mourning, with a long flowing veil.

Mr. Charles H. Wynne testified, that during the riot yesterday, he saw the prisoner, then dressed in colors, with a chicken bonnet, in the act of going into Mr. Ezekiel's store; he accosted her politely, and knowing her requested her to go home, as it was no place for her; she insisted that she would go in, and threatened to blow his brains out if he interfered; her son, it was, who sold the pants to the boy Hopkins.

Mrs. Bell stated that she did not go into the crowd to take anything, but to look after her son, and to keep him from getting into a scrape as he was very bad.

The prisoner was sent on to the Hustings Court.

The case of Thomas Samani [Thomas Samanni, Jr.], William G. Lusk, and James Hampton, charged with aiding in the riot, was called up.

Mr. Charles H. Wynne testified that he saw Thomas Samani aiding a crowd of women to break in the door of Mrs. Minna Sweitzer's [also, Mena Schweitzer] store on Franklin street, below the market, he was the only man engaged in the assault upon that store; just as the door gave way, from the repeated blows of Samani and the women, witness seized Samani by the collar and carried him to Castle Thunder.

Mrs. Sweitzer testified that Samani and a parcel of women broke into her store with hatchets, breaking the door and windows; she lived in the house.

Mr. Jos. Taylor testified that he saw W. J. Lusk get into the window of a store just below Randolph's book store, and pull the women up into the window; after the door of the store was broken open and the crowd rushed in, Colonel [John B.]Baldwin called on the citizens to put down the riot, and [witness] rushed forward with others, and tried to hem the rioters in the store; women rushed out with shoes which we took from them; a number of satchels were also thrown out of the store, which we gathered up and threw back; the prisoner started to come out of the store, and witness exclaimed "here is the ringleader," and seized him; prisoner had a large hickory stick with which he attempted to strike witness; witness was positive that prisoner was the man who aided the women to get into the store.

Mr. C. H. Wynne testified that he assisted Mr. Taylor to arrest the prisoner; he fought so violently that he had to put a pistol to his head and threatened to shoot him; when prisoner found resistance useless, he denied that he had any connection with the riot, and said he was a patient, in very bad health, at the Winder hospital.

Prisoner is a tremendous muscular fellow, who might sit for a picture of health.

Mr. C. H. Wynne testified that he had arrested James Hampton, a youth of fifteen, with a lard firkin full of coffee, which he had stolen from either Pollard & Walker's or Tyler & Son.

The Richmond Bread Riot

The case of Benjamin Slemper, a German belonging to the City Battalion, was called.

Mr. L.[Lafayette] H. Fitzhugh, Sergeant-at-Arms of the Confederate States Senate, testified that he was standing near Knote's [Knott's] shoe store when it was broken into by the mob; the mob was pouring in through the broken windows; witness saw the prisoner and an Irishman get in through the window; witness went into the store and seized the prisoner and the Irishman; after a struggle, the Irishman got away; witness handed prisoner over to another citizen, and went back and arrested another rioter; Slemper stated, in answer to questions, that he was not a regular member of the Battalion, but was serving as a temporary substitute.

All these prisoners were sent on to the Hustings Court.

The case of Mary Jackson, a huckster in the market and the leader of the women's riot was called. The prisoner was a good specimen of a forty-year-old Amazon, with the eye of the Devil.

Mr. John [James] P. Tyler, Clerk of the Second Market testified that he had for some time heard there to was to be a meeting of the women; Mrs. Jackson told him the intention of the women was to go in a body to the provision stores and demand goods at Government prices; they meant to take them; did not advise Mrs. Jackson on the subject; witness on Wednesday night informed the Mayor that there was going to be a meeting of the women; never informed the Mayor that Mrs. Jackson had said the women were going to take goods from merchants or anything of that sort.

Mr. A.[Augustus] A. Hughes testified that he heard Mrs. Jackson tell two women in the market that the goods of merchants were to be taken at Government prices; though he believed it to be a joke, tried to discourage the idea of violence; Mrs. Jackson said it was no joke, and asked me to lend her a pistol; I told her I would; she said she meant to be armed, and that she would be assisted by the military in Richmond; Mrs. Jackson stopped and communicated the plan to some twenty women; had no idea of lending her a pistol; regarded the whole matter as a joke.

Officer [William A.] Griffin testified that the first he heard of this affair was from Mr. Tyler; on the morning of the riot Mrs. Jackson accosted him in the market, and told him "he'd better keep out of the street today; as the women intended to shoot down every man who did not aid the women in taking goods;" advised her to go home and behave herself; Officer [William N.] Kelley [Kelly] came up also and advised her to behave; during the riot saw Mrs. Jackson on the corner of 1st and Broad streets with a bowie knife in her hand; she said in the market that morning that she "would have bread or blood;" when he saw her on Broad street she was in the midst of an excited crowd of women; walked up to her; Mr. [Edwin H.] Chalkley came up at the same time and took her in custody; she had the bowie knife under her shawl with a piece of paper around it.

Officer Kelley heard Mrs. Jackson make the threats about taking the merchant's goods; went to her and told her the people of this town would not stand anything of the sort, and that if she persisted in it she would get into trouble; hoped what he had said would influence her; the next he heard of her she was under arrest; there was present a woman who would prove that Mrs. Jackson had told her that every woman who did not join the riot would be mobbed.

Mr. Robert F. Redford testified that he saw Mrs. Jackson in the market on Thursday morning between eight and nine o'clock, with a bowie knife and a six barrelled pistol; the pistol was not loaded at the time.

The prisoner was sent on the Hustings Court. She is the same party who, two weeks ago bought two veals at the toll gate for one hundred dollars, and offered the same for sale at two hundred and fifty dollars on the same morning.

Recorder Caskie here relieved the Mayor.

Dr. Thomas M. Palmer was charged with unlawfully engaging in an unlawful and riotous assembly, and then and there by his presence and language to encourage and incite the said assembly in the unlawful and riotous conduct and not dispersing when lawfully commanded, and participating in the said riot.

Dr. Palmer was a middle aged, portly man, in blue uniform, and is the surgeon at the Davenport hospital.

Governor [John] Letcher testified when he commanded the mob to disperse, the prisoner remarked to him that "there was a power be-

The Richmond Bread Riot

hind the throne mightier than the throne;" the rest of the crowd dispersed, but the prisoner remained and still refusing to depart; was ordered into custody; when asked what that power was he said, the people.

Mayor [Joseph Carrington] Mayo did not know what had passed between Governor Letcher and Dr. Palmer; when he came up to the corner of 15th and Main, ordered the crowd to disperse; all dispersed except Dr. Palmer, who declined to do so; said "I hold in my hands the laws of Virginia, and in their name, I order you to depart;" he still refused to go and was ordered into custody; he was arrested by citizens; after being arrested he said if he was released he would go, and witness agreed to release him, but on the affidavit of the Governor, made Thursday night, he had issued a warrant for Dr. Palmer's rearrest.

Mr. Andrew Jenkins testified that the Governor went down to the corner of 15th street and ordered the crowd to disperse; the crowd dispersed except the prisoner, who refused to leave, and told the Governor there was a power behind the throne greater than the throne, and that that power was the people; the Governor ordered him into custody; didn't know whether prisoner knew who the Governor was; Governor told prisoner he would be participating in the riot by standing where he was.

Mr. Peyton Johnston corroborated the previous witnesses; when the Governor ordered prisoner into custody and several citizens put their hands on him, then the prisoner made the remark that there was a power behind the throne greater than the throne; I told the prisoner that was the Governor of Virginia, and that (for Mr. Mayo had just come up) was the Mayor of the city. During the riot dwelling houses were broken into.

Mr. Robert S. Pollard testified that during the riot he attempted to close his doors, when they were broken in with hatchets and his goods taken; it was a store, not a dwelling house.

Lewis Lichenstein [Lichtenstein] testified that during the riot his sister's Mrs. Sweitzer's, store and dwelling house was broken into; he saw the mob break in the windows and door with hatchets; Mrs.

The Richmond Bread Riot

Sweitzer and her family lived in that house; a great quantity of goods were taken.

The Steward of the hospital testified that he had heard the conversation between Dr. Palmer and the Governor; there was a large crowd about the corner; the doctor had been on the corner not more than five minutes before the Governor came along; there were two military officers from Florida with the doctor; shortly after the conversation with the Governor the doctor returned to the hospital.

The Recorder said this was a very important question; the law declared that a person present at a riot who refused when called upon either to assist in suppressing it or to depart, was participating in the riot; the question with him was what kind of a riot prisoner was engaged in. As there was doubt on this point he would continue the case to the following day, and in the meantime admit the accused to bail.

The Mayor resumed his seat.

Mary Elizabeth Foy, an Irishwoman, was brought into court on the charge of inciting a riot.

Mr. Julius A. Hobson testified that an hour before he was near the place where the Christian Association were dispensing food to the poor; this woman was in a crowd of women; heard her say the food they gave was not worth coming after; that she intended to go into the stores and take it; that the riot was kept out of the papers to keep the Yankees from knowing it, but that the Yankees should know all about it before night; she also said in a loud voice that if they didn't intend to give her something to eat why didn't they send her to the North; Mr. Sydnor, with the intention of relieving the woman if she was deserving and needy asked her name; she said her name was none of his business; afterwards she said she lived in Cottage row; a young man coming up said he saw her coming out of a store with goods on Thursday.

The woman denied that she had said anything alleged against her; she was poor, &C.

Mayor - There is no reason why there should have been any suffering among the poor of this city; more money has been appropriated than has been applied for. It should be, and is well understood,

The Richmond Bread Riot

that the riot yesterday was not for bread; Boots are not bread, brooms are not bread, men's hats are not bread, and I never heard of anybody eating them. Take your seat.

At this point the remaining cases were continued, and the Mayor adjourned the court.

Mrs. Mary Woodward, a genteel looking woman, asked to be bailed on account of sickness.

Officer [Benjamin M.] Morris and Captain [James B.] Pleasants, testified that they had arrested Mrs. Woodward and Mrs. Wesley [Wasley] with a dray load of flour and bacon, which they had taken during the riot.

In consideration of her sickness the Mayor bailed her in seven hundred dollars, Mrs. Louisa Woodward, her mother in law, who it was proved was well off, becoming her security.

Elizabeth [Kate] Ammons, the suspicion of her being engaged in the riot being slight, was bailed for appearance to—day.

Mrs. Jacobs was bailed because she had a young child at home.

Mrs. Champion applied for bail on the ground that she had three little children. The Mayor bailed her, but told her she had better have been at home with her children on Thursday than roaming about the streets.

Mrs. Taliaferro [alias Sarah Coghill or Coghil], a childless old woman, was admitted to bail on account of her advanced age, the Mayor remarking that she was old enough to know better than to be caught in such a scrape. This woman's husband is making good wages in a Government workshop.

Mrs. Jackson's husband desired to become her bail, alleging that he owned seven thousand dollars worth of real estate. He was declined as bail on account of his relationship.

Alexander Jennings was bailed, it appearing most probable that he had, while aiding in attempting to suppress the riot, been arrested under misapprehension.

A German woman named Barbara Idoll, being *enciente*, was bailed. Her husband owns a house and lot, and she has been making $25 a week as a tent maker.

A number of other women were permitted to go home to their families.

Just as the court adjourned, Mrs. Isabell Hold [Ould] was arrested on the City Hall steps and brought in, and the Mayor resumed his seat.

Officer [Caleb] Crone testified that the prisoner was talking on the Hall steps; she said she approved of the riot.

Dr. Maddux testified that he heard her say she advocated the riot; that she had rather take goods than to beg; that she wished the Yankees would come here and sweep the city.

Mayor — Where are you from?

Mrs. Hold — I am from England.

Mayor - Has your husband got a British protection?

Mrs. Hold - Yes. I did not think I was doing any harm. I was just standing there talking. I did not think I was going to get into any trouble. The prisoner was committed for examination this morning.

NOTE — The Mayor will resume the investigation of the riot cases at nine o'clock this morning. At the same hour Recorder Caskie will hold court in the Sergeant's office, to dispose of the ordinary police cases.

CITY INTELLIGENCE

Charges of Theft. — Margaret [Martha] Mudd was arrested yesterday by officers Pleasants and Ellis, charged with entering and robbing the store and commission house of Messrs. Tyler & Son, Cary street. - Joseph Johnson, Robert W. McKinney and Patrick Henry were arrested, charged with aiding and abetting in the robbery.

The parties were held for the Mayor.

***DAILY RICHMOND EXAMINER* - Monday Morning, April 6, 1863**

THE COURTS
THE RIOTERS

MAYOR'S COURT - April 4, 1863. - The Mayor this morning resumed the investigation of the riot cases, all the ordinary police

The Richmond Bread Riot

cases having been handed over to Recorder Caskie, who held court in the Sergeant's office.

The court room presented an appearance never approached in strangeness, except upon the previous day, when the riot cases were first called. - The male rioters, fifteen or twenty young men of the veriest rowdy class, occupied the prisoner's boxes on each side of the bar. Some of them seemed to regard the affair as a good piece of fun; others, however, evidently took a graver and more sensible view of the matter. The female prisoners, thirty, perhaps, in number, more of whom were clad in furs and silk than calico, were ranged round the court room outside the bar, sitting on barrels of flour, piles of bacon, and piles of dry goods. The goods recaptured from the rioters filled the balance of the space of the room not occupied by policemen and lawyers, a flock of the latter being gathered like vultures by the scent of the prey. It were idle to attempt an enumeration of the various articles of merchandize gathered together. Everything that ever was to be found in a flourishing country store and many things beside were here collected; flour, bacon, sugar, coffee, candles, silk, cloth, brogues, balmorals, cavalry boots, ladies' white satin slippers, children's embroidered dresses, wash tubs, men's shirts, pocket handkerchiefs, bowie knives, stacks of felt hats, clothes pins, unfinished tailors and shoemakers work, etc., etc.

We published yesterday the names of the rioters then in the court room and think it unnecessary to repeat that list. The parties, except those absent on bail, were in court. The following persons were arrested for riotous conduct on Friday: Martha Good [Goode], Sarah Radford, Martha Goode, Martha A. Cardona, Martha Mudd, Margaret McCarthy [Macarty], Joseph Johnson, Robert W. McKinney and Patrick Henry.

We were in error in saying that any of the cases had been sent on to the Hustings Court; the Mayor reserved his decision in all the cases.

In our account of the investigations we shall follow the course of the court. The reader would do well to bear in mind that a great number of the names given by the parties accused are assumed. On the day of the riot the many women disguised their persons and assumed aliases which they retained during the examination.

Robert W. McKinney, of Atkinson's Battalion, was called to the bar.

Officer Crone testified that this man and others were collected in a large crowd near the old market; Colonel French requested them to disperse; this man went off grumbling; a few minutes afterwards encountered him in a crowd of women on Franklin street; heard him say to the women, "G-d-n it, why don't you go to the cage and tear it down, and go into the stores and take what you want, and I'll back you"; took him into custody; prisoner was intoxicated.

The prisoner was ordered to sit down. Prisoner stated that he was so drunk on Thursday that he did not recollect anything that happened.

Alexander Jennings was called up.

L. H. Fitzhugh testified that on the day of the riot, after he had arrested a Dutchman and carried him off and returned to Mr. Knote's [Knott's] store, saw the prisoner standing against the wall, swearing he would kill the first man who came to him; Mr. Knote, his clerk and another gentleman were trying to take him; they said he was one of the leaders; witness arrested the prisoner and took him out into the street; prisoner called on the mob to rescue him; prisoner repeatedly said he had marked witness and would "fix him."

Mary Jackson, the huckster, was recalled. On the previous day it had been proved that she was arrested on Broad Street with a bowie knife under her shawl.

Mr. Joynes [John Beauchamp Jones], clerk of the Secretary of War, testified that on the evening preceding the riot saw Mrs. Jackson near the New Market; had known Jackson from her frequent application at the war office for a discharge for her son; she said there had been a meeting of three hundred women on Oregon hill to organize to demand bread at Government prices and if they did not get it they would take it; she said the Mayor had been informed of the intended movement, and had threatened to break it up, but if he attempted it he would get a ball put through him; as she said the Mayor had been

The Richmond Bread Riot

informed of the movement witness did not think it necessary to communicate what she had said.

Mayor — It may be well for me to state that I had heard nothing of such design on the part of the women.

The Mayor then gave his opinion in the case and remanded Mrs. Jackson to answer for felony before the Hustings Court, refusing bail.

Mrs. [Mary] Johnson, a toothless old woman, with a most determined phis, was called up.

Colonel Bassett French testified — On the morning of the riot was at the Governor's house; this woman came with a mob of women; asked her what she wanted; she said they wanted bread, and bread they would have or die; told her she was not proceeding in the right way to get bread; told her the Governor was at the Capitol and left her; this is certainly the woman.

Robert S. Pollard testified — On Thursday morning a mob of women came to my store; attempted to keep them out; this woman headed the mob; we attempted to shut the door; it was broken open with hatchets and axes; this woman was the first to enter the store; had a scuffle with her at the door; in a moment the store was full; they took three thousand dollars worth of bacon, a large quantity of brooms, shoes, hats, and a large box of soda.

Mr. Salmon deposed — Was standing in Mr. Pollard's door; heard this old woman demand bacon.

This case was continued to Tuesday morning.

Alexander Jennings was recalled for further examination.

Mr. Fitzhugh repeated his testimony; Mr. Knote said Jennings was the man who led the rioters into the house and stood at the window and dealt out papers of needles to the women; Jennings said he had gone in there to disperse the mob; this Mr. Knote's clerk denied; did not see either of the Messrs. Tompkins' there.

Mr. Knote testified that he had put shutters on the doors of the store; the mob demolished the windows; I think I saw Mr. Jennings at the window with the mob, but am not certain; after the mob had somewhat dispersed, I saw him at the lower end of the store; asked him if they were never going to be satisfied; he said he was helping me; I was very much excited, and had been knocked down when the mob burst in and was stunned for a considerable period; recollect asking some one who was in the window to throw out some things to appease the mob, and at the same time I handed that person a box of ten thousand needles; I don't recollect who that person was; a couple of hours after the excitement was over, Jennings came back to the store and made threats; seemed to have a spite against us on account of his arrest; can't remember the words he used.

Mr. James W. Johnson was in the street; saw Jennings in the window throwing the things out; the windows had been demolished and the panel of the door cut through; after the excitement was over Jennings came into the store and said he was hurt; I said you are the man who was throwing the things of the window; Jennings said you are a d——n——d liar; I told him he was a robber and a scoundrel; I did not know that Mr. Knote had told any one to throw things out; I don't know whether Mr. Knote told him to throw them out; after he had been bailed, Jennings came back with Mr. Tompkins, and they pronounced the charge made against him as false.

Mr. Herbert Tompkins deposed — I was standing on a coal cart in front of Knote's store; the mob were trying to break in; Mr. E. B. Spence was trying to keep them out; a member of the City Battalion got Mr. Spence down; I ran to the assistance of Mr. Spence; I am certain the man was a member of the City Battalion; he used to be in the State guard; after Mr. Spence was relieved, went to the window of Knote's store; Mr. Jennings was throwing things out; he called to me, and he and I helped to clear the store of the mob; after Mr. Jennings' arrest, Mr. Knote expressed regret, and acknowledged that he had told him to throw the things out to appease the mob.

Mr. Shephard, an old gentlemen, clerk at Knote's, testified that Jennings was about the first person who entered the store; was engaged putting things out of the window; as I threw things out of the window into the store Jennings handed them over my shoulder to another man in the window, who distributed them to the mob; the man in the window said hand up those blank books; I said for God's sake don't, they can't possibly be of any use; Mr. Knote was in the other window on the other side of door; I did not hear him tell Jennings to throw things out; Jennings was near me; Knote may possibly have given the direction; Jennings was throwing out needles, socks, shoe strings, &c.; when at last I told Jennings to stop; he stopped; after it was all over Mr. Knote said, "Gentlemen, is there no one who will help me to arrest this man," meaning Jennings; a gentleman, who may have been Mr. Fitzhugh, I didn't see his face, seized Jennings and carried him off; there were some few women in the mob, but most of the mob were men; (in answer to the Mayor) they were not in search of bread or provisions; there was nothing eatable in our store.

Mr. Robert Tompkins saw the mob at Knote's store; Mr. Jennings was nearest the door, apparently endeavoring to put the mob back.

Mr. Shephard recalled — After the store was cleared, the cry was raised, "the police has come, its all up," and immediately a shower of goods was thrown back into the store, things that had been stolen from our store and many things stolen from other stores.

The case was continued to Monday, and the accused admitted to bail.

Sarah Coghill, *alias* Martha Taliafero, and Mary Butler, were called up.

Officer Morris testified that he, Captain Pleasants and Mr. [John O.] Hall, arrested the prisoners on Thursday morning coming up Fourteenth street towards Main; they all had articles of merchandize in their hands, bacon, brooms, &C.

Mr. Hall corroborated his testimony.

The prisoners were sent on to answer for a misdemeanor before the Hustings Court at the May term, and bound over to keep the peace.

Mr. Robert F. Barnett, who swore that he owned several houses and lots in the city, went bail for his sister, Mrs. Mary Butler.

Old Mrs. Taliafero [Taliaferro, Coghil, Coghill], being well-to-do in the world, and herself the owner of real estate, found no difficulty in giving bail.

Henry Cook was called. A small boy in the crowd answered "he ain't here; he was bailed out yesterday and said he wan't coming back."

John Jones, *alias* Orvell Jones, was called up. — Prisoner was a pop—eyed, red headed man of forty.

Officer Griffin testified that on the day of the riot he arrested the prisoner on Cary street, near the Columbian Hotel, with twelve hats filled with coffee, some dry goods, bacon, candles and other things wrapped up in a lady's shawl; Mr. Martin Lipscomb first gave information of the man and said he had stolen the goods from Pollard & Walker and was guarding them with a knife.

Lieutenant Adrian Vannerson said he saw the prisoner with the goods; he was standing guard over them with an open knife; saw officers Griffin and Adams arrest him.

Jones stated that he was walking up Cary street when he met Mrs. Enroughty and Mrs. Jordan, from Rockett's old field, and they asked him to take care of the things for a few minutes; while he was guarding them he was arrested.

The case was continued.

George Jones [alias Orvell, Virgil Jones], a man in the uniform of the City Battalion, but not a member of that corps, was called up, but his witnesses not being present, his case was continued till Monday.

W. J. Lusk, whose case was examined on the previous day, was sent on to the Hustings Court. This was the party who busied himself lifting the women into Knote's store, and when arrested pleaded that he was a patient at the Winder hospital and in dreadful health.

Thomas Samani [Samanni] was sent on to the Hustings Court and bail refused. This party distinguished himself by breaking into the widow Sweitzer's. He is the same who has been rendered notorious by his connexion with more than one forgery case. He is a native of Richmond, of wealthy parentage.

Miss Elizabeth C. Ammons was called, but the witnesses not being present, the case was continued till Monday. The accused was handsome and handsomely dressed, furs, fine bonnet and all that.

The Richmond Bread Riot

Eliza Jane Palmeter was called up. The prisoner was a girl of fourteen, who, for two years has been a notorious thief and street walker.

Officer [Walter T.] Bibb testified that he arrested her on Thursday in a wagon loaded with flour, bacon, twelve hats and a number of brogues; when prisoner saw him she jumped off the wagon and ran.

Mr. John T. Hicks testified that on the day of the riot the mob broke into his store and took all he had, boots, shoes and hats; the hats taken from the prisoner were his property.

The prisoner was sent on.

John D. Lowry was called up for examination. Prisoner was a stout man of fifty. He lives on Cary street, near Rahm's foundry, and keeps a house — well, say a cookshop and shoe store, for that it purports to be.

Officer [John D.] Perrin stated that on the day of the riot, understanding that bacon had been carried to Lowry's, went there with Mr. Bibb; Mrs. Lowry said there had been no bacon brought there; Lowry coming in said some bacon had been brought there by the girl Palmeter; found the bacon, two middlings, in a chest upstairs in Lowry's chamber, with women's underclothing over it; no one had yet claimed the bacon.

The case was continued till Monday.

Martha Jamison alias Martha Fergusson, a dweller in Penitentiary bottom, was bailed to appear on Tuesday next.

Frank Wohleb alias Frank Wallip [also, Wallis], a German huckster in the market, and Margaret Macarty, an Irish woman, with a most tremendous brogue, were called up for examination.

Lieutenant [Lewis M.] Carter, of the night watch, testified that on the day of the riot he arrested the prisoners on the corner of Thirteenth and Cary Street; they each had a middling of bacon; the man said the woman was his wife, and that she had given him the meat; the woman offered witness the meat if he would let her go.

Margaret Macarty stated that a man gave her the middling; she did not give Wallip any meat; she never saw him before; she had a husband, whose name was Kennedy.

The Richmond Bread Riot

Wallip stated that a woman he didn't know gave him the meat in the street to carry home; he didn't tell the officer that Mrs. Macarty gave him the meat.

The case was continued.

Sarah W. Champion, from below Rocketts, was called up for examination.

Watchman Hall testified that he arrested the woman on the day of the riot on the corner of Twenty—Fifth and Marshall streets, with three pair of men's shoes, some unfinished shoe makers work and a lot of candles; she said she got them from up town; when asked if she was in the riot, she at first said she was, but when arrested denied it and said the goods were given to her.

At the instance of the prisoner, the case was continued till Tuesday.

Minerva Meredith was called up for examination. The prisoner is full six feet high, rawboned and muscular, and about forty years of age. She was well dressed.

Mr. Henry Myers, steward of the city hospital, testified that on the morning of the riot he had a wagon load of beef for the patients of the hospital; Mrs. Meredith and a crowd of women surrounded the wagon; he told them the beef was for the sick at the hospital; Mrs. Meredith went off up the street, and an Irish woman and a one eyed woman jumped into the wagon, and he jumped out; the women carried the wagon and beef off; hadn't seen the beef since; had known Mrs. Meredith for years.

Mr. G.[George] W. Gretter saw a woman like Mrs. Meredith standing on the corner of Main street and Locust Alley, inciting the women to violence; was not certain Mrs. Meredith was the women, as she had a sister.

Mrs. Meredith — It was me. I was there.

Mr. Adcock testified that during the riot he saw Mrs. Meredith surrounded by a crowd of women, pass down Main street near Knote's shoe store; she was apparently very much excited, and had a pistol uplifted in her hand; she was talking, but I was too far off to hear what she said.

The Richmond Bread Riot

Mr. Orange Bennett said he saw Anne Meredith, sister of the prisoner, on Main street during the riot, and at first thought it was Minerva Meredith; but when he saw the prisoner here he was convinced that the woman he saw was not Minerva Meredith.

Mrs. Meredith — I was the woman that had the pistol.

The case was continued till Tuesday morning.

Mrs. Lane, from Henrico, was called up.

Dr. Maddux testified that he heard this woman and others discussing the riot on the City Hall steps; this woman said she approved of the riot and should have been in it if circumstances had permitted; that she wished they had come upon Broad street and swept every store on it; that the Yankees had been very near here once and they could get here again whenever they choose; she said if she had been in the riot she would have got a calico dress certain; asked if she was in favor of the Yankees; she declined to answer; there were two girls in the Court room who heard all she said.

Miss Harris was called up as a witness but seemed very unwilling to testify. She had heard Mrs. Lane say she would like to have a calico dress, but didn't hear her say anything else.

The other girl was called up but said she had heard nothing at all; she said she would like to have a calico dress herself.

Mrs. Lane denied that she had used any of the language attributed to her; she came to Court as a witness against Mrs. Ould.

Mrs. Isabella Ould, the English woman, was called up. She is the party arrested on the previous day for using incendiary language on the City Hall steps.

The prisoner was dressed in all the hues of the rainbow.

It was fully established by the evidence of several gentlemen that she had publicly expressed her approbation of the riot.

The Mayor, after explaining to Mr. Ould that his British protection did not authorize his wife to incite, by language or otherwise, people to riot and lawlessness, required her to give security in the sum of five hundred dollars to keep the peace and be of good behavior.

At this point, the hour of four o'clock, P.M., having arrived, the Court adjourned.

The Richmond Bread Riot

RICHMOND WHIG - April 6, 1863

The Riot

In deference to the weak suggestion of authorities who are scarcely less afraid to acknowledge a disagreeable truth than the despotism at Washington, the papers of this city forebore to make mention of the riot which occurred on Thursday morning last.

When Fort Donelson fell, the news was kept back from the people for nearly a week, and to repeated inquiries made at the War Office, the answer was given that the Government was in possession of no intelligence. This was to have been expected from the person then at the head of the War Department, but under this new *regime* the people had a right to expect, did expect, courage and common sense. To suppose that in a city containing nearly a hundred thousand people, every tongue and every pen could be checked, in obedience to the request of any human being whatever, and because the newspapers were silent—to believe, for an instant, that the throng of "special correspondents" would pass over the most precious item that has fallen into their nets since the war began—to hope that the courts would close their doors and investigate crime in secret session—to dream that passengers leaving by the cars, farmers going out on horseback, women in buggies and hucksters in chicken carts, would one and all be stricken dumb, or, retaining possession of their speech, would refuse to tell their wives, children, friends, neighbors and gossips the marvellous story of the great "bread" riot—the breaking open of stores—the calling out of the military—the appeals of old citizens—the repeated reading of the riot act by the Mayor—the eloquent harangue of the President in a furniture wagon to a crowd of innocent men, squares away from the scene of female burglarism in broad daylight—to suppose that all this could be suppressed by any agency conceivable, much less the mere silencing of the papers, is, to say the very least of it, the silliest expectation that ever entered the brains of men outside of strait-jackets.

The Richmond Bread Riot

This timidity, or want of common sense, or whatever it may be called, must be regarded as by far the worst part of the business. The riot itself is an nothing compared to it. If the authorities who rule this Confederacy are so pusillanimous as to fear the truth, whatever it may be, or so deficient in intellect as to suppose that such a thing as a female riot could occur in Richmond, at any time of the day or night, and not be known outside of the city limits, then are we just as badly off as if starving. We are not starving, nor are on the verge of it; but the ostrich system of hiding the head behind a leaf whenever danger is near, or thought to be near, does obtain in our councils; and there, and there only, is the only real trouble perceptible in this whole matter.

Happily, these daylight burglaries are undergoing judicial investigation; a great part of the stolen goods has been reclaimed; the ringleaders are being arrested; they will be tried and punished; a full account of the affair, from its obscure origin to its disgraceful culmination, will be made public; and the exaggerations that have gone to the country will be counteracted.

That there was any just ground for the shameful disturbance of Thursday, no one believes. The more it is looked into the more causeless it appears. Doubtless there is much suffering in the city. But the fund voted the poor was by no means exhausted; the churches were willing and abundantly able to relieve distress; private benevolence had not once been appealed to. No petition, no remonstrance had been made; yet, on a sudden, a hundred or a hundred and fifty well-dressed, plump-cheeked women led by a virago, who is known to have made a fortune by market-gardening, and cheered by a rabble of gamblers and ruffians, who are protected here by the special toleration of the Confederate, State and Municipal governments, that misrule this unhappy city— all of a sudden this throng of courtesans and thieves assembles in the Capitol Square, organizes and proceeds to break open stores, to get what forsooth? Not meat and bread, but boots, shoes, silk dresses, tobacco, jewelry, brooms, and the like. These, the Mayor, in his investigation last Friday, suggests permanently[?] are not articles of food. But there is a proof more convincing than any yet given of the absurdity and falsehood of the plea, that

The Richmond Bread Riot

this row was occasioned by suffering for food or clothing, and that is the fact substantiated by every housekeeper in the city, that, notwithstanding high prices and scarcity of provisions, there have been fewer applications for charity than in any previous winter for many years. The entire absence of beggars at a time like this, and in a city so crowded by idlers as Richmond, is very notable. The writer of this article can testify, that during the whole winter he has encountered but two beggars, one of whom, an obvious imposter, wanted to fight because his veracity was doubted, while the other set upon him with the stunning petition for "a quarter to buy a catechism?" The truth is, this petticoated foray was political in its origin; as the simultaneous disturbances in other cities indicates, and as the evidence before the Mayor will yet prove.

If there be a soul of good in things evil, this ridiculous affair may be turned to account. It ought to put a stop to hoarding, to suppress speculation, to induce producers to bring in supplies, to make the government facilitate transportation, and to clean out the gamblers, loafers and ruffians, stock, lock and barrel.—Let Congress at once pass a law requiring every man to show that he is engaged in some honest useful calling or else go into the army forthwith. In this way the five and twenty gambling houses that feed every day nearly as many thousand idlers, and thereby run up the price of provisions, will be swept away. And let our high officials display a little courage and a little reason. The people are not afraid of unpleasant truths, why should they be? Let them not attempt impossibilities. But, the reports in the papers will go to the country and encourage other riots! Better a correct account in print than a thousand exaggerations from as many tongues and private letters. If the riots occur, put them down; it is easily done. But, the Yankees will get hold of it. Certainly! What if they do? Let them make the most of it; they are going to do their worst, any way. Better a thousand fold that the Yankees should ply their lying arts with all the aid the disaffected here can give them, than that the people should see that the government of Jefferson Davis is timorous about any thing on earth. The people are manly; so should their government be, and put a bold calm face on every-

The Richmond Bread Riot

thing. If anything could be "kept back," the fate of Ananias should warn us of the folly of attempting it. Have we gotten so deep in the mire of a sneaking, evasive, alternately truckling and bullying policy, as not to be able to turn around and face Yankees and females combined? Or shall it go to the country that the Confederate government is scared out of its wits because a parcel of women broke open a store and stole a pair of shoes.

The following remarks by a looker on, are very just and true as far as they go;

To the Editor of the Whig:

I happened to be a spectator of a portion of the doings of the mob of "Holy Thursday." I did not witness the organization on Capitol Square, or see the outrages committed in Cary street. When I reached the "scene of action" entrance was just being forced into 117 Main street, which, with the shoe store adjoining, was sacked. Mr. Baldwin addressed the mob, which comprised, perhaps, five thousand males and as many hundred females and in response to his promises, many hundreds of boots and shoes were thrown back. Soon after this, the riot act was read and the military came on. A section of the crowd had, in the meantime, taken possession of the old market, whither the military followed them leisurely.

I think it is all-important to call attention to one or two points connected with this outbreak. The mob, which was got under the name of a woman's bread riot, was in reality, a man's plundering riot. The females, a fraction of whom were respectable, were all comfortably clad, and many of them were bedizened out in finery, which was not wanted to show their trade.—— Those "ladies," as the worthy Mayor addressed them, were of home production as well as of foreign growth. The indications were that they had been stimulated to the part they were acting not by want, but by the thousands of ruffians who stood around them, and who hoped to secure, by means of them, both safety and plunder. Who can describe a mob gathered in Richmond, and of the vilest of the vile dregs which the war has been causing to flow into the city for so many months? The substitute who has sold himself to dozens of regiments, the expelled of the Tigers, the

The Richmond Bread Riot

Plug Ugly of Baltimore, the ignoble army of skulkers, the unclean company of Mississippi wharf-rats, the abhorred fellowship of the deserters, the off-scourings of Penitentiaries, the Yankee emissary, the select villains of many nations, were no doubt all there. Hunger was the ostensible cause of the riot. But neither the butcher nor the baker suffered. Stores containing provisions escaped, while those containing dry goods, boots and shoes, and, above all, fancy articles were sacked. No. 117 Main street, which, while kept by Mr. Rouss, was the cheapest store in the city, was attacked because it was known there were fine goods within. It was not a rising against extortion, but for plunder and open robbery.

Mr. Editor, there is a vast, and, it is feared, an increasing sum of misery arising from destitution now in Richmond. But it is not believed that the mob of "Holy Thursday" represented that misery. It represented rather the vice, the profligacy, the prostitution, the crime of the city, the elements which wage eternal war against society, and against which society must wage eternal war. Elements which, finding the times favorable for an outbreak, and which being no doubt prompted and paid by spies in our midst, took advantage of this opportunity to rob in the day, what they generally steal in darkness. These stimulated, under false pretences, some really respectable people, who, with their children's children, will loathe the memory of this day. And their mischief, has been accomplished. But, I repeat my belief, that this mob did not represent the suffering part of this community. I may mention, in illustration of this, two examples that came under my observation. While the mob was at its full, I saw a man, excellently dressed, fat and stout, pass by your office door. On his head were three hats, a demijohn, apparently full, was over his shoulder, in one hand was a ham, in the other a pair of fine boots. On the outskirts of the mob, trying to get through, I saw, a little later, a poor woman. She wore neither flowers, feathers, crape shawls, nor hoops, like the rioters. Her clothes were thin and so was her face. In her arms she carried a baby, and by her side walked another little one. She told me she had a helpless old mother at home, that her husband's pay of eleven dollars a month was their all, but that she would rather beg in the streets than join the rioters.

The Richmond Bread Riot

DAILY RICHMOND EXAMINER - Tuesday, April 7, 1863

THE COURTS

MAYOR'S COURT - April 6, 1863. - The Rioters. - The Mayor resumed investigation of the riot cases.

John Jones, the pop—eyed, red—headed man of forty, was called up. This is the party that it was proved on the previous day was arrested on riot Thursday, standing guard with a knife over twelve hats full of coffee, in the door of Tinsley & Tardy.— Jones was remanded to answer for felony, and bail was refused.

Alexander Jennings was called up for further examination.

Colonel T. P. August testified that the accused was a member of his regiment, and had been since the beginning of the war; could recollect no impropriety on the part of Jennings; was greatly astonished when he heard that Jennings was engaged in the riot.

Mr. C. W. Purcell deposed — On the day of the riot I saw Jennings in Knotts' store; Mr. Johnson was accusing him of aiding the rioters and throwing things out of the store; Jennings denied or evaded the charge and Mr. Johnson called him a thief; then two gentlemen came up and arrested Jennings.

Mr. Johnson recalled — When I called him a thief Mr. Knotts seized him by the collar, and Mr. Fitzhugh and another gentleman came up, and taking hold of Jennings carried him out, Mr. Knotts going with them; in a moment Mr. Knotts returned and said he had let Jennings go; it is now my impression that Jennings was told by Mr. Knotts to throw things out of the window.

Mr. L. H. Fitzhugh deposed — I helped to arrest Jennings and brought him out into the street; then Jennings called upon the crowd to rescue him, and the crowd rushed upon us; Mr. Knotts let go and ran back into the store and left me alone with Jennings who would have been rescued, but that a stout gentleman, with heavy whiskers, came to my assistance and said, "I have seen the whole of this affair and I'll help you"; I never heard Knotts say any thing about author-

The Richmond Bread Riot

izing Jennings to throw things out to the mob until he said it in court.

Mr. Knotts - I told some one to throw a box of needles, hoping to appease the mob until the officers could come up; I don't recollect who I told

Mayor - I regret that any citizen of Richmond should encourage a riot by throwing out things to the mob. I will say here that it is reported that Maj. Griswold told me that this riot was about to occur, and I take occasion to pronounce the report absolutely false. Mr. Knotts, on your utter failure to recollect anything at all, I shall discharge this young man. Before you have persons arrested in future, you had better be certain of your charges. As Jennings has threatened violence to Mr. Fitzhugh, I shall require him to give security to keep the peace.

Jennings gave the necessary security and was discharged.

George Jones alias Orvell Jones alias Virgil Jones, was called up.

He was in the uniform of the City Battalion, but not a member of that corps. He was discharged from the Battalion three months ago for endeavoring to bribe one of the guards at the Government lithograph establishment to steal Treasury notes.

Captain William L. Maule — On the day of the riot I heard that the prisoner was engaged in the affair; I heard that he was seen entering one of the stores; I went to look for him and arrested him on Main street.

Sergeant Harris, of the City Battalion, deposed. I saw Jones on the street and went down with him into the neighborhood of Pollard & Walker's; there he separated from me; the women made an ineffectual attempt on the door; I was looking on and saw Jones take a hatchet from a woman's hand and attack the door; under his efforts and those of others the door gave way; when I came down street with him he said nothing to indicate that he meditated engaging in the riot.

Corporal John M. Jackson, of the City Battalion, deposed — I met Jones during the riot; he told me he was the first person who entered Pollard & Walker's; that he had been handing bacon out to the ladies.

The Richmond Bread Riot

Another member of the Battalion testified that he saw Jones take a pair of boots from a man in front of Hicks' and give them to a woman.

A young woman testified that while the stores were being broken open Jones was talking to her on the other side of the street; he advised her to go home; he said he was going to take things from men and give them to the women.

Private William Smith testified that he saw Jones take things from the men and give them to women; he said it was bad enough for the women to take the things.

Jones was remanded for felony and bail was refused.

Sarah Farrand, from North Carolina, was sent on to answer for a misdemeanor. This is the party whose husband keeps a family grocery near Mayo's bridge, and where were found nine pair of shoes and other goods stolen during the riot.

Mrs. Mary Woodward was called up. She was a young woman, perhaps of eighteen, pretty and handsomely dressed.

John S. Caskie appeared as counsel for the accused.

Officer Morris deposed — On the day of the riot this lady and another came up Thirteenth street from towards Cary, sitting in a furniture wagon loaded with two barrels of four, a barrel of soap, and eighteen pieces of bacon; the woman with her was Mrs. Wasley.

Mayor — As Mrs. Wasley's case is continued to tomorrow, I will continue this case.

Mr. Caskie — We have a witness we would like heard.

Mr. Burnett, clerk at West & Johnston's, testified that seeing this lady in distress in the crowd on the day of the riot, he assisted her to get into a furniture wagon to get out of the crowd; her hair was disheveled; her bonnet off, and she was evidently in great distress; the wagon had gone but a short distance when I saw it arrested; put her on the wagon in Cary street.

Officer Morris — When I first saw Mrs. Woodward on the wagon it was coming up Thirteenth street, between Main and Cary; I stopped the wagon at Spence's corner and told the women not to get out; this man, Burnett, ran up and helped this woman off the wagon

The Richmond Bread Riot

and started with her down the street; I stopped her; she struck me in the face, and Burnett seemed disposed to interfere, when Mr. Johnston came up.

Officer Kelly — I did not see this woman until she was in this room; I was utterly astonished; I went up to her and said, "Great God, you wan't in that crowd"; she said, "Yes, I was"; I said, "Well, if you were, it was not for the want of anything to eat," for I know her family to be well off; I said to her, "Where's your husband"; she said he was in the country; I said, "Well, you don't suppose he will ever have anything to do with you after this"; she said, "Oh, yes he will — he don't care anything about it."

Mayor — I prefer to continue this case.

The case was continued to the following day.

Barbara Idol, German, red headed and *enciente*, was called up. She was from Rocketts, where her husband owns real estate.

Officer Kelly deposed — On the day of the riot I arrested this woman in the passage over Sinton's hardware store, with a ham of bacon and some other things, which she said had been given to her in the street by another woman.

Mrs. Idol stated that she had been up to the Young Men's Christian Association, where she had got some rice and other things, and was coming down Main street, when a lady gave her a ham.

She was sent on for misdemeanor.

This concluded the riot cases set for the day. The remaining cases will be taken up to—day.

Note — The parties in these cases sent on for felony, will be tried before Judge Lyons; those sent on for misdemeanor will be tried before Judge Meridith, in the Circuit Court of the city of Richmond.

RECORDER'S COURT — April 6, 1863 — The case of Thomas M. Palmer, Surgeon of the Florida Hospital, charged with participating in the riot of last Thursday, was called up, pursuant to continuance.

Messrs. G. W.[George Wythe] Randolph and J. H. Gilmer appeared as counsel for the accused.

Governor Letcher and other witnesses repeated their testimony, given last Friday.

After hearing the evidence and the argument of counsel, the Recorder sent the prisoner on to be tried before the Judge of the Circuit Court of the City of Richmond for being present in Main street during the riot on Thursday last and refusing to depart when lawfully commanded so to do by John Letcher, Governor of Virginia, and Joseph Mayo, Mayor of the city of Richmond. The accused was admitted to bail in the sum of $1,000, to appear before the Circuit Court on the first day of May to answer for the said offence.

DAILY RICHMOND EXAMINER - Wednesday, April 8, 1863

THE COURTS

MAYOR'S COURT - April 6, 1863. - The investigation of the riot cases was continued. Ten men and fifteen women were in custody.

Peter Blake, a young man of twenty, was called up.

Officer Perrin testified - On the day of the riot I arrested two women breaking into Mrs. Sweitzer's; they resisted so violently that I called on a Mr. Levy to assist me; as soon as Levy took hold of the woman this man seized him by the throat; I went to Mr. Levy's assistance and the prisoner ran; I caught him and put him in Castle Thunder.

The accused was remanded to answer for a misdemeanor.

Francis Brown, a tall young man, was called up.

Captain [James B.] Pleasants deposed - On the day of the riot, understanding that some boots had been carried into the "Our House," I went in there; I found this young man putting on a pair of cavalry boots; he had put on the right boot; I took the man in custody; on the way to the cage he told me he had taken them from a man in the street to carry back to Mr. Knotts' store, from which they had been stolen.

Joseph McKinney, of the city battalion, testified he was with Brown on the day of the riot; a man came along with a pair of boots;

The Richmond Bread Riot

Brown took the boots from him and made several ineffectual efforts to carry the boots back to where they belonged; could not get to the store for the crowd; went into Charley Hunt's and asked the bar-keeper to keep the boots; the bar-keeper refused to have anything to do with them; Mr. Brown then said he would put the boots on, and if they fitted him he would wear them back and pay for them; just as he put one boot on the policeman arrested him; Brown is a shoemaker; works on Government work; have known him for years; he has always borne a good character; he was intoxicated on the occasion referred to.

Mayo deposed - Saw Brown with the boots; he said he was going to carry them back where they belonged when the crowd returned.

Brown was sent on for misdemeanor.

Mrs. Mary Jacobs, Jewess, was called up.

The accused is a young woman. Her husband keeps a dry goods store in the house formerly occupied by Thedeorick Robinson. He is the same party who being some time since committed to jail on the charge of receiving stolen blankets, was garroted by the jail birds.

Officer [Edwin H.] Chalkley deposed - On the day of the riot I understood some things had been carried into Mr. Jacobs' store; I tried to get into the store but it was shut; I went round the back way and saw Mrs. Jacobs; I told her that I had heard that some things that had been stolen had been brought into her house; she denied it, but on my finding two bundles of cotton cloth and three shoes in the room in which she was, she said they had been brought in by a woman who worked for her and lived in Rocketts; I asked her to let me go into the store; she said the store was locked and her husband had carried the key off, but that there was nothing in there; I told her I had heard some bacon had been carried in there; she denied it, but still refused to let me go in; I asked Mr. P.[Patrick] H. Butler to go to the Mayor and get authority to break the door open; as soon as Mr. Butler left, Mrs. Jacobs produced the key and let me into the store; there I found a large box containing hats, soldiers' shirts, ladies' white slippers, six pieces of calico, a middling of bacon, some candles, and three large corn brooms, all hid behind the counter; on finding these

I asked her where they came from, she said a woman that she did not know had brought the things in there.

P. H. Butler corroborated the testimony of the previous witness.

Mrs. Jacobs - I was standing at my door, and Mrs. Mildred Emory came and asked me to keep the things for her; I didn't know that there was any bacon in the things.

Mildred Emory being called up, admitted that she had left the things at Mrs. Jacobs' to be taken care of.

The case was continued till Wednesday, and Mrs. Jacobs bailed in the sum of $1000, her husband going her bail. He alleged that he owned "a large store and niggers."

Subsequently the Mayor agreed to re-hear Mrs. Jacobs' case on to-day week, and she was bailed in $3500.

Mrs. Margaret Mudd was called up.

Captain Pleasants testified that he heard that women were breaking into Tyler's store; went up there and found this lady; she was in the back part of the store, talking with a gentleman.

G. W. Gretter deposed - Friday, about eleven o'clock, a crowd of women came down Main street and stopped near H. W. Tyler's store; this woman was in front, with a man dressed in blue uniform; the party advanced towards Tyler's store; I went there and told this young woman, who was in front, to go away - that she could not come in; she advanced to the door; I caught her and pulled her into the store; she got away and ran out, but came back again, and I caught her again; then the young man with her caught hold of me; I threw him off and drew my pistol and told the crowd not to attempt to enter the store; if they did I would shoot the first one, this woman made no effort to take anything in the store.

Mrs. Mudd was discharged.

Mrs. Martha Jamieson [Jamison], of Penitentiary Bottom, was called up.

Officer Kelly deposed - I got information that there were goods in Mrs. Jamieson's house stolen in this raid; I went there and found two barrels of flour and several hams, which had evidently been in the house a considerable time; on a cupboard I found two lots of but-

The Richmond Bread Riot

ter answering the description of butter lost by Tyler & Son; an empty barrel with butter sticking inside of it was found in her back yard; the barrel had the initials on it and the weight, corresponding to the memorandum furnished by Mr. Tyler to the police; Mrs. Jamieson said she was in the riot and that two young men brought the barrel of butter to her house and divided it there; "T.W.S.182" were the marks on the barrel. Lieutenant Carter deposed - On the day of the riot I saw a crowd at Mrs. Jamieson's house, and heard that some of the stolen goods had been carried to her house; I informed Mr. Kelley, and we went together to the house; the balance of my testimony as to what we found in the house is identical with Mr. Kelley's; when I was carrying Mrs. Jamieson to jail she asked me to go by Tyler & Son's; I went there with her; she appealed to Mr. Tyler's clerk, to know if she did not try to prevail on the mob not to destroy his goods; the clerk said she had done so; Mrs. J did not say that she took any part in the riot, but merely that she was in the crowd.

Mr. Kelley - Mrs. Jamieson told me that Mrs. Jackson had told her that if she did not join in the riot that her house would be mobbed.

Mr. S. N. Tyler testified that while his store was being sacked a woman did intercede with the crowd to spare the goods; Mrs. J. may have been that woman; a Mrs. Mays was in the store that day, who has not been arrested; she dropped a ring in the store bearing the initials of her name before she was married.

Sarah Wright and Martha Goode, from Sheep Hill, a locality at the west end of Leigh street, were called up.

Captain Pleasants testified that on the day of the riot he arrested the parties on Thirteenth street, with sundry pieces of bacon in their hands.

The prisoners were sent on to answer for a misdemeanor.

Sarah Champion, from Rocketts' old field, it being proved that she was found in the street with a lot of men's shoes and unfinished shoemaker's work, which she said she got in the riot, was sent on to answer for a misdemeanor.

John D. Lowry, keeper of a cook and shoe shop on Cary street, on whose premises, it had been proved on a previous day, bacon

The Richmond Bread Riot

stolen during the riot had been found, was sent on to answer for felony.

Mary Woodward and Mary Wasley were called up. Woodward is young and pretty; Wasley old and hard featured. These are the two women officer Morris arrested on top of a furniture wagon loaded with bacon, flour, &c.

Officer Morris testified - When I stopped the wagon I arrested Mrs. Woodward; she struck me and drew this pistol on me; then Mrs. Wasley jumped out of the wagon and attempted to escape, but some citizen arrested her; Mrs. Wasley had a hatchet.

An old gentleman named Johnson stated that he saw Mrs. Woodward at Tyler's store, and believing she was not engaged in the riot, asked her to help me to dissuade the women from further violence, and helped her upon a box for that purpose.

Mrs. Wasley - I have no witness at all; Mr. Morris has told the truth; I come from the country; a parcel of men took me and put me on the wagon with Mrs. Woodward; I went up to the Church on Oregon Hill to the meeting on Wednesday night, and was authorized to come up the next day and bring a hatchet.

Mayor — Unfortunately for all of you who were on the wagons on that occasion, they were loaded wagons.

Mrs. Woodward, Sr., Deposed - On the morning of the riot my daughter had on an every day sack and a skirt she had been wearing all the winter; she heard that morning there was to be a woman's meeting on the Square, and went down through curiosity to see what was going on.

Mrs. Woodward was discharged; Mrs. Wasley's case will continue till Friday morning.

Minerva Meredith was sent on for misdemeanor and bailed.

The court adjourned.

We are requested to state that Mrs. Ould, required to give security to keep the peace for using incendiary language on the City Hall steps, was, on a reconsideration of her case by the Mayor, released from bond.

The Richmond Bread Riot

DAILY RICHMOND EXAMINER - **Thursday, April 9, 1863**

THE COURTS

MAYOR'S COURT — PRESENT RECORDER CASKIE - April 8, 1863. - Mrs. Sarah Davis, of Oregon Hill, was charged with receiving a lot of shoes and calico, stolen from some person unknown. Officer Kelley testified that he went to Mrs. Davis' house with a search warrant; he asked her if she had any of the goods stolen during the riot; she said she had some shoes which she had picked up in the street; on search found two pair of new shoes and an odd shoe and a piece of new calico; the calico she said belonged to her sister.

Mrs. Lucy Bernard, sister of the accused, testified that the calico belonged to her, and that she had left it at her house.

Mrs. Davis was sent on to the Hustings Court to answer.

CITY INTELLIGENCE

Receiving Stolen Goods. - Sarah Davis was on Tuesday lodged in the cage by Officer Kelly, on the charge of receiving a lot of shoes and calico, knowing the same to have been stolen.

[The following was submitted to the Examiner by officials of the Belvidere Hill Baptist Church where the women met on April 1 to plan their confrontation of the merchants:]   A CARD

It having been publicly stated that the riotous assemblage of females which last week disturbed our city, was organized at a meeting held in the Belvidere Hill Baptist Church, situated on Oregon Hill and this statement being calculated to injure this church in the estimation of both the religious and order loving portion of the community, the following fair exposition of facts is deemed proper, if not necessary.

The financial resources of the church being limited, a sexton, whose whole time may be employed in attending to the house of worship, cannot be engaged and therefore a brother consents to keep it in order for public worship, while through the day he is obliged to pursue his mechanical avocation. While this brother was away at work, his wife, then sick in bed, was applied to for the key, as had been done on former occasions, when a funeral or marriage service was to be performed, and she knowing nothing of the intended meeting, gave the key to the child who had been sent for it.

The crowd first tried to get the Methodist meeting house on Oregon Hill, to hold the meeting in, and but for the sexton being on the spot, and his determined refusal, the probability is the meeting would have been held there.

So far as known to this church, not one of the members knew of the meeting being held in our meeting house, and nothing, beyond mere rumor, of its being held at all, until after it was in progress, and no interference then could have availed for the dispersion of the crowd. This must be obvious to all who consider how little the resistance offered by those who had not only houses, but their valuable contents to defend, effected.

Presented, on behalf of the church, by order passed at a called church meeting held April 5th, 1863.

J.F. Cottrell, Clerk, *pro tem.* W. H. Fonderden [William H. Fonerden], Pastor

DAILY RICHMOND EXAMINER - Saturday, April 11, 1863

THE COURTS

MAYOR'S COURT - Friday, April 10, 1863. - Mrs. Martha Marshall, from Oregon Hill, was charged with being engaged in the riot of the 2d instant.

William Mitchell testified that he went with officers Kelly and Williams to the house of Mrs. Marshall's husband, a shoemaker on Oregon Hill; asked him if any stolen goods had been brought there; Marshall said there had not; on search, found a shoulder of bacon, a lot of butter, two hats, and a lot of candles; whilst he was searching the house, Mrs. Marshall ran out and hid herself in an outhouse; when drawn from her concealment, she said the articles found were her share of the riot booty; that a wagon load of things had been sent over to Oregon Hill and divided, and that the goods found were her share of the booty.

Mrs. Marshall was sent on to answer for a misdemeanor before Judge Meredith.

Mrs. Elizabeth Goode, from Rocketts, was charged with being engaged in the riot of the 2d.

Watchman Vaiden testified that he arrested Mrs. Goode on the day of the riot with a lot of men's socks, which she said had been given to her.

Mrs. Goode - I was in the crowd on Main street, near Mr. Knote's store; the Jew store next door was broken into; the Jew was giving the ladies things; I had a calico dress in my hand, and some one snatched it away; the Jew then gave me the socks.

I. Marcuse, merchant, deposed - My store is next below Knote's; it was broken open on the day of the riot and one side entirely stripped; I gave the women some things in the hope of appeasing them; I think I recollect this woman's going off with a lot of men's socks; these socks are some of our goods.

John Jones, from Rocketts, the red-headed, pop-eyed rioter, was called up. His case had been reconsidered to allow him to introduce as witnesses Mrs. Enroughty and Mrs. Jordan.

The prisoner, it will be recollected, was arrested on the day of the riot whilst standing guard over twelve hats full of coffee and other plunder.

Mrs. Anne Enroughty, from Rocketts, testified that on the day of the "furse," she and Mrs. Jordan were going up Cary street, and saw Jones standing guarding a lot of things; being very warm, she asked him to take care of her shawl until she came back; she never took anything at all; she came up to return work to Weisiger's, and only looked on at the riot.

Mrs. Jordan, also from Rocketts, corroborated the previous witness' testimony.

Mrs. Elizabeth Goode, the accused in the preceding case, was called as a witness for the Commonwealth, and deposed - I know

The Richmond Bread Riot

Mrs. Enroughty well; have known her all my life; on the day of the riot saw her coming up Twelfth street with her lap full of things; a roll of plain merino or some other goods was sticking out; I heard she made two turns home; carried her first load home and came back for more.

Mrs. Enroughty - My God, you didn't see me at all that day; I never did know you at all. I heard that you carried a whole lot of goods home yourself.

Mrs. Goode, Enroughty and Jordan were sent on for misdemeanor; Jones was sent on for felony.

Note. - Miss Elizabeth Ammons requests us to say that her name was used (in place of her own) by Miss Kate Ammons, at the trial of the rioters.

DAILY RICHMOND EXAMINER - Monday, April 13, 1863

THE COURTS

MAYOR'S COURT - PRESENT RECORDER CASKIE. - April 11, 1863. - Mrs. Sarah Champion, one of the rioters, was called to the bar.

The prisoner was a good-looking woman of thirty-five and lives in Rocketts. She is the party who was found on the day of the raid with a lot of men's shoes and unfinished shoemaker's work, which she told the officer who arrested her that she had taken from a shoe store on Main street. When arrested she was with a number of other women and seemed to be hunting for more plunder. The unfinished shoemaker's work belonged to James Knott, whose store was broken into and sacked on the day of the riot.

Mrs. Champion was sent on for felony.

Mrs. Frances Kelly, rioter, was called up. She was a tall, well-dressed woman of forty.

Mr. Fleming Griffin testified - On the day of the riot, whilst the disturbance was at its height, saw Mrs. Kelly come out of Pollard & Walker's with a large ham of bacon in her hand; had known the prisoner many years, and could not be mistaken in her identity.

The Richmond Bread Riot

Mrs. Frances Smith saw Mrs. Kelly in the riot, with a hatchet in her hand; did not see her with any goods.

Officer Griffin testified that he saw Mrs. Kelly in the market on the morning of the riot, running around in a very excited manner, apparently getting the crowd together; she and Mrs. Jackson were together; saw her, later in the day, go into the Capitol Square with the crowd of women.

The prisoner, the goods being valued at over $20, was remanded to the Circuit Court to answer for misdemeanor.

This concludes the examination of the riot cases. All the parties arrested have been discharged or sent on for trial before the higher courts. From the beginning of the examination a glaring incongruity forced itself upon the attention of the reporter - the large amount of means at the command of the parties charged with being engaged in a "bread riot." All, with a solitary exception, whose cases admitted of it, have been able to give bail; all, with the aforesaid exception, have had counsel, employed at enormous fees; and many of them have retained their counsel at a fee of five hundred dollars to appear for them before the higher courts. Several of the women deposited from three to five hundred dollars in the hands of parties to induce them to go their bail.

LATEST FROM THE NORTH:

FREDERICKSBURG, April 12th, 1863. - New York journals to the 9th instant are received. The following is a summary of the principal features of the news:

THE YANKEE ACCOUNT OF BREAD RIOTS IN RICHMOND

Information of the riot in Richmond has reached the North, as the Examiner predicted would be the case, through the return of prisoners. The following is a *verbatim et literatim* copy of the *Herald's* dispatch, headings and all:

IMPORTANT NEWS - SERIOUS BREAD RIOT IN RICHMOND - THREE THOUSAND WOMEN ATTACK THE GOVERNMENT AND PRIVATE STORES - THE MILITIA ORDERED

The Richmond Bread Riot

OUT BUT FAIL TO RESTORE ORDER - JEFF. DAVIS AND OTHER HIGH OFFICIALS SPEAK TO THE WOMEN AND RESTORE PEACE.

BALTIMORE, April 7th, 1863. - Colonel Stewart, of the 2nd Indiana regiment, one of the fourteen United States officers just released by the rebels, who has arrived here, makes the following statement:

On Thursday last he saw from his prison window in Richmond a great bread riot, composed of about three thousand women, who were armed with clubs, stones and guns.

They broke open the Government and private stores and took bread, clothing, and whatever else they wanted. The militia were ordered out to check the riot, but failed to do so.

Jeff. Davis and other high officials made speeches to the infuriated women and told them they should have whatever they needed.

They then became calm and order was once more restored.

All the released Union officers confirmed this statement.

The Herald has no editorial remark on the object, excepting a paragraph in the "situation" article, as follows:

"The bread riot which took place in Richmond on Thursday is very significant of the condition to which rebellion is reduced. If the people of that city are compelled to break open the public stores to obtain bread, what must be the state of the inhabitants of those districts which produce but little food, and raise mainly cotton and tobacco. Virginia is the most fruitful grain-raising State in the South, and is to the eastern portion of it, what Tennessee and Kentucky are to the west, and if the want of food manifests itself in such a demonstrative fashion as to bring out a hungry mob of three thousand women into the streets of the Capital, we can readily imagine how dire must be the distress of the other States."

[The following editorial carried by the *Examiner* on April 13, 1863, responded to the riot news carried in the *New York Herald*:]

The reader will perceive in the summary of intelligence from the United States that the story of that *chauferie* of the criminal popula-

The Richmond Bread Riot

tion in this city, commonly known as the riot, was carried North by the paroled prisoners who went off next day, with every exaggeration and addition which their malice and invention could suggest. This fact is of no real consequence, however disagreeable it may be to those weak persons who are rendered unhappy by "what people will say!" It is of little importance what enemies say to our disadvantage so long as it is a falsehood. We know the truth ourselves, and the country is able to abide it.

At the same time it is impossible not to entertain a sentiment of fresh indignation against the wretches, who have taken advantage of their country's embarrassed situation to bring this scandal upon it. - They are now in the hands of the law. It would be improper to prejudge the evidence. But while we shall carefully refrain from doing so, it is perfectly legitimate to express the hope, if the evidence supports the accusation on which they are imprisoned, that the heaviest penalties of the law will be enforced without distinction, and without false mercy, on everyone of them.

Those who have examined the sketches of these examinations before the Mayor will have seen that so far from being in starvation, the males and females engaged in this villainy were rioters because of their riotous living; children of Belial, "flown with insolence and wine"; that many of them were not only above want, but possessed of ample means to engage, by large fees, the carrion crows of the bar to claw them from the clutch of justice. Indeed, some of the accused have been able to produce certificates of high character, &c., elsewhere. Let us hope that the judges and juries by whom they must be tried will fix their eyes only on the law and the testimony to their acts on the streets of Richmond on the day of its disturbance. What the courts have to decide is the credibility of the witnesses, the nature of the acts which they witnessed, and the penalty, if any, affixed by the law of the land to those acts.

If they have been guilty of the crimes, their punishment must follow, or this community and the whole country will suffer for the crime of their impunity. Their offense is new in the Southern States, and could not have been committed here at all but for the general

The Richmond Bread Riot

disorder attendant on a war. Hence the community is not yet fully certain as to the proper means of dealing with it. But it is a common crime in other countries; and experience has proven that there are but two ways of repressing it. One is, to seize the first opportunity to punish the criminals in the act, by an unhesitating application of the public force. The other is to arrest the perpetrators and bring them to justice in all its severity, without the least indulgence or distinction, so that the example may deter others. In Richmond the first method was not chosen. But the second means of repression is still within reach. It is highly important to the public safety that it should be sternly employed.

RICHMOND DAILY EXAMINER - Thursday, April 16, 1863

THE COURTS

HUSTINGS COURT - PRESENT RECORDER CASKIE AND ALDERMEN - April 15th, 1863. - Mrs. Mary Jackson, Thomas Samani and Benjamin Slemper, rioters, were severally examined for their participation in the unlawful proceedings of the 2d instant, and the court having heard the evidence in their cases, sent the parties on for trial before Judge Lyons.

Mrs. Jackson is the reputed prime mover and chief instigator of the riot; Slemper, who is a German, was prominent in the assault upon Knotts' store, and Samani distinguished himself by his successful efforts to break into the shop of the widow Sweitzer. When these cases come up for trial before Judge Lyons a correct report will be made of the evidence.

MAYOR'S COURT - April 15, 1863. -

Melinda Emory, Martha Smith, Jennett Williams and Mary Jacobs, a Jewess, were charged with being engaged in the riot of the 2d of April.

Mr. Gustavus Myers appeared as counsel.

Mrs. Jacobs' husband keeps a large dry goods store on Main street. He is the party who was garroted and robbed sometime since in the city jail, where he had been put on the charge of receiving stolen blankets.

The Richmond Bread Riot

Officer Kelly testified that on the day of the riot was informed that stolen goods had been carried into Jacobs'; the store was locked up; went round the back way and saw Mrs. Jacobs; she said nothing had been brought there, and that the keys had been carried off by Mr. Jacobs; she afterwards produced the key and opened the store; found in the store a middling of bacon, half-dozen soldiers shirts, six or eight pairs of shoes, some candles and other things, all in a dry goods box at the rear end of the store; Mrs. Jacobs said the things had been brought there by a woman that she did not know.

David, Jacobs' clerk, testified that the three women, Emory, Smith, and Williams had brought the things into the store about nine o'clock; they were in the habit of leaving their things there; didn't know what it was they brought in; was busy waiting on two customers at one time; Mr. Jacobs was out; when informed of the riot, Mr. Jacobs shut up the store and went away.

Mary Jacobs was sent on to answer before Judge Meredith for misdemeanor, and was bound over in the sum of five hundred dollars to keep the peace for twelve months. Mrs. Smith was discharged; Mrs. Williams and Mrs. Emory were sent on to Judge Meredith.

Miss Laura Gordon was charged with being engaged in the riot of the 2d April. The accused was young and neatly dressed.

Lawrence Martin, a boy about 12 years of age, was sworn as a witness, and deposed. - On the day of the riot I was on Cary street, near the Columbian; the mob had broke into Pollard & Walker's; I saw Miss Gordon in the riot; she gave me a shoulder of bacon and asked me to carry it up to her house on Oregon Hill; I started with it, and when I got by the Dispatch office Mr. Caskie told Mr. George Wilde to arrest me and carry me to the City Hall. Mr. Wilde carried me to the City Hall, and I was put into jail where I remained for thirteen days; I didn't know exactly where Miss Gordon's house was, but knew she lived in Oregon Hill, and knew I could find it; I knew Miss Gordon; I knew her when she used to live in Sidney.

Mr. Wilde testified that on the day of the riot, in obedience to the order of Recorder Caskie, he had arrested Lawrence Martin; Martin had two pieces of bacon, one of which he said had been given him by a lady, and the other he had taken on the invitation of an old gray headed gentleman, who was standing on a barrel addressing the rioters and encouraging them; the boy said he was an orphan and gave witness to understand that he had eaten little or nothing for four years; he said the lady who gave him the bacon to carry was so heavily loaded with brooms and other plunder that she could not carry it herself.

Dr. [Erasmus] Powell was sworn - Saw Miss Gordon about 8 o'clock on the day of the riot; she said she was going on the square to see the fun; about 12 o'clock saw her about the Spotswood Hotel, going up Main street; she had no plunder that could be seen; it may have been eleven o'clock when I saw her last; have known Miss Gordon about eleven months; never heard anything against her; have been attending her sister-in-law; on the day of the riot she had that hat or flat on; don't know how she was dressed otherwise.

Mr. Sweeney sworn - Known the family ten years; all very respectable people.

Mr. August sworn - Knew nothing about the young lady; knew her father, who was a man of high character.

At this point the case was adjourned.

THE DAILY RICHMOND EXAMINER - Monday, April 20, 1863

THE COURTS

MAYOR'S COURT - April 18, 1863. - Mrs. Margaret A. Pomfrey, of New Kent, was charged with being engaged in the riot of the 2d April, and stealing bacon from Messrs. Pollard & Walker.

Mrs. P. had been brought from New Kent by a policeman sent after her by the Mayor.

Mr. Robert S. Pollard sworn, deposed - On the morning of the riot, whilst the women were robbing my store, I recognized Mrs. Pomfrey, and asked her, "is it possible, Mrs. Pomfrey that you are robbing me too;" she had some bacon and carried it off.

Mrs. Pomfrey - I was passing by Mr. Pollard's and was shoved in by the crowd.

The Richmond Bread Riot

Mayor - The crowd did not shove you out of Rocketts. Hasn't she been living in Rocketts?

Mr. Green - Yes, sir. She lived in Port Mayo.

Mrs. Pomfrey - I heard they were going to distribute some provisions to the ladies, that's why I came up to town that morning.

Mayor - Nothing more clearly proves the character of that "bread riot" than that you, owning a farm and negroes in the county of New Kent, should be engaged in it. You will have to give bail to appear to answer for misdemeanor before Judge Meredith.

DAILY RICHMOND EXAMINER Tuesday, April 21, 1863

THE COURTS
HUSTINGS COURT - JUDGE LYONS - April 20, 1863

Mary Jackson, the huckster and reputed arch instigator of the women's riot of the 2d of April, sued out a *habeas corpus*, asking to be admitted to bail. She alleges in her petition that she is illegally detained in jail, being entirely innocent of the charges against her. Her application will be heard on Thursday next.

DAILY RICHMOND EXAMINER - Thursday, April 23, 1863

STORY OF A RICHMOND "REFUGEE" - HIS VERSION OF THE BREAD RIOT - WHAT HE SAYS OF MILITARY AFFAIRS, &C.

The *New York Herald* publishes the following as "the statement of a refugee from Richmond."

"Considerable excitement had prevailed in Richmond for some time in consequence of the exorbitant prices and rumours of a popular movement had been in circulation for several days. Females had begged in the streets and at the stores until begging did no good, and many had been driven to robbery to sustain life. On the morning of the 2d incident, a large meeting, composed principally of the wives and daughters of the working classes, was held in the African church,

The Richmond Bread Riot

and a committee appointed to wait upon the Governor to request that articles of food should be sold at Government prices. After the passage of sundry resolutions the meeting adjourned, and the committee proceeded to wait upon Governor Letcher. That functionary declined to take any steps in the matter, and upon urging the case the ladies were peremptorily ordered to withdraw. The result of the interview was soon made public, when a body of females, numbering about three hundred, collected together and commenced helping themselves to bread, flour, meat, articles of clothing, &c. The entire city was at once thrown into consternation. The stores were closed, the windows barred, doors bolted, and every precaution taken against forcible entries; but hatchets and axes in the hands of women rendered desperate by hunger made quick work, and building after building was rapidly broken open. The destruction commenced on Cary Street, above Fifteenth street, and was becoming general in that section of the city, when the City Guard, with fixed bayonets, arrived at the scene of operations. A few individuals attempted to resist the women, but without success. One man who struck a female was wounded in the shoulder by a shot from a revolver, and the threatening attitude of those armed with hatchets, &c. intimidated others from attempting force. The Mayor soon appeared, and, mounting a stool on the sidewalk, proceeded to read the Riot Act. During the reading of that document a portion of the crowd suspended operations, but no sooner had the Mayor concluded than the seizure of provisions commenced again more vigorously than before. At this juncture an attempt was made to arrest the more violent; but the party immediately scattered, and, entering Main street, resumed operations. Governor Letcher then appeared, and, mounting a vehicle in the centre of the street, addressed the throng, characterizing the demonstration as a disgrace and a stigma upon the city, and announcing that but five minutes would be given them in which to disperse. If in that time the order was not complied with, the troops would be called upon to act. Again the crowd broke up, and in a few minutes burst into the stores on Franklin street. But little damage was done here, however, and the riot finally subsided, but not until after the arrest of about forty of the women and the promise of the Governor to relieve the wants of the destitute. A large amount of bread and bacon was carried off, and all engaged in the riot succeeded in getting a good supply of provisions. Steps have been taken to provide for the immediate wants of some of the families; but great suffering still prevails and is daily increasing. Another uprising is feared, and precautionary measures for its suppression have been instituted; but great uneasiness is felt throughout the city, and merchants are adding to the strength of doors and shutters in every possible manner. The effect of this riot upon the troops about Richmond was very demoralizing.

The authorities are much exercised over it, and the greatest vigilance is enjoined upon the police force. The leading men of the city attempted to circulate the report that the women were "Irish and Yankee hags," endeavoring to mislead the public concerning the amount of loyal sentiment in the city, but miserably failed. The fact of their destitution and respectability was too palpable, and the authorities are forced to admit the conclusion that starvation alone incited the movement."

DAILY RICHMOND EXAMINER - Friday, April 24, 1863

THE COURTS

HUSTING'S COURT - JUDGE LYONS - April 23. - This court heard the application for bail of Mrs. Mary Jackson, the huckster and alleged instigator of the women's riot, of the 2d April, 1863, who was then in custody of the jailor of the city, on the charge of inciting and participating in said riot.

Mr. E.[Eaton] Nance appeared as counsel for the accused.

The prisoner is an athletic woman of forty, with straight, strong features, and a vixenish eye. She was dressed in a silk dress, plaid shawl, nun's bonnet, with a long cape and black kid gloves.

As we have very recently published in full the Commonwealth's evidence in this case as elicited during the examination before the Mayor, more than a brief statement of the facts is upon this occasion unnecessary.

The Richmond Bread Riot

For ten days previous to the riot, Mrs. Jackson had been telling people in the market that there was to be a meeting of the women in relation to the high prices. At an early hour on the day of the riot Mrs. Jackson told several persons that the women were going to demand goods from the merchants at Government prices, and if their demands were not acceded to they intended to take them forcibly. At the time of uttering that threat she had in her hand a six barreled pistol and a bowie knife. She told officer Griffin that the women intended to have bread or blood, and that they were prepared and determined to shoot down every man who attempted to frustrate their plans. Mrs. Jackson was not known to have stolen anything during the riot, but was arrested, while the lawless proceedings were at their height, on the corner of First and Broad streets, in a crowd of excited women, with a bowie knife in her hand. The crowd in which she was found had just before broken into a store on Broad street, below Fourth.

Mr. Redford, huckster, was introduced as a witness for the accused. Had known Mrs. Jackson seven years; she sold in the market next to his stall; she lived on a small farm beyond the new fairgrounds; the road to her house was dangerous; many robberies had been committed on it; she sometimes brought bacon to market, and had a knife to cut it; on the morning of the riot she brought nothing to market to sell; she left the market about eight o'clock; saw her next about eleven o'clock on Franklin street, near the Custom House; she was in a crowd of women; the riot was then over; did not see any knife in her hand then; asked her where she was going; there was such an uproar that I couldn't hear her reply.

Mr. Jacob L. Woodson sworn - Saw prisoner on the morning of the riot, just as the women were starting down from the Square; the crowd of women were two hundred yards ahead of her; I said to her, "I thought Jackson always led his army, and your army's ahead of you;" she said she "was sick of the business - had enough of it;" she was following along after the crowd; this was between nine and eleven o'clock.

Mrs. Jamieson, a tall, swarthy looking woman, was sworn for the defence. - I was present at the meeting on Oregon Hill; all were

The Richmond Bread Riot

women there except two boys; the object of the meeting was to organize to demand goods of the merchants at Government prices, and if they were not given, the stores were to be broken open and goods taken by force; Mrs. Jackson addressed the women; she said she didn't want the women to go along the street like a parcel of heathens, but to go quietly to the stores and demand goods at Government prices, and, if the merchants did not grant their demands, they were to break into the stores and take the goods; she went up in the pulpit and said this; the meeting was held in the Baptist Church on Oregon Hill; pretty near every one in there was talking at once; she further said that they were to meet the next morning at nine o' clock, and to be sure and leave their children at home; she said they were not to break open the doors until they had first demanded goods at Government prices and given the merchants time to consider.

Cross-examined by Mr. Nance - If you wouldn't bother me, I would tell the whole thing; I never could tell anything, beginning in the middle; I was washing in my yard, and Mrs. Jackson came by and told me that the women were going to hold a meeting to arrange about demanding goods from the merchants at Government prices; she said there were three hundred women engaged in it who worked at Weisiger's (Government clothing establishment), and that she had sent word to all the women in Hanover that they must come to town and participate in the proceedings; she asked me if I would not engage in it; I told her I did not know whether I would or not; she said that all the women who did not engage in the movement were to be mobbed; I told her I was not afraid of any one women, nor two neither, mobbing me, but that I might go; on the day before the riot, some women from the country came by my house and asked if that was Oregon Hill; I told them no, that that was Penitentiary Bottom; they then asked me if I could tell them where they could find Mrs. Jackson; that she had appointed to meet them on Oregon Bill; after that I saw a great number of women all going over to Oregon Hill, and I got my bonnet and went over; Mrs. Jackson went up into the pulpit, and said what I have stated; but all the women talked at once, and all said just as much as she did; I was in the crowd on the Capitol Square; it was at my instance that the crowd went to the Governor;

The Richmond Bread Riot

the women wanted to go straight to the stores, but I told them it would never do to go to breaking into the stores without letting somebody know what we were doing; I went to the Governor's house; he wasn't there and we went over to the Capitol; I went up stairs to see him; I don't know how many pair of stairs I went up; I didn't count them; but they were a great many; I was so confused I hardly knew what I was about; the Governor was not in his office; when I came down the Governor was making a speech; I don't know what he said, but heard him say something about dispersing the women with the bayonet if they did not go home; I don't know whether Mrs. Jackson was on the Square or not; she might have been there; there was such a crowd and hubbub, and I was so confused, that I didn't recognize anybody; when I got down on Cary street a store was broken open, and the women were coming out with great turns of meat, brooms, and hats; Mr. Mayo was standing in a buggy, reading his book; he told the women to go home, and I went as straight home as I could ride to the gallows in an omnibus if I was going to be hung; I wish to God that Mrs. Jackson and all the rest of them had been at the bottom of Jeames [James] river, before I ever had anything to do with them.

A woman, who lives near the Market, testified - Early on the morning of the riot Mrs. Jackson came to my house; she came up stairs into my room, and said she was going downtown, but had left a knife down in my dining room, which she would call for when she came back; I did not see the knife; about twelve o'clock I saw her at my house; she said she had come for her knife; still I did not see the knife; she told me how the women had been carrying on downtown and reprobated the whole proceedings.

At this point, in the absence of material witnesses, the further hearing of the case was postponed till Saturday, and the prisoner remanded to jail.

The Richmond Bread Riot

DAILY RICHMOND EXAMINER - **Monday, April 27, 1863**

THE COURTS

HUSTINGS COURT - JUDGE LYONS - Saturday, April 25, 1863. -Pursuant to continuance the Court resumed consideration of the application for bail of Mrs. Mary Jackson, rioter. It will be recollected that this woman who was confined in jail awaiting a trial for felony, for instigating the riot of the second of April and participating in the same, alleged, in her petition for a *habeas corpus*, that she being innocent of the offences charged against her, was illegally detained in jail, and prayed that the Judge would hear the evidence in her cause and allow her the privilege of bail, if the suspicion of her guilt should appear light. On Thursday the case was partially heard, and in the absence of a witness deemed material, continued until this day.

Mr. Leonard Chamberlayne, the witness aforesaid, appeared and was examined. He had heard Mrs. Jackson speak of the intended outbreak; had heard her exhort various women in the market house to join in the combination for the riot; when he attempted to dissuade the women from the scheme, Mrs. Jackson demanded of him, in a very threatening manner, "what he had to do with it;" he told her he had nothing to do with it, and she said "it was very well for him;" on the morning of the riot he saw Mrs. Jackson collect together the women about the market house and start down town with them.

The Judge, the evidence being concluded, refused to bail the prisoner, not thinking the suspicion of her guilt light, and not believing that her health would be endangered by confinement.

The Richmond Bread Riot

DAILY RICHMOND EXAMINER - Tuesday, April 28, 1863

THE COURTS

MAYOR'S COURT - Monday, April 27, 1863. - William J. Lusk, one of the rioters of the second of April, having been on a former occasion unanimously sent on to Judge Lyons' Court was reexamined.

Mr. Alexander Taylor testified that on the day of the riot he saw Lusk get into the smashed in window of Knotts' shoe store, and help a number of the female rioters into the store; witness arrested Lusk, when he resisted violently, and only ceased to fight when he found further resistance unavailing; he then declared himself a patient of the Winder Hospital, in very infirm health.

Lusk was sent on to Judge Meredith's Court to answer for a misdemeanor.

Pursuant to continuance, the investigation of the case of Laura Gordon charged with being engaged in the riot of the 2d of April was resumed.

Mr. Crawford appeared for the accused.

Mrs. Smith testified that on the day of the riot she saw the accused going home with a hat and a large pair of course red brogues in her hand; didn't recollect what kind of dress she had on; didn't see her with any gaiters; she and I went along home together.

Mrs. Nancy Garrison sworn - I went to Miss Gordon's on the day of the riot; saw this pair of gaiters lying on the bed; asked her to give them to me; she said she couldn't do it; I told her I would take them; she said I could, that they were too large for her; I took them home and found they were too large for me; I did not pay for them; she said when she wanted the money she would call on me; she gave me this handkerchief; I saw no brogues.

Mrs. Virginia Holloway sworn for the defence - I was with the accused on the day of the riot; we met about nine o'clock on the plank road and came down to the Square together; we went into the Square by the bell house gate; walked all through the Square; some-

The Richmond Bread Riot

body was speaking on the Capitol steps; didn't know who it was; heard it was the Governor; we went out of the Square by the same gate we went in; went down to Cary street to avoid the crowd; I was so bewildered I hardly know which way we went; went straight up Cary street to Sydney; she picked up the shoes on 7th street and was about to throw them away; I told her not to throw them away, and she took them home with her; she had no brogues or hat.

A sister of the accused testified that she met her coming home; she had these black gaiters, and said she picked them up on Seventh street.

Mrs. Sarah Barnett sworn - Laura Gordon occupies a part of my house; when she came home on the day after the riot she said, "look-a-here what I found," and showed these gaiters; she had no hat or brogues.

Mrs. Dickerson sworn - I went down street to get a couple of apples at the confectionary near the Postoffice; I saw Laura Gordon and her sister standing on the corner of Ninth and Main street; this was between ten and eleven o'clock; Laura was complaining of being sick; she was trembling and looked nervous; I heard afterwards that she went into the Square and sat until she got better, and then came home; she had neither hat, brogues nor gaiters in her hand when I saw her.

Mr. Alexander Taylor testified that the accused was not the party he arrested on the day of the riot.

The accused was sent on to Judge Meredith's Court.

DAILY RICHMOND EXAMINER - Wednesday, April 29, 1863

THE COURTS

MAYOR'S COURT - Tuesday, April 28, 1863. - Andrew J. Hawkins was charged with being engaged in the riot of the second of April.

Mr. A. J. [Judson] Crane appeared as counsel for the accused.

Mr. C. R. Mason, distiller, sworn - Saw the prisoner in the crowd near Mr. Gretter's store; Mr. Gretter was remonstrating with one of the women on account of their conduct; when Mr. Gretter turned off the prisoner asked her why she "did not talk to him (Gretter) right;" she answered that she was but a woman; thereupon I asked him if he was one of the mob; he said he was; I asked him his name and he gave it to me; he then asked me what I wanted with his name; I told him I desired to report him; several other persons then crowded around and the prisoner came to me and said that I had misunderstood him; that he had not said he was one of the mob, but that he was one of the party; I don't know what he meant by the distinction between mob and party; I saw the prisoner commit no act of violence; there was no rioting at that particular place when prisoner made the aforementioned remark; I understood his remark to the woman an encouragement to the mob.

W.[William] T. Trueman sworn - On the day of the riot when the riot was somewhat over, Mr. Gretter was remonstrating with a woman who was in the mob and whom he had been in the habit of assisting charitably; the prisoner encouraged the woman to talk boldly to Mr. Gretter, and told her to "talk to him (Gretter) like a man"; when spoken to by Mr. Mason, the prisoner openly avowed himself one of the rioters; I went for a policeman and had the prisoner arrested. I think it was between 12 and 1 o'clock when this conversation occurred.

Mr. [James H.] Peay testified that he was foreman of the Confederate shoe shop; on the day of the riot the prisoner was at work in the shop until 12 o'clock, M.

A German testified that between 12 and 1 o'clock on the day of the riot he went out of the shoe shop to see how the fun was going on; saw accused near Mr. Gretter's; heard him say he had nothing to do with the riot.

An Irishman saw the accused at the same time and place; heard him say he did not approve of the women's proceedings, but that they ought to have something to eat; that he had always been able to take care of his family.

Mr. Trueman recalled - The prisoner first proclaimed his being one of the rioters; I have no doubt on this point; but after Mr. Mason asked him his name he seemed to think that he was to be held responsible for his declaration, and then denied that he had any connexion or sympathy with the rioters.

Hawkins was sent on to answer before Judge Meredith for a misdemeanor, and admitted to bail in the sum of five hundred dollars.

DAILY RICHMOND EXAMINER - Saturday, May 2, 1863

THE COURTS

CIRCUIT COURT OF RICHMOND - Present JUDGE MEREDITH - Friday, May 1, 1863. - The Grand Jury for this Court brought in true bills of indictment against the following parties, charged with participating in the famous "women's bread riot" of the second of April,1863: William J. Lusk, Sarah Farrand, Barbara Idle, Mary Woodward, Mary Wasley, Martha Jamison, Laura Gordon, Elizabeth Ammons, Ann Bell, Margaret A. Pomfrey, James Hampton, Frances Kelly, John D. Lowry. Peter Blake, Sarah Mitchel, Francis Brown, Andrew J. Hawkins, Thomas M. Palmer, and Martha Burnett.

The Court will proceed with these parties severally from day to day.

DAILY RICHMOND EXAMINER - Monday, May 4, 1863

THE COURTS

HUSTINGS [CIRCUIT] COURT - JUDGE MEREDITH - May 2 - Wm. J. Lusk and Mrs. Anne Camp, were tried for participating in the riot of the 2d April, and found guilty. Lusk was fined one hundred dollars and sentenced to the city jail for twelve months. Mrs. Camp was fined seventy-five dollars. The Judge has not decided upon the term of her imprisonment.

The Richmond Bread Riot

DAILY RICHMOND EXAMINER - Wednesday, May 6, 1863

THE COURTS

HUSTINGS [Circuit] COURT OF RICHMOND - JUDGE MEREDITH - May 5, 1863. - Mrs. Barbara Idle was tried for participation in the Riot of the 2d of April last and acquitted.

Dr. Palmer was arraigned for using language calculated to encourage the rioters on the 2d of April last, and not departing from the scene when commanded by the Governor of Virginia. His counsel moved to quash the indictment. The motion was argued, and the Court took time to consider of its judgment.

DAILY RICHMOND EXAMINER - Thursday, May 7, 1863

THE COURTS

HUSTINGS [CIRCUIT] COURT - JUDGE MEREDITH - May 6th, 1863. -In the case of Dr. Thomas M. Palmer, mentioned on yesterday, the Court quashed two counts of the indictment, and the Attorney for the Commonwealth, with the advice of the Court, entered a *nolle prosequi*.

Laura Gordon, charged with being engaged in the riot of the 2d of April, 1863, was found guilty by the jury and fined $25. Before the court had given its judgment as to her term of imprisonment in the jail, the prisoner attempted to make way with herself by taking an ounce and a half of laudanum. Two doctors and a stomach pump were procured, and her life saved. She was taken home by her friends, but is still, technically, in the custody of the sheriff.

Martha Jamieson, charged with being engaged in the riot of the 2d of April, 1863, was tried, found guilty, and fined ten dollars by the jury, and sentenced by the court to twenty-four hours imprisonment in the city jail.

The Richmond Bread Riot

DAILY RICHMOND EXAMINER - Friday, May 8, 1863

THE COURTS

JUDGE MEREDITH'S COURT - May 7. - Minerva Meredith, rioter, who was tried and found guilty, was fined $100 and sent to jail for six months.

Peter Blake will be tried today.

DAILY RICHMOND EXAMINER - Saturday, May 9, 1863

THE COURTS

JUDGE MEREDITH'S COURT - May 8, 1863.- Martha Barnett and Sarah Mitchel [Sally Mitchell] were severally tried for participating in the riot of the 2d of April, found guilty, fined $5 and sent to jail for thirty days.

Ann Enroughty was put on trial for participating in the same riot, but the jury, at a late hour, not being able to agree upon their verdict, were adjourned to the following day.

Peter Blake was tried for participating in the said riot, and the jury finding him not guilty, he was discharged.

DAILY RICHMOND EXAMINER - Monday, May 11, 1863

THE COURTS

JUDGE MEREDITH'S COURT - May 9, 1863. - Mary Wasley, charged with being engaged in the riot of the 2d of April, was put upon trial.

This is one of the women who were arrested on the day of the riot on top of a furniture wagon loaded with bacon, brooms, &c., stolen from Pollard & Walker's.

The jury having heard the evidence, found the prisoner guilty, and fined her $25. The judge sentenced her to thirty days imprisonment in the city jail, but in consideration of the fact that she had an infant at the breast and two small children suffering with pneumonia, let her off with four hours imprisonment.

Martha Marshall was also charged with complicity in the riot of the 2d of April, was tried, found guilty and fined one dollar, and, also having a young infant, was only given four hours imprisonment.

DAILY RICHMOND EXAMINER - Wednesday, May 13, 1863

THE COURTS

JUDGE MEREDITH'S COURT - May 12, 1863. - John E. Lowry, charged with being engaged in the riot of the 2d of April, 1863, was put upon his trial.

The accused is a short, thick, oleaginous looking man of about fifty, who keeps a nondescript sort of an establishment, half shoe shop and half hotel, on Cary street, below Fourteenth.

Mr. Crane appeared for the defence.

From the evidence it appeared that about noon of the day of the riot, officers Perrin and Bibb being informed that some of the goods stolen during the riot had been carried to Lowry's, they went there to investigate the matter. Lowry himself was not at home, but his wife denied that anything had been brought there. Lowry then coming in, admitted to the officers that two pieces of bacon had been brought to his house by a girl of depraved character, named Mary Palmeter. The officers followed Lowry up to the second floor of his house, where he produced two shoulders of bacon from a box containing female wearing apparel. The officers searched the house, but found nothing else.

Messrs. Pollard & Walker identified the bacon as some stolen from them during the riot.

The defence introduced witnesses to prove that Lowry was absent from home when the girl brought the meat there, and that he knew nothing of it until after she had left.

The evidence having been concluded, Mr. Tazwell, for the Commonwealth, opened the case. He said the law had fixed a very light punishment for riot at most the extent being a fine of $100 and twelve months' imprisonment; and asked the Jury, in consideration of the fact that this was a woman's riot, and that therefore the men aiding them should be more severely dealt with than they, to give the prisoner the extent of the law. There could be no doubt of his guilt. He knew the character of the girl Palmeter, and he knew that the riot was going on. He, therefore, must have known that the bacon was taken during the riot.

Mr. Crane contended that his client not being at home at the time of the leaving of the meat by Palmeter, he could not be held responsible as having received it. There was nothing but the bacon to connect him with the riot. It had been shown that he was absent from home when it was brought there. As well might any gentleman living ten miles in the country, at whose house a piece of bacon stolen in the riot had been left, be held as guilty of the riot.

After a short retirement the Jury found the accused guilty and assessed his fine at $100.

Counsel for the defense moved to set aside the verdict, and the Judge took time to consider the motion.

DAILY RICHMOND EXAMINER - Friday, May 15, 1863

THE COURTS

JUDGE MEREDITH'S COURT - May 13, 1863. - It will be recollected that on the previous day the Judge took time to consider the motion of counsel to set aside the verdict by which Lowry was found guilty of riot and fined one hundred dollars. The Judge set aside the verdict upon the ground that the Commonwealth had failed to make it appear that the two pieces of bacon, received by the accused from the girl Palmeter, was part of the spoils of the riot. There was no proof that the goods were taken during the riot; if he had been prosecuted for receiving stolen goods it was possible he might have been convicted; he, the Judge, could therefore, grant the accused a new trial.

The Richmond Bread Riot

Upon the rendering of this judgment, the prosecuting attorney entered a *nolle prosequi*, and the accused was discharged.

Mrs. Margaret A. Pomphrey [Pomfrey], of New Kent, charged with being engaged in the riot of the 2d of April last, was put upon her trial.

Mr. A. J. Crane appeared for the accused. Mr. Crane addressed the jury. He desired to tell them what Mrs. Pomphrey expected to prove. On the morning of the riot she, who was a woman of means, was going to the post office, when she saw a crowd at Pollard & Walker's; went there and saw the woman taking bacon; thinking *bona fide* that the Young Men's Christian Association, who had been distributing rice, were distributing bacon, she went in took a piece of bacon, but put it down when remonstrated with by Mr. Pollard. - Mr. Crane said this was what he expected to prove, and if he did prove it, he should ask the acquittal of his client.

Mr. R. H. Pollard sworn - On the morning of the 2d of April a great crowd of women came in a noisy and turbulent manner to my store; I attempted to shut the door, when the women made an attack on it with axes and hatchets; I then let go the door, and an excited crowd of seventy or eighty rushed in and began to take bacon, tea, brooms, etc.; I appealed to them to desist, and got upon a barrel for that purpose; among the first of the crowd who came in I recognized Mrs. Pomphrey; she had two pieces of bacon, and was going out with it; knowing her very well, I said to her, "why, Mrs. Pomphrey, is it possible that you too are robbing me!" she replied she was "obliged to do it," and went out with the bacon.

Cross examined — Mrs. Pomphrey's reputation is good in the neighborhood in which she lived in New Kent; I don't recollect her smiling when I told her to put down the bacon; I think she was one of the crowd who came to my door and made a noise and broke in; I believe she was.

A female sworn for the defense, testified that she went with Mrs. Pomphrey to the post office on the morning of the riot, and left her there and went home; did not see Mrs. P. until evening, when she returned home; she brought no bacon home with her; Mrs. P. moved from New Kent on account of the advance of the Yankees.

The Richmond Bread Riot

Another female testified that on the day of the riot, about noon, she met Mrs. Pomphrey on the street and walked home with her; Mrs. Pomphrey had no bacon or other goods with her.

Dr. Vaiden testified that he had known Mrs. P. in New Kent, and practiced in her family; she bore a good character for honesty and industry, and had two sons in the army.

The evidence having been concluded, Mr. Crane asked the Judge to give the jury the following instructions:

"That if, from the evidence in this case the jury shall believe that the accused entered the store of Pollard & Walker, and then and there took, against their consent two pieces of bacon, without, however, participating in the noise within or without the store, and without aiding in the breaking in of the door, then that the prosecution cannot be sustained."

The Commonwealth's Attorney also submitted instructions, whereupon an argument sprang up as to the definition of riot, during which, Mr. Crane read the following:

"A riot is a tumultuous disturbance of the public peace by three or more persons assembling together of their own authority, with an intent mutually to assist one another against any who shall oppose them in the execution of some private object, and afterwards executing the same in a violent and turbulent manner, to the terror of the people, whether the act intended is lawful or not - (1. Hawk.)"

Mr. Tazewell denied that this was a complete definition of riot, as any person joining rioters subsequently to their assembling, was as guilty as they.

The court gave the jury instructions, which were Mr. Crane's, essentially modified.

The Commonwealth's Attorney declined to argue the case, but desired to say a few words as to the amount of fine. In his opinion, the maximum punishment fixed by law for riot was very mild - one hundred dollars fine and twelve months imprisonment. The accused, in this case, was proved to have been a woman of means and respectability. She had had advantages of moral education, and was therefore more disgraced and more culpable than many other participants. He asked that the jury would impose the maximum fine, the guilt of the accused being clear.

Mr. Crane regretted that the attorney had nothing new to say. He had said the same thing in every one of these cases - the guilt of the accused was clear and the jury must assess the maximum fine. He had said the same in two cases, one of which was discharged by the jury and in the other the verdict had been set aside by the Court. What were the facts of this case as shown by the testimony? Mrs. Pomphrey, in returning from the Post office, saw a crowd at Pollard & Walker's, and, through curiosity, went there. There she saw bacon being distributed, and, thinking it a free barbecue, proceeded to help herself, and declined to put down the bacon when told to do so by Mr. Pollard. Whether she heard what Mr. Pollard said was doubtful, owing to the noise and tumult. Yet the attorney would have the accused punished to the extent of the law. Ladies of the first respectability in Richmond had accidentally got into that riot and could not get out without assistance. In conclusion, Mr. Crane stated that the poor women engaged in this unhappy riot had been hunted down with inevitable pertinacity and vigor, while the men who instigated them had been unmolested.

Mr. Tazewell said he had yet to hear a tittle of evidence going to prove that men had instigated the women to this riot. From his association with a number of these cases, he was convinced that no man had anything to do with the organization of this miscalled bread riot - some had joined the riot after its organization. Counsel mentioned that ladies had gotten into this riot against their will. Does any one suppose for a moment that if one of these ladies had been carried by the crowd into Mr. Pollard's store, that she would have taken two pieces of bacon? Certainly not. The first and only effort of a lady would have been to get out of the riot as soon as possible. Mr. Crane had stated to the jury that he, the attorney, always said the same thing in these cases. There was, he admitted, much truth in the remark. These cases were all similar, the guilt the same and the punishment fixed by law the same. Consequently it was plainly his duty to say in all cases pretty much the same. Not so with the brilliant orator on

The Richmond Bread Riot

the other side. He always said something new, something for the entertainment of the bar, the jury and the court.

The case was then given to the jury who, after a brief retirement, brought in a verdict of guilty, and assessed her fine at fifty dollars, and the Judge sentenced her to thirty days imprisonment in the city jail.

Mary [also, Lucy] Duke was put on trial for riot on the 2d of April.

The accused was a finely dressed woman of forty, with a quantity of rouge on her face.

George Watt sworn - Saw the accused in the riot at P.[Philip] K. White's, on Main street; when the crowd went round to Sweitzer's on Franklin street, I followed them; saw the women crowd round Mr. Sweitzer's door; saw a chuckle headed Irishwoman assail the door with an axe; I rushed forward and seized the axe; three or four men then seized me; the accused was in the crowd pushing back the persons who were attempting to put down the riot; she drew a navy revolver and leveled it at the gentlemen who were endeavoring to quell the riot; in the confusion some one got the pistol from her; after I had extricated myself from the crowd, the accused came to me and demanded her pistol; I told her I did not have it; she said I had it and should give it up forthwith; a gentleman standing by assured her I did not have it; I then told her if I could get the pistol I would return it to her; I asked her what was her name, she replied with a *vim*, "My name is Mary Duke!" I told her where my store was, and that if she would call during the week and I could get the pistol, I would return it to her. The next day a man named Lampkin called at my place and asked for the pistol, which he said belonged to him.

Mr. Pratt testified that he saw Mrs. Duke several times on the day of the riot; he was with her at her house on the day of the riot; he did not believe she was in the riot; she borrowed the pistol from Mr. Lampkin ten days before the riot; some bacon was brought to Mrs. Duke's on the day of the riot by her son; her son said he bought the bacon at the market house; the proper name of the accused is Lucy Duke.

Mr. Lampkin sworn - Well, I lent her the pistol ten days before the riot took place; I was at her house one night, and the negro woman came in and said there was a drunken man down stairs; I went down and saw a man lying with his head on the steps; some weeks before, some man had attempted to break into the house, and she said she was afraid to stay alone; she asked me to lend her a pistol, and I lent it to her.

The case was submitted without argument.

The jury found the accused guilty, and assessed her fine at one hundred dollars, and the Judge sentenced her to six months imprisonment.

James Marshall, charged with riot on the 2d of April, was found not guilty and discharged.

Elizabeth Ammons, charged with rioting on the 1st [2d] of April, was put upon her trial.

The accused was young and pretty - indeed, decidedly the best looking of all the rioters.

Officer Morris testified that on the day of the riot he arrested the accused coming from the direction of Mrs. Sweitzer's store, which had been broken into, with shoes, suspenders and other goods in her hands.

The jury, after long deliberation, being unable to agree, were discharged.

DAILY RICHMOND EXAMINER - Friday, May 15, 1863

THE COURTS

HUSTINGS COURT - May 14, 1863. - Present Recorder Caskie and Aldermen.

Mrs. Frances Kelly, charged with being engaged in the riot of the 2d of April, 1863, and stealing one hundred dollars worth of bacon from Pollard & Walker, was called to the bar for examination.

Messrs. Crane and Wooten defended the prisoner.

Mr. Crane moved to quash the certificate of the Magistrate, by which the accused had been committed and sent on, on the ground that it set forth that she was sent on both for felony and misdemeanor - larceny and felony [riot]. If she was a rioter the court had no jurisdiction. By statute the Circuit Court alone had jurisdiction in riot cases.

The court quashed the certificate of commitment not upon any ground advanced by the counsel, but for the reason that the words "with intent to commit larceny" had been omitted.

The accused was re committed for examination by the Mayor.

DAILY RICHMOND EXAMINER - Thursday, May 28, 1863

THE COURTS
HUSTINGS COURT - JUDGE LYONS - May 27, 1863. -

Virgil Jones, indicted for breaking and entering the store of Pollard & Walker, during the riot on the 2d day of April, and stealing one hundred pounds of bacon, was put upon his trial.

The prisoner was a young man of twenty-one or two years of age, who might have been good looking but for the extraordinary smallness of his eyes. His young wife sat near him at the bar.

Mr. Crane appeared for the defense.

Mr. Robert S. Pollard sworn — On the morning of the riot, when the crowd was pressing on my door, I attempted to shut it, but axes being freely used upon the door, and some of them being near striking me, I gave way, and permitted the door to swing open; the crowd then rushed in and took goods to the value of four thousand dollars; the crowd brought in their axes and hatchets; I cannot swear that I saw the prisoner there.

Thomas H. Harris sworn — I saw the prisoner in the crowd of rioters; I spoke to him and he went down to Pollard & Walker's with the crowd, and I lost sight of him for a moment; when the attack was made on Pollard & Walker's I got upon a wagon, and looked over the heads of the crowd; the women were attacking the door with axes and hatchets, but as they were working without any system, they made little progress; I saw the prisoner take a hatchet out of the hands of a woman and attack the door. I saw him strike at the door; I was in a position to look over the heads of the crowd; I saw the prisoner

The Richmond Bread Riot

distinctly; I had known him for several months; I don't recollect to have seen him enter the store; I have been a member of the same company in the City Battalion with the prisoner; I have never had a difficulty of any kind with him; there were four or five or more hatchets displayed in front of the door.

Mr. Pollard recalled — The goods were taken from my presence and I was appealing to them all the time to desist.

John M. Richardson, member of the City Battalion - On the day of the riot I met the prisoner near the corner of the Columbian Hotel; he told me his hands were very greasy, and explained this circumstance by saying that he had been in Pollard & Walker's, handing out bacon to the ladies; he said he was the first man that entered the store; I had very little conversation with him; this was between nine and ten o'clock; the crowd was then moving down Cary street. Witnesses were then sworn for the defense.

Miss Virginia Thurston sworn - I met the prisoner going down Cary Street, [between] eight and nine o'clock on the day of the riot; he was looking for his wife, and said he did not want her to be in the crowd; his hands were not greasy, and he had nothing in his hands; I met him between Thirteenth and Fourteenth streets, nearly opposite Pollard & Walker's.

Mr. Smith sworn - Saw the prisoner take boots from men during the riot, and give them to the ladies; Jones said it was bad enough for women to take the things much less the men; he said he was going to take things from the men and give them to the women; when Pollard & Walker's store was entered I was standing on a wagon looking on; I did not see Jones enter the store, but would have seen him if he had been there; I didn't see him close to Pollard & Walker's, but saw him close to Hicks' boot and hat store; the prisoner was discharged from the City Battalion for attempting to bribe a sentinel at the lithograph office, where they make Confederate money.

Mr. Drew sworn - I saw the prisoner on the day of the riot on Main street; he was taking no hand in the riot; 'twas after ten o'clock when I saw him.

Mr. Wilson sworn - During the riot I was on the opposite side of the street from Pollard & Walker's; I heard the hatchets but could not see who was using them; I didn't see the prisoner there; I can't say he was there, or was not there.

Mr. Mullen saw Pollard & Walker's door broken open; he was up stairs over the store, looking down out of a window; I didn't see the prisoner there; saw nothing but women; only saw three women with hatchets; I am acquainted with the prisoner, and would have recognized him if he had been there.

Mr. Palmer, City Battalion, sworn - A few minutes after Pollard & Walker's was broken open, I saw Jones, and he told me he didn't approve of the proceedings, and was trying to put down the riot; I was with him off and on for an hour; I was not with him all the time; I was with him when he was arrested.

John Jones, a rioter, was brought from the City Jail and sworn - Saw the prisoner all the time Pollard & Walker's was being broken open; he did not cross Cary street till the door was broken open; I never saw him with any bacon.

To Tazewell - I was put in jail for standing on the street, minding some things for some ladies during the riot; they charge me with stealing and receiving stolen goods; I was going up the street when two ladies called me and asked me to mind their things, some hats, coffee, candles and shoes; I had a knife in my hand cleaning out my pipe preparatory to smoking.

Another individual from the jail testified that he saw Pollard & Walker's broken open; no men were engaged in the breaking, they were all women.

Mr. Pollard recalled - Men and women both assailed my door with hatchets, and when the door was broken open men and women both entered.

Several witnesses testified to the good character of the accused.

Lieutenant Garret of the City Battalion, sworn as to the character of the accused - I know nothing of him except that he was a member of my company, and was discharged for stealing; his reputation in the company is that of a dishonest man; he was discharged for stealing Confederate notes; he was not tried before a civil tribunal but his dishonesty being proved to the satisfaction of the commandant, he was discharged.

The Richmond Bread Riot

Mr. Richardson recalled - I met the prisoner near the corner of the Columbian; he said his hands were greasy, that he had been in Pollard & Walker's store handing out bacon; I know the prisoner well and never had any difficulty with him.

Mr. Harris recalled - I know the prisoner well; I saw him during the riot take a hatchet from a woman and strike at Pollard & Walker's door; I never had any difficulty with the prisoner; his reputation in the company from which he was discharged is not good.

After argument, the case was given to the jury, who, after brief deliberation, brought in a verdict of guilty, and sent the prisoner to the penitentiary for three years.

DAILY RICHMOND EXAMINER - Saturday, May 30, 1863

THE COURTS

JUDGE MEREDITH'S COURT - May 29, 1863. - Francis Brown, a very tall young man, said to be from Baltimore, was charged with participating in the "women's bread riot" of the 2d of April last.

Messrs. [Daniel] Ratcliffe and [J.L.C.] Daner appeared for the accused, Mr. John S. Caskie for the Commonwealth.

Captain James B. Pleasants, of the night-watch, sworn - While the riot was in progress I learned that a man had gone into the Our House, on thirteenth street, with a pair of cavalry boots; I and officer Morris went into the house, and there found the accused sitting down trying on the boots; he had put the right boot on; I took the boot off his foot and carried him and the boots to the watch house.

A private in the City Battalion testified that during the riot, he saw the accused take the boots from a man and attempt three times to carry them back to the store from which they had been stolen, but owing to the denseness of the crowd, he was unable to reach the store; accused then said he would take the boots into the Our House and leave them with the bar keeper until the riot was over, and then return them to the owner; the barkeeper of the Our House, however, refusing to have anything to do with the boots, the accused said he would try them on, and if they fitted him, he would wear them and pay the owner for them; while he was trying the boots on an officer came in and arrested him; witness knew the accused well; had known him for four years; saw him take no part in the riot, so far from it, heard him condemn the men who were participating.

The jury found the prisoner guilty, and fined him fifty dollars. The Court sentenced him to four months imprisonment in the city jail.

Andrew J. Hawkins, a man of forty, indicted for aiding and comforting the rioters on the 2d of April was put on trial.

Mr. Crane appeared for the accused.

Mr. Caskie for the Commonwealth.

Mr. C. R. Mason testified that on the day of the riot, about twelve o'clock, Mr. George Gretter was remonstrating with a woman for being engaged in the riot; a large crowd was standing about; the prisoner spoke to the woman and asked her why she did not speak to Mr. Gretter "like a man;" witness asked prisoner why he did not speak to Mr. Gretter himself; just then Mr. Gretter turned away; prisoner replied that he would have spoken to him if he had not gone away; witness asked prisoner, "are you one of the rioters?" Prisoner replied, "yes, I am one of them;" In a few minutes afterwards when there was some talk of arresting the prisoner, he came to witness and said, "you misunderstood me, I did not say I was one of the rioters;" witness considered prisoner's language as encouraging to the women to continue the riot.

Mr. W. T. Trueman sworn - heard the prisoner say he was "one of them," and presumed that he meant he was one of the rioters; when someone spoke to him prisoner said, "what can they do about it, they can't eat me;" a lieutenant in the crowd told him they could do something with him; I went for an officer and had him arrested.

Several witnesses were introduced for the defence, who testified that they saw the accused on Main street on the day in question, but did not hear him use the language attributed to him, and did not see him participate in the riots; he was a shoemaker, well able to provide for his family and of good character. It was also proved that the accused was at work in the Government shoe shop till about twelve o'clock, M.

The jury acquitted the prisoner, being satisfied that at the time he made use of the language imputed to him the riot had ceased; and that though he had said he was one of the rioters, he could not have been in the riot, having been in the Government shoe shop all the morning.

DAILY RICHMOND EXAMINER - Thursday, June 4, 1863

THE COURTS

HUSTINGS COURT - JUDGE LYONS - June 3, 1863. - Thomas Samanni, indicted for unlawfully and riotously assembling with three or more persons, on the 2d of April, to the disturbance of the peace of the Commonwealth, and then and there breaking and destroying, in part, the dwelling house of Minna Sweitzer, to the great terror of the said Minna Sweitzer, and of all persons passing along the highway.

The accused is too well known in the city to require a description.

Mr. Crane appeared for the defense.

Mrs. Sweitzer, Charles H. Wynne, Morris Kaufman, and Lewis Letchenstein [Lichenstein], were heard as witnesses for the Commonwealth.

Mrs. Sweitzer deposed - On the 2d of April a crowd of persons broke in the door of my store and took all of my goods; I was so much alarmed that I did not recognize anyone; I live over the store, but you have to go outside to get upstairs; there is no way to get up stairs without going out of doors.

Mr. Wynne deposed - On the day of the riot I saw a crowd of persons around the door of Mrs. Sweitzer; I saw Samanni standing on the sill of the door with his hand against the door, evidently, to my mind, making demonstrations against the door; I made my way through the crowd to him; when I got to him the panel of the door was split; I cannot swear that he split it; I arrested him; he made no

The Richmond Bread Riot

resistance, and only said, when I took him away, that "he would not stand by and see any one strike a woman;" I saw no one about to strike a woman; when I took him away the door was not open.

Cross-examined - I did not see the door yield to his hand, but it is my firm conviction that his hand split the panel of the door; if I had waited a few seconds he would have broken into the store; there were other persons hammering on the door.

Mr. Letchenstein deposed - On the day of the riot, when the crowd assembled around Mrs. Sweitzer's door, I entered her store by going through her dining room in the rear; persons were then breaking in the store window and door; they broke in and robbed the store; Mrs. Sweitzer is my sister, and I am well acquainted with her house; there is a door leading from the store upstairs, but it is locked up.

Morris Kaufman deposed- On the day of the riot I saw the crowd pressing against Mrs. Sweitzer's store; I pushed through the crowd and got to the door; the prisoner was standing against the door, and a woman was hacking on it with a hatchet; I pushed the woman away, when the prisoner said, "don't strike any of these women," and took the hatchet from her and hacked away upon the door; I then pushed him away, when he handed the woman the hatchet again and she renewed the attack on the door; by this time some of the crowd were breaking into the window, and I started to the window; just then a gentleman, that I cannot now recognize, came through the crowd and arrested the prisoner; while the gentleman was carrying the prisoner off, I noticed that the door was open; the door was opened by breaking in a panel and removing the bar.

Cross-examined - I am positive that the prisoner is the man who was at the door and told me not to strike the woman; I saw him hack the door with the hatchet.

The jury found the prisoner guilty, and sent him to the penitentiary for two years. Counsel are preparing a bill of exception.

The Richmond Bread Riot

DAILY RICHMOND EXAMINER - Friday, June 5, 1863

THE COURTS
HUSTINGS COURT - JUDGE LYONS - June 4, 1863. -

John Jones, the pop-eyed red headed man, indicted for aiding and abetting in the riot of the 2d of April, and stealing a quantity of hats, coffee, shoes, &c., and also indicted for receiving stolen goods, was put on his trial.

Mr. Danner appeared for the accused.

Having twice previously published in full the evidence in this case, we will on this occasion only make a brief recapitulation of the facts.

During the progress of the riot on Cary street, while the stores of Tyler & Son, Pollard & Walker, and John T. Hicks, were being robbed, Mr. Adrien Vannerson informed Officer Griffin that a man was standing on Tardy & Williams' corner, guarding a quantity of goods. On repairing to the spot, Griffin found the prisoner standing with a large pocket knife in his hand, over some goods that were covered with a shawl. Griffin caught hold of the shawl to raise it, and see what it concealed, when the prisoner told him very gruffly, "not to touch those things." Griffin then told the prisoner he was in custody, and arrested him. There were concealed under the shawl a number of hats filled with coffee, a dozen pairs of shoes, some candles, and other articles of less value. After he was arrested, the prisoner declared that the goods were not his, but had been left in his charge by a Mrs. Enroughty or a Mrs. Jordan.

The jury found the prisoner guilty of receiving stolen goods, and ascertained the term of his confinement in the Penitentiary at one year.

Counsel entered a motion for a new trial.

The Richmond Bread Riot

***DAILY RICHMOND EXAMINER* - Wednesday, June 17, 1863**

THE COURTS

MAYOR'S COURT - June 16, 1863 - Mrs. Francis Kelley was charged with being engaged in the riot of the 2d of April last.

It was, in evidence, that the prisoner was seen with Mrs. Jackson at the market house at an early hour on the day of the riots; that she was seen to enter the Capitol Square and leave it with the mob of women and go down to Cary street; that she was seen to assail the store house of Pollard & Walker with an axe, and after the store had been broken into, to emerge therefrom with a very large ham of bacon.

The Mayor, in deference, as he said, to an opinion held by Judge Lyons on this subject, sent the prisoner on to the Hustings Court to answer for felony.

***DAILY RICHMOND EXAMINER* - Thursday, June 18, 1863**

THE COURTS

JUDGE LYONS' COURT - June 17, 1863. - Benjamin Slemper, charged with breaking and entering the store of James Knotts, on the 2d of April, 1863, and stealing sundry pairs of shoes, was led to the bar for trial.

The prisoner was one of the women's bread rioters of the memorable second of April last. He is a young German, who says he has been in America two years, and in the City of Richmond one year. Since his arrest and confinement in jail, a friend and fellow countryman of his, named Rosey, has stolen and sold all of his property and gone North, leaving the prisoner without the means wherewith to hire counsel. When arraigned he plead quilty.

Mr. Lafayette H. Fitzhugh, Sergeant at Arms of the Confederate Senate, was the principal witness for the Commonwealth. He testified that he saw the prisoner, being apparently one of the most active and desperate of the rioters, break into the window and enter the store of Mr. Knotts, and that he, the witness, pushed through the crowd into the store and arrested him and an Irishman both having boots and shoes in their possession; the Irishman succeeded in getting away, but he carried the prisoner to the Mayor's office, whence he was sent to jail.

The jury found the prisoner guilty, and sent him to the Penitentiary for three years and eight months.

DAILY RICHMOND EXAMINER - **Monday, June 22, 1863**

THE COURTS

JUDGE LYONS COURT - June 20th, 1863. - John Jones, the pop-eyed, red headed man from Henrico, indicted for stealing coffee, shoes,&c., during the riot on the 2d of April, 1863, was led to the bar for trial.

It will be recollected the prisoner was tried for this offence and convicted at the last term of the Court, but the verdict was, because of some irregularity, set aside, and a new trial granted, by Judge Meredith, who was then presiding.

The evidence against Jones was that during the riot he was found on the corner of Thirteenth and Cary streets, with a large amount of riot goods in his possession.

The jury acquitted the prisoner of grand larceny, but the Judge sent him back to be examined by the Mayor for riot.

DAILY RICHMOND EXAMINER -**Tuesday, June 23, 1863**

THE COURTS

MAYOR'S COURT - June 22, 1863 - John Jones, the pop-eyed man of destiny, was examined on the charge of being engaged in the "woman's bread riot" of the second of April last, and sent on to Hustings [Circuit] Court.

The Richmond Bread Riot

DAILY RICHMOND EXAMINER - Wednesday, June 24, 1863

THE COURTS

JUDGE LYONS COURT - June 23. - Sarah Champion was charged with stealing a pair of shoes, an odd shoe and some unfinished shoemaker's work on the day of the women's riot.

It appeared from the evidence that on the day of the riot, the prisoner was met on Marshall street with the shoes, &c., in her hands, which she said had been given to her down town, but there was no proof that she had been personally engaged in the riot, or was at any time near the scene of action. She was acquitted.

DAILY RICHMOND EXAMINER - Tuesday, August 18, 1863

THE COURTS

MAYOR'S COURT - August 17, 1863. - Mrs. Jackson, charged with being engaged in the riot of the 2d of April, 1863, was surrendered into court by John N. Davis and Alice Perdue as former bail, and thereupon gave as bail Charles W. Allen in a similar amount.

DAILY RICHMOND ENQUIRER - Saturday, October 10, 1863

CITY INTELLIGENCE

A PARTICIPANT IN THE RIOT SENTENCED TO THE PENITENTIARY. - Mrs. Mary Jackson [Johnson], an old lady about sixty years of age, was arraigned for trial in Judge Lyons' Court, yesterday, charged with being engaged in the disgraceful riot in this city on the 2d of April.

The accused was ably defended by Messrs. Ratcliffe and Hall, but the evidence was of such a conclusive character that the jury brought in a verdict of "guilty," and ascertained the term of her imprisonment in the penitentiary at five years.

From the evidence in the case, it appears that on the morning of the riot she headed the mob, and marching to the Governor's Mansion, demanded "bread or blood." Colonel French, aid to the Governor, informed her that that was not the proper place to come for either "bread or blood." She then marched down the street, at the head of the riotous procession, and coming to the store of Pollard & Walker, entered and took therefrom a large quantity of bacon, flour &c. Mrs. Jackson [Johnson] has hitherto been regarded a highly respectable old lady. She has two children, one a daughter married and residing in this city, the other having attained his majority, and now serving his country in the army of Northern Virginia.

DAILY RICHMOND EXAMINER - **Monday, October 12, 1863**

JUDGE LYONS' COURT - Mrs. Mary Johnson, a woman of sixty years of age, was tried for stealing bacon from Pollard & Walker's store during the women's riot last April, and, being convicted, was sent to the penitentiary for five years.

It appeared from the evidence she was spokesman of the excited crowd of women who went to the Governor's on the morning of the 2d of April, and that she said she "would have bread or blood;" that she was subsequently seen assisting to beat in the door of Pollard & Walker with an axe; and that after the said door was broken open she was seen issuing from the store and making off with a quantity of Pollard & Walker's bacon.

The prisoner in this case has been inaccurately spoken of by a city paper as Mary Jackson. Mary Jackson was the prime instigator and great ringleader of the riot, but she was too smart to commit any overt act which might fix a felony upon her. She incited many foolish women to steal and plunder openly, but was very circumspect in her own actions. It being found that no charge of felony could be sustained in her case, she was sent to Judge Meredith's Court to be tried for a misdemeanor, and though it was fully established by the testimony of Mrs. Jamison and others that she was at the bottom of the whole movement, which resulted in such a waste of property and has brought grief to so many homes, it is more than probable that, if she is not acquitted altogether, she will get off with some merely nominal punishment.

We may here mention that five parties have been sent to the penitentiary for the parts borne by them in the riot, viz: Flemper [Benjamin Slemper], Luck [William J. Lusk], and another man, and old Mrs. Johnson.

RICHMOND DISPATCH **- Saturday, November 14, 1863**

LOCAL MATTERS

Circuit Court of Richmond. - JUDGE MEREDITH had the following criminal cases before him on yesterday:

In the case of Ann Enroughty, one of the April rioters, a *nolle prosequi* was entered.

RICHMOND DISPATCH **- Monday, November 16, 1863**

LOCAL MATTERS

Richmond Circuit Court. - JUDGE MEREDITH disposed of very little criminal business last Saturday. In the case of John Jones, who was indicted as one of the April rioters, a *nolle prosequi* was entered, and he was discharged.

DAILY RICHMOND EXAMINER **- Saturday, November 21, 1863**

THE COURTS

[VIRGINIA] SUPREME COURT OF APPEALS - Friday, November 20, 1863.- Thomas Samanni, who was convicted at the last April term of Judge Lyons' Court of participating in the riot and breaking the door of the store house of Mrs. Minna Sweitzer, and sentenced to two years' confinement in the penitentiary, to which an appeal was taken, was to-day tried in the Supreme Court of Appeals, and the decision of Judge Lyons was affirmed and Thomas Samanni was sent to the penitentiary.

DAILY RICHMOND EXAMINER - Monday, February 11, 1864

THE COURTS

HUSTINGS COURT - Before Recorder Caskie and Aldermen - Wednesday, February 10, 1864. - Frances Kelley [Kelly], charged with being engaged in the "women's riot" of the second of April, 1863, and breaking into the store of Robert S. Pollard and stealing fifty pounds of bacon, was examined and sent on for final trial before Judge Lyons. This party would have been examined months ago, but having been admitted to bail by the committing magistrate, she ran off to Lynchburg, and there, under an assumed name, was employed as a matron in a hospital, a position she lost by misconduct. Some three weeks ago the gentleman who had gone bail for her hearing of her whereabouts, went up and brought her to this city.

DAILY RICHMOND EXAMINER - Tuesday, March 1, 1864

THE COURTS

HUSTINGS COURT - BEFORE JUDGE WILLIAM H. LYONS - Monday, February 29, 1864 - Frances Kelly, indicted for breaking and entering the store of Pollard & Walker, on the 2d of April last, and stealing a ham of bacon, was put on trial.

This was one of the rioters of the famous "woman's riot," of the 2d of April, 1863. She was a tall, fine-looking, dark-haired woman of forty, dressed in deep mourning, with the exception of her bonnet, which had a border of frayed white silk around the crown.

Mr. R.S. Pollard testified that about nine o'clock on the morning of the 2d of April last, a mob of women, men and boys battered in the front door of his store, which he attempted to close against them, and carried off four thousand six hundred dollars' worth of bacon,

The Richmond Bread Riot

besides a quantity of other merchandise. He could not identify the prisoner at the bar as one of the parties who broke into his place.

Officer Griffin stated that on the morning of the 2d of April, about eight o'clock, he saw the prisoner in the Second Market in the company with Mrs. Jackson. Mrs. Jackson told him that the women were going to have a riot, and that they would have bread or blood - and if any policeman attempted to interfere with them, he should be shot down. He could not swear that the prisoner heard these remarks, but she was near enough to have heard them if she had been listening. In the course of an hour after these remarks of Mrs. Jackson, he saw the prisoner and Mrs. Jackson with the rioters in the Capitol Square.

Mr. William Ready said that whilst the attack was being made on Pollard & Walker's store, he saw the prisoner battering in the store door with a hatchet. He was positive as to seeing the prisoner battering in the door with a hatchet. Whilst she was so battering someone caught hold of her and she turned around, and witness looked full in her face. Knew prisoner previously and recognized her. Was not more than fifteen or twenty paces distant from her.

Mr. Fleming Griffin had known prisoner for years. On the day of the riot, whilst Pollard & Walker's store was being sacked, he saw the prisoner come out of the door with a ham of bacon in her arms. Had not a doubt that prisoner was the identical woman he saw come out of the store with the ham in her hands. This concluded the testimony for the Commonwealth.

Mrs. Louisa Langford and Mrs. White, a daughter of the prisoner, were examined for the defense.

Mrs. Langford stated that, on the morning of the riot she went down with prisoner to Weisiger's with work. They passed Pollard & Walker's whilst the riot was going on, but took no part in it. The prisoner had no hatchet, and did take a ham of bacon in her hand whilst passing through the mob, but she did it only to oblige a small boy who asked her to hold it a minute; and after holding it a minute she gave it to a man who asked for it, and who put it into a wagon. Weisiger's being closed, she and prisoner returned home together. Prisoner wore on that day the same bonnet she wore in court.

Mrs. White stated that, on the morning of the riot she came down with prisoner as far as the Powhatan House. The rioters were then in the Square. She and prisoner went into the Square to see what was going on. Prisoner did not know Mrs. Jackson. Prisoner did not have on a long-eared bonnet. She had on the same bonnet and was dressed in the same clothes she was then wearing in court.

A man testified that he had known Mrs. Kelly many years, and that she had always borne an irreproachable character.

Officer Griffin recalled - knew Mrs. Langford very well, and would not believe her under oath.

Mr. Flemming Griffin recalled - Prisoner on the day of the riot did not have on the same bonnet she was wearing in Court.

The case was then given to the jury, who in a few minutes, brought in a verdict of, "guilty," and, under the misapprehension that having found her guilty, they were obliged to send her to the penitentiary, they ascertained the term of her imprisonment in the penitentiary at one year.

Upon the rendition of the verdict the prisoner gave way to most boisterous grief, which for a time, stopped the business of the court. She, after a while, having gotten comparatively quiet, the Judge informed the jury that, on reading over the indictment, he found that the article with which the prisoner was charged with stealing was of less value than twenty dollars, and that, therefore, the jury might have punished her by confinement in the city jail.

Thereupon the jury again withdrew, and quickly brought in a verdict ascertaining the term of her imprisonment in the city jail at one month. The court then adjourned.

Appendix D: City of Richmond Hustings Court Minutes

Minute Book, No. 28

Monday, April 13, 1863; page 395

Mary Johnson, who stands charged with a felony by her committed in this, that on the second day of April in the year 1863, at this city and within the jurisdiction of this court, she did, in the daytime of that day, by force and violence, she the said Mary Johnson being then and there armed with a dangerous weapon, then and there break and enter the storehouse of Robert S. Pollard and Joshua Walker, partners trading under the style of Pollard & Walker, and them the said Pollard and Walker in bodily fear feloniously did put, and a large quantity of bacon, to wit, one hundred pounds, of the value of one hundred dollars, of the goods and chattels of the said Pollard and Walker, from the person and against the will of the said Pollard and Walker, feloniously did steal, take and carry away; and in this also, that she the said Mary Johnson, on the day and year last aforesaid, at this city, in the day time of that day, did break and enter the storehouse aforesaid, and did then and there from said storehouse feloniously take, steal and carry away a large quantity, to wit, five hundred pounds of bacon of the value of five hundred dollars, of the goods and chattels of said Pollard & Walker, was this day led to the bar in custody of the sergeant, and the court having heard the evidence are of opinion that the said Mary Johnson ought to be tried for the said offense before the Judge of this court. And she is thereupon remanded to jail. Depositions of the witnesses for the commonwealth taken down in writing and filed. And S. Basset [Bassett] French and Robert S. Pollard recognized in the sum of three hundred dollars each, with condition for their appearance before the Judge of this court, on the first day of the next May term of the said court to he holden by the said Judge, to give evidence on behalf of the commonwealth against the said Mary Johnson, and not to depart thence without the leave of the said Judge.

The Richmond Bread Riot

Monday, April 13, 1863; Page 396

Virgil Jones, who stands charged with a felony by him committed in this, that on the second day of April in the year 1863, at this city and within the jurisdiction of this court, he did feloniously, in the daytime of that day, by force and violence, he the said Virgil Jones bring then and there armed with a dangerous weapon, then and there break and enter the storehouse of Robert S. Pollard and Joshua Walker, partners trading under the style of Pollard & Walker, and them the said Pollard and Walker in bodily fear feloniously did put, and a large quantity of bacon, to wit, one hundred pounds, of the value of one hundred dollars, of the goods and chattels of the said Pollard and Walker, from the person against the will of the said Pollard and Walker, feloniously did steal, take and carry away; and in this also, that he the said Virgil Jones, on the day and year last aforesaid, at this city, in the daytime of that day, did break and enter the storehouse aforesaid, and did then and there from said storehouse feloniously take, steal and carry away a large quantity, to wit, five hundred pounds of bacon of the value of five hundred dollars of the goods and chattels of said Pollard and Walker; was this day led to the bar in custody of the sergeant, and the court having heard the evidence, are of opinion that the said Virgil Jones ought to be tried for the said offence before the Judge of this court. And he is thereupon remanded to jail, Depositions of the witnesses for the commonwealth taken down in writing and filed.

And Robert S. Pollard, Thomas H. Harris and John M. Richardson recognized in the sum of three hundred dollars each, with condition for their appearance before the Judge of this court, on the first day of the next May term of the said court to be holder by the said Judge, to give evidence on behalf of the commonwealth against the said Virgil Jones, and not to depart thence without the leave of the said Judge.

Tuesday, April 14, 1863; Page 402

Sarah Champion, who stands charged with a felony by her committed in this, that on the second day of April 1863, at this city and within the jurisdiction of this court, she the said Sarah Champion and divers other persons whose names are unknown did feloniously and riotously assemble themselves together, to the terror of the public, and did feloniously and riotously break and enter the storehouse of James Knotts, and she the said Sarah Champion did, with the said other persons so riotously assembled, make an assault upon him the said James Knotts, and him the said James Knotts in bodily fear did feloniously put, and one pair of shoes of the value of fifteen dollars, one shoe of the value of two dollars, three pair of upper leathers for shoes of the value of fifteen dollars, and five candles of the value of fifty cents, of the property, goods and chattels of the said James Knotts, against the will and consent of the said James Knotts, feloniously did steal, take and carry away, was this day led to the bar in custody of the sergeant, and the court, having heard the evidence, are of opinion that the said Sarah Champion ought to be tried for the said offence before the Judge of this court. And thereupon the said Sarah Champion is remanded to jail. Depositions of the witnesses for the commonwealth taken down in writing and filed. And James Knotts, John 0. Hall and Alexander C. Orange recognized in the sum of three hundred dollars each, with condition for their appearance before the Judge of this court on the first day of the next May term of this court to be held by the said Judge, to give evidence on behalf of the commonwealth against the said Sarah Champion, and not to depart thence without the leave of the said Judge.

Wednesday, April 15, 1863; pages 406-09

Benjamin Slemper, who stands charged with a felony by him committed, in this, that on the second day of April 1863, at this city and within the jurisdiction of this court, he did feloniously, in the day time of that day, by force and violence break and enter the storehouse of James Knotts, and did then and there feloniously put the said James Knotts in bodily fear, and did then and there by force and violence, from the person of the said James Knotts and against his will, feloniously take, steal and carry away a quantity of boots and shoes of the value of fifty dollars, of the goods and chattels of said Knotts; and in this also, that the said Benjamin Slemper, on the day and year

The Richmond Bread Riot

last aforesaid, at the city aforesaid, did feloniously take, steal and carry away divers other pairs of shoes and boots of the value of fifty dollars, of the goods and chattels of said James Knotts; was this day led to the bar in custody of the sergeant, and the court having heard the evidence is of opinion that the said Benjamin Slemper ought to be tried before the Judge of this court for the said offence. And he is thereupon remanded to jail. Depositions of the witnesses for the commonwealth taken down in writing and filed. And James Knotts, Lafayette H. Fitzhugh and Charles Norton recognized in the sum of three hundred dollars each, with condition for their appearance before the Judge of this court on the first day of the next May term of this court to be holden by the said Judge, to give evidence on behalf of the commonwealth against the said Benjamin Slemper, and not to depart thence without the leave of the said Judge.

Thomas Samanni and William J. Lusk, who stand charged with a felony by them committed in this, that on the 2d day of April in the year 1863, at this city and within the jurisdiction of this court, they the said Thomas Samanni, William J. Lusk and a certain Mary Johnson, being free white persons, together with other evil disposed and riotous persons unknown, did feloniously, unlawfully and riotously assemble and gather together to disturb the peace of this commonwealth, and being so assembled and gathered together, the dwelling house of one Minna Schweitzer did in part feloniously injure and destroy, to the great disturbance and terror of the said Minna Schweitzer and of the people in the neighbourhood then residing, were led to the bar in custody of the sergeant, and the court having heard the evidence is of opinion that the said Thomas Samanni ought to be tried for the said offense before the Judge of this court, and that the said William J. Lusk be acquitted and discharged of the same. And the said Thomas Samanni is thereupon remanded to jail. Depositions of witnesses for the commonwealth taken down in writing and filed. And Minna Schweitzer, Charles H. Wynne and Lewis Lichenstein recognized in the sum of three hundred dollars each, with condition for their appearance before the Judge of this court on the first day of the next May term of this court to be held by the said Judge, to give evidence on behalf of the commonwealth against the said Thomas Samanni, and not to depart thence without the leave of the said Judge.

Thomas Samanni and William J. Lusk, who stand charged with a felony by them committed in this, that on the 2d day of April 1863, at this city and within the jurisdiction of this court, they did feloniously by force and violence break and enter, in the daytime of that day, the storehouse of Minna Schweitzer and feloniously put her in bodily fear, and from her person and presence and against her will feloniously take, steal and carry away a large quantity of dry goods, to wit, two hundred yards of homespun cotton goods, four hats, divers pieces of calico, divers pairs of mens boots and shoes, a large quantity of pocket handkerchiefs, stockings, gloves and socks, pantaloons, coats, shirts, combs, and divers pieces of sheeting containing three hundred yards, and of the value of one thousand dollars, of the goods and chattels of Minna Schweitzer; and in this also, that the said Thomas Samanni and William J. Lusk, on the day and year aforesaid, divers articles of dry goods, towit, two hundred yards of domestic homespun, three hundred yards of sheeting, divers articles of mens wearing apparel, towit, boots and shoes, shirts, pantaloons and coats, all of the value of seven hundred dollars, of the goods and chattels of Minna Schweitzer, did feloniously take, steal and carry away; were this day led to the bar in custody of the sergeant, and the court, having heard the evidence, is of opinion that the said Thomas Samanni ought to be tried for the said offence before the Judge of this court, and that the said William J. Lusk be acquitted and discharged of the same. And the said Thomas Samanni is thereupon remanded to jail. Depositions of the witnesses for the Commonwealth taken down in writing and filed. And Minna Schweitzer, Charles H. Wynne and Lewis Lichenstein recognized in the sum of three hundred dollars each, with condition for their appearance before the Judge of this court on the first day of the next May term of this court to be holden by the said Judge, to give evidence on behalf of the commonwealth against the said Thomas Samanni, and not to depart thence without the leave of the said Judge.

Mary Jackson, who stands charged with a felony by her committed, in this, that on the 2d day of April 1863, at this city and within the jurisdiction of this court, Thomas Samanni, William J. Lusk and Mary Johnson, being free white persons, together with many other evil disposed and riotous persons unknown, did feloniously, unlawfully and riotously assemble and gather together to disturb the peace of this commonwealth, and being so assembled and gathered together, the said Thomas Samanni and William J. Lusk the dwelling house of one Minna Schweitzer did in part feloniously injure and destroy, to the great disturbance and terror of the said Minna Schweitzer and of the people in the neighbourhood then residing, and that the said Mary Jackson, before the felony aforesaid was committed in form aforesaid, on the day and year last aforesaid, did feloniously incite, counsel, aid and abet the said Thomas Samanni and William J. Lusk to do and commit the said felony in manner and form aforesaid, was this day led to the bar in custody of the sergeant, and the court having heard the evidence is of opinion that the said Mary Jackson ought to be tried for the said offence before the Judge of this court. And she is thereupon remanded to jail. Depositions of witnesses for the commonwealth taken down in writing and filed. And Minna Schweitzer, Charles H. Wynne, Lewis Lichenstein, William N. Kelley, Washington [William] A. Griffin, James P. Tyler and Augustus A. Hughes recognized in the sum of three hundred dollars each, with condition for their appearance before the Judge of this court on the first day of the next May term of this court to be held by the said Judge, to give evidence on behalf of the commonwealth against the said Mary Jackson, and not to depart thence without the leave of the said Judge.

Friday, April 17, 1863; Pages 417—18

John Jones, who stands charged with a felony by him committed in this, that on the 2d day of April in the year 1863, at this city and within the jurisdiction of this court, he did feloniously have and receive twelve hats of the value of one hundred dollars, of the goods and chattels of John T. Hicks, two pair of shoes of the value of twenty dollars, of the goods and chattels of some person unknown, ten pounds of coffee of the value of thirty dollars, of the goods and chattels of John Tyler & Son, two shoulders of bacon of the value of twenty five dollars, of the goods and chattels of some person unknown, and one lot of candles of the value of ten dollars, of the goods and chattels of some person unknown, then lately before that time feloniously taken, stolen and carried away by some person unknown, he the said John Jones then and there well knowing the said goods to have been feloniously taken, stolen and carried away; and in this also, that on the day and year aforesaid he the said John Jones twelve other hats of the value of one hundred dollars, of the goods and chattels of John T. Hicks, two other pair of shoes of the value of twenty dollars, two other shoulders of bacon of the value of twenty five dollars, and one other lot of candles of the value of ten dollars, of the goods and chattels of some person unknown, and ten pounds of coffee of the value of thirty dollars, of the goods and chattels of John Tyler & Son, feloniously did steal, take and carry away; was this day led to the bar in custody of the sergeant, and the court having heard the evidence is of opinion that the said John Jones ought to be tried for the said offence before the Judge of this court. And he is thereupon remanded to jail. Depositions of the witnesses for the commonwealth taken down in writing and filed. And Mitchell L. Adams, Washington [William] A. Griffin, Adrien Vannerson and John T. Hicks recognized in the sum of three hundred dollars each, with condition for their appearance before the Judge of this court on the first day of the next May term of this court to be held by the said Judge, to give evidence on behalf of the commonwealth against the said John Jones, and not to depart thence without the leave of the said Judge.

Thursday. May 14, 1863; pages 452—53

Frances Kelley, charged with a felony by her committed in this, that on the 2d day of April in the year 1863, at the City of Richmond, and within the jurisdiction of this Court, she did, with divers other persons whose names are unknown, feloniously and riotously assemble themselves together to the terror of the public, and did feloniously

The Richmond Bread Riot

and violently break and enter the storehouse of Robert S. Pollard and Joshua Walker partners under the firm of Pollard and Walker, and a large quantity of bacon of the value of one hundred dollars, of the goods and chattels of the said Robert S. Pollard and Joshua Walker, partners as aforesaid, feloniously and violently did take, steal and carry away - was this day led to the bar in the custody of the Sergeant, and thereupon the said Frances Kelley moved the Court to quash the Certificate of the committing magistrate, for error apparent on its face, which motion the Court sustained, and order that said certificate be quashed, but that the said Frances Kelley be retained in custody and be carried before the Mayor or some other justice of the peace of this City, to be examined for the said offence.

Minute Book No. 29

Wednesday, February 10, 1864, Page 123

Frances Kelly, who stands charged with a felony by her committed in this, that on the 2d day of April in the year 1863, at the City of Richmond, and within the jurisdiction of this Court, she did, with Margaret A. Pomfrey, Mary Johnson and a large number of other persons, towit: to the number of two hundred, unlawfully, violently and tumultuously assemble themselves together in the public streets of the said City, to the terror of the good people of this Commonwealth, and to disturb the public peace, and that the said Frances Kelly being one of the said persons so unlawfully and riotously assembled did at the said City, on the Day and year last aforesaid, riotously and feloniously break and enter the storehouse of Robert S. Pollard and Joshua Walker, with intent to commit larceny therein, and a large quantity of bacon, to wit: fifty pounds of bacon of the value of seventy five dollars, of the goods and chattels of the said Robert S. Pollard and Joshua Walker, feloniously did take, steal and carry away; - was this Day led to the bar in the Custody of the Sergeant of this City, and the Court having heard the evidence, are of opinion that the said Frances Kelly ought to be tried for the said offence before the Judge of this Court. And the said Frances Kelly is remanded to jail. And Fleming Griffin, Robert S. Pollard and W. A. Griffin severally entered into a recognizance in the sum of three hundred Dollars each, for their appearance.

Appendix E: Richmond Newspaper Articles of 1888-1889 and later

Richmond Dispatch, December 16, 1888, Our Richmond Mobs
Richmond Dispatch, December 30, 1888, Bread Riot of 1863
Richmond Dispatch, January 20, 1889. Bread Riot, Again
Richmond Dispatch, April 28, 1889, Hon. Jeff'n Davis
Richmond Times-Dispatch, October 10, 1909,
    The Richmond Bread Riot
Richmond Times-Dispatch, October 24, 1909,
    Richmond During Bread Riot Days

The Richmond Bread Riot

***THE RICHMOND DISPATCH* - Sunday, December 16, 1888, Page 2**

OUR RICHMOND MOBS
SOME EXPERIENCES IN THIS CITY WITH
UNRULY MASSES

THE BREAD RIOT

April 1[2] 1863, occurred in Richmond what is commonly called the "bread riot," though as a matter of fact many of the people engaged in it were willing to take anything they could lay their hands on; and though some of them were no doubt honest though much misguided people, crazed almost by the woes laid on them by the war, the majority were coarse women, and two of them paid the penalty of their misdeeds by being convicted of robbery and were sent to the penitentiary.[167]

The incidents of this remarkable affair have never yet been written up in truly historical style, though they deserve to be.

The best account at hand is below given. It is the relation of the Hon. John W. Daniel, an eye-witness, but he never wrote it for publication. In 1878 he was traveling on a Chesapeake and Ohio car, and to while the hours of the night away he described the mob to Dr. Moffet and Hon. John Paul. Without knowing it he had another listener - a reporter of the New York Sun - which enterprising individual sat with open ears, and as soon as possible thereafter wrote out what he had heard. While most of the publication is in the reporter's own language, Major Daniel said when he saw it that it was substantially correct. The reporter probably misquotes the Major in attributing to President Davis the commands to Captain Gay, of the Public Guard. That company was a State organization in State service. The mob was violating a State law, and it is safe to presume that Governor Letcher or the Mayor (very likely the Governor) managed all those little details, which, with the presence of the State Guard, disposed of the most remarkable mob in the history of Richmond.

The Richmond Bread Riot

MAJOR DANIEL'S STORY

The Major said that when Harper's Ferry was captured at the beginning of the war all the available machinery for the manufacture of arms was taken to Richmond. Hundreds of workmen and their wives and daughters had been employed in the arsenals and machine-shops, and they followed the machinery to the capital in search of employment. They got it. For a time they were regularly paid in good money, and everything moved smoothly.

But as the currency depreciated they began to suffer. The money received by the workmen would not support their families. As the war progressed Confederate notes became almost valueless. The wages of the workmen would not purchase food for their families. They protested, but in vain. They were too patriotic to organize a revolution. Their women, however, formed a secret society, based on communistic principles. They seem to have held that their husbands were working for the Confederacy, and that the Confederacy was the only safety of the grocers and shopkeepers. Without clothing and provisions their husbands and sons must stop work. This would cut off necessary munitions and supplies, the Government would fall, and all be involved in one common ruin. To avoid this a general division of food and clothing must be made.

While standing in Main street one morning the Major witnessed an extraordinary scene. Hundreds of women suddenly appeared. The broad avenue was filled with them. They came filing in from the cross-streets by platoons, and began to sack the stores. Hollow-eyed and gaunt with hunger, nobody dared resist them. A crowd of men hung upon the outskirts, offering no interference and expressing no sympathy for the shopkeepers. The women took the stores in line, one after the other. They proceeded systematically. The goods were piled upon wagons drawn by horses driven by female sympathizers. Not a word was spoken. The work was done with terrible earnestness. When the mob entered a grocery a certain percentage of them piled the goods upon the outstretched arms of the others, and they were borne to the streets and dumped into the wagons. The women had it all their own way. Neither soldiers nor police were in sight. Mean-

The Richmond Bread Riot

while the crowd increased. Other women heard what was going on, and flocked to Main Street for a share of the plunder. Not a man joined them, and for a long time no one made an effort to stop them. At last Colonel Baldwin, of Virginia, jumped upon a dry-goods box, and made an impassioned appeal for law and order. He might as well have talked to the wind. No one paid the least attention to him. The women went on with their sacking, and the bystanders drowned Baldwin's voice with their whoops and cheers.

"While I was gazing at the scene," said the Major, "I saw a captain of a cavalry regiment, with whom I had a slight acquaintance. We were both in uniform. We agreed that something ought to be done to restore order and stop the robbery. At his suggestion we stationed ourselves at the door of a store already overrun. In a few seconds a virago tried to pass us. I can see her now. Her cheeks and lips were red, but she had a pinched, starved look, and an eye like a hawk. She carried in her arms a half dozen bars of yellow soap, a piece of dress silk, a long box of stockings, and some raisins and herrings. I said:

'Madam, I beg your pardon; but you are forgetting yourself. These goods are not yours. You have not paid for them, and you will not be permitted to leave this store with them.'

"She looked at me," said the Major, "in a wild way, as though endeavoring to comprehend what I had said, and then went to the counter and threw down the goods. As she came back she deliberately took me by the arm and slung me from her with such force that I went spinning around like a top, and struck the front of the building so hard that it took the breath out of me. She then quietly gathered up her load from the counter and walked out. The Alabama captain looked at me and laughed, but kept his hands in his pockets and said nothing. I told him I thought we were out of place, and he nodded. We concluded after that to remain simple spectators.

"Meanwhile the women were approaching near the Old market. Certain people down there were credited with great wealth. It was said that they had made barrels of money out of the Confederacy, and the female Communists went at them without a qualm of conscience. The shopkeepers, however, had heard what was going on

The Richmond Bread Riot

above and tried to protect themselves. They put up their shutters, barricaded their doors, ran upstairs, and watched the proceedings from the second-story windows. But the women were not dismayed. While some of them ran for axes, others found a long piece of scantling and used it as a battering-ram. The first door flew open amid the cheers of the outsiders, followed by a wail of sorrow. 'Oh, mine kott! mine kott! I ish ruined, I ish ruined!' was the cry. But they made no further defence. Indeed it would have been dangerous for them to attempt it, for if one of the female robbers had been hurt the crowd of husbands and brothers would surely have avenged it.

"And so," said the Major, "the spoilation continued. At last a rumor ran through the street, 'The Governor is coming.' It proved true. Down the hill came Governor Letcher, accompanied by his staff and a few friends."

Then a second rumor spread over the crowd. The President was coming. This also proved true. President Davis rode down, followed by a Captain Gay and the Public Guard. He mounted a wagon and everybody was silent. I had seen him several times but had never heard him speak, so I forced my way within ten feet of him and stood spell-bound. It was the most eloquent speech I ever heard. Tall and slender, he swayed with emotion like the willow in the wind. His words were carefully chosen. He spoke of his experience in the Mexican war, and, while expressing his deepest sympathy with the sorrows and sufferings of the children of the Confederacy, sternly maintained the necessity of law and order.

The Major heard that many of the women stopped pillaging, and gathered at a distance listening to the words that they could catch. At the close of his speech the President(?) took out his watch and gazed at it long and earnestly.

"Captain Gay," said he, "order your men to load with ball cartridges."

The order was obeyed, and the ringing of ramrods was heard. The crowd began to give way.

"Captain Gay," said the President,(?) still looking at his watch, "if this street is not cleared within five minutes, order your men to fire down the street until it is cleared."

The Richmond Bread Riot

The scene was on Franklin street near the Old market, not on Main. I first saw the mob on Main near the old American Hotel.

Mr. Davis rode away. Within three minutes there was not a soul in sight but the Guards. The mob funnelled itself into the side streets. Those nearest the President gave the information to those in front and rushed against them with the force of a wave. "They are going to fire!" The words were heard by the pilferers in the stores. They knew the character of Jefferson Davis and of Governor Letcher and they knew the reputation of old Captain Gay. Where Davis would not flinch from giving an order Gay would not flinch from obeying it. The women dispersed as quickly as they came and that was the end of the Female Commune. They never held another meeting.

THE RICHMOND DISPATCH - Sunday, December 30, 1888, Page 2

BREAD RIOT OF 1863
Reminiscences of a Memorable Period of Our War History

A MOB OF WOMEN
Military Called Out to Disperse Them
How it was Done, an Unsolved Question

Two weeks ago there was published in this paper an account of memorable mobs in Richmond, the most remarkable of which was that known as "the bread riot." This occurred on April 2, 1863, and in the beginning was composed chiefly of women who clamored for bread, and who in their extremity thought it right and proper to break into stores and warehouses and help themselves not only to food but to shoes, clothing, and other valuables.

It was the fashion of that period to style these women "termagants," "viragoes," &c., and no doubt many tough characters were among them; but these were days when wives, mothers, and daughters had to support the families of soldiers, and provisions were ter-

The Richmond Bread Riot

ribly scarce and high, and it requires no imagination to understand that desperation must have seized many who, under favoring circumstances, would not have dishonored their sex. However that may be, the women started out to pillage the stores, and gangs of men followed them and helped them and the town was in great excitement and the shopkeepers with big stocks in much alarm. The result was that the Public Guard had to be called out. It was only by threatening to fire into the crowd that the riotous and roguish men and women were dispersed.

Restrained by fear of giving information of our straitened circumstances to the public enemy the newspapers of that day had precious little to say about the affair. Some of them did not mention it at all. Others referred to it briefly. The Examiner made full reports of the examination by the Mayor of those who were charged with theft. In one case Governor Letcher testified that when he commanded the mob to disperse the prisoner (Palmer) remarked to him that "there is a power behind the throne mightier than the throne." The rest of the crowd dispersed, but the prisoner remained and still refused to depart, and was thereupon ordered into custody. When Palmer was asked what the power was he said the people.

Mr. Andrew Jenkins testified that the Governor "went down to the corner of Fifteenth street" and ordered the crowd to disperse. The crowd dispersed except the prisoner.

Reputable witnesses now living declare that it was not Governor Letcher but President Davis who dispersed the mob. Some others attribute this action to Mayor Mayo. Here is direct contradiction.

Now the question is, Who gave the mob five minutes to disperse or be fired into? Was it President Davis, Governor Letcher, or Mayor Mayo? When that point is settled the next question is, Whereabout in the city did this occur? To the solution of these problems the following eye—witnesses, all intelligent gentlemen, speak at the request of the Dispatch:

The Richmond Bread Riot

SPEECH OF PRESIDENT DAVIS

Mr. D. S. Doggett: The day before I left for the Valley to join a cavalry command I had occasion to pass through Capitol Square on my way up—town, and as I approached the Washington Monument I saw a number of women congregated about it. Asking someone what it meant and getting no satisfactory answer I passed on. After awhile returning by the same route and missing the crowd I inquired what had become of it and was told that what I had seen was the beginning of the riot then in progress about the Old market. Upon learning this I ran down Main street and up Seventeenth to Franklin, where I encountered the mob.

On reaching the corner I saw Mr. John B. Baldwin standing in the door of a shop driving back the infuriated women as they attempted to plunder it. He was a large man, and his stalwart figure never appeared to better advantage than on that occasion, when, with his sleeves rolled up and stern determination upon his manly features, he stood between the frenzied mob and the frightened vender of boots and shoes and cheap clothing.

While this scene was being enacted some one shouted that the soldiers were coming, and sure enough the Public Guard, with Captain Gay at their head, were seen marching rapidly up Seventeenth street.

At this unexpected turn of affairs the mob took to their heels and dashed up Franklin street with the soldiers after them. When they reached the intersection of Governor and Franklin streets, whether out of breath or reassured, they stopped as if determined to resist any further advance on them by the military. At this juncture his Honor Joseph Mayo, Mayor of the city, ordered the mob to disperse, giving them five minutes in which to do so, and telling them if they didn't the soldiers would be commanded to fire on them.

Then old Captain Gay stepped forward and with tears streaming down his cheeks besought the rioters to go peaceably to their homes, and spare him the pain of turning his guns upon the bosoms of his own people.

But this dread alternative never became necessary, for just as the Captain finished speaking President Davis clambered into a cart

The Richmond Bread Riot

which was standing at Binford & Porter's corner (now Rountree & Brother's),[168] and for a few seconds calmly - one might say mournfully looked into the faces of that turbulent throng. When he spoke his voice was quiet and his tones were gentle. A hush fell upon the crowd. He didn't upbraid them, he didn't threaten them, but in thrilling words he told them that was not the way to redress their grievances, and begged them not to fasten a reproach upon the fair name of Richmond. His remarks were few, but when they were ended the rioters had stolen away as if ashamed of their conduct.

NOT DAVIS BUT LETCHER

Mr. George I. Herring: You say in your issue of the 21st that there is great conflict of authority as to when the bread riot ended and where it was that President Davis halted the mob with a speech, &c. It was not President Davis, but Governor Letcher who made the speech. Captain Gay, with a detachment of the Public Guard, had just arrived, and the Governor told the mob if they did not disperse at once (I think he gave them five minutes) he would order Captain Gay to fire into the crowd. This occurred on Main street between Fourteenth and Fifteenth, very near or just in front of Thomas R. Price's store. I was doing business at the time a little lower down on the opposite side from Price's and on the same square, and heard the speech and saw the mob disperse.

SAW A CANNON

Mr. James H. Binford, now of Rocky Mount, Va.: I was in Richmond on furlough during the bread riot. I was on Main street, near Richardson & Co. s carpet store, between Fourteenth and Fifteenth streets, when the cannon was brought out and stationed near the St. Charles Hotel, pointing up Main street. Orders were given for the mob to disperse. As soon as the order was given I stepped into Richardsons's store, and in five minutes the crowd had dispersed in every direction. This I think ended the riot, at least I never heard of any demonstration afterwards.

The Richmond Bread Riot

E. B. Spence, Clothier, No. 1300 Main Street, corner of 13th Street, where one 1888 newspaper correspondent stated that Jefferson Davis addressed the remnants of the Mob (E. B. Spence side door).

The Richmond Bread Riot

PRESIDENT DAVIS SPEAKS AT ANOTHER PLACE

Mr. W. W. Davies, who was the messenger in the office of President Davis: Did President Davis address this mob more than once? I think not, and if not the locality was at the northwest corner of the custom-house, in which at that time the offices of the Executive Department (State and Treasury departments) were, I then being messenger in attendance upon President Davis. President Davis mounted a barrel of rice, which was rolled out of the old Madison House, near the corner of Tenth and Bank streets and adjoining the custom-house, from the northwest corner of which he addressed the mob. After the address the rice was distributed to them. This I saw from the top of the portico on a line with our department (the Executive). After the address was ended the President came to the department and his office in quite an excited frame of mind, and on the following morning I had quite a long talk with him upon the general impression caused by this riot and his action in the matter.

FROM THE NEWSPAPER SCRAP-BOOK

Major G. A. Baskerville: In my war scrap-book there is somewhat of a detailed account of the so-called "bread riot" of April 2, 1863. The scraps were taken from the Examiner of April 3, 1863, and subsequent dates during the trials before the Mayor's Court.

During the reading of the riot act by Mayor Mayo the Public Guard, Lieutenant Gay commanding, arrived on the ground, halting about midway the square between Fourteenth and Fifteenth streets, and were stationed ready for action on either side of the street. Soon after the reading of the act and the arrival of the guard the riot subsided. I think I saw Governor Letcher with the Mayor. I did not see the President. My recollection is that he started for the scene, but yielded to persuasion and returned to his office. In this I may be mistaken, but am certain he was not there at the time the riot act was read, nor after that time, as there was no occasion.

The Richmond Bread Riot

THE ELOQUENCE OF PRESIDENT DAVIS

Mr. W. G. Bentley, of Norfolk: Having noticed that there is a controversy about the location of the point where President Davis checked and dispersed the mob of women at the time of the bread riot in Richmond during the war, I wish to contribute what I can to the solution of that fact.

I was at the time on duty in Richmond in the service of the Confederate army, and my recollection of the matter, of which I was an eye-witness, is that Mr. Davis met the mob, entirely composed of women, near the intersection of Cary and Thirteenth streets, just after they had broken open and partially sacked the house formerly and afterwards occupied by Messrs. Tyler & Son, in which there were at the time of the mob supplies belonging to the Government.

I do not think that Mr. Davis dispersed them by threats, but mainly by promises to look into their grievances, which he did to their satisfaction. It was the eloquence of Mr. Davis, together with the confidence of the women in his willingness and ability to do them justice, which quelled the disturbance.

DAVIS, LETCHER, AND MOUNTED POLICE

Dr. A. S. McRae: During the progress of the bread riot in Richmond, in company with the late Dr. Junius Archer, of Bellona, Dr. D.S. Hancock, and Mr. Austin E. Moore, both of Chesterfield, I was standing in the door of the grocery store of which Mr. Moore was the proprietor, which was located a door or two below where the Columbian Block now stands. We were in constant apprehension of an attack upon this well-filled store by the mob. We did not have to wait very long before a crowd of three or four hundred men and women gathered in front of the store, yelling and shouting as if maddened by liquor and determined upon serious mischief. They immediately demanded the surrender of the store and announced their determination to break into it if the door was not opened. Mr. Moore showed a great deal of nerve and firmness, and with a six—shooter in his hand told them that he would defend his property at the risk of his life. There were standing in about ten or twelve feet of us several stout, rough-looking men, with axes in their hands. Mr. Moore's evident determination to shoot the first person who attempted to break down the door held them at bay until Mr. Joseph Mayo, the Mayor of the city, and President Davis rode up at the head of fifteen or twenty mounted police. Mr. Mayo read the riot act, and then told them that he would give them five minutes to disperse, and that if they did not do so he would fire upon them. They immediately rushed down Cary street and scattered in various directions. My recollection is that they did not afterwards reassemble or do any further damage. They had previously broken into a number of stores.

I am entirely confident in the statement that Mr. Davis was present on that occasion. This is all that I am able to state of my personal knowledge about this, one of the most exciting and alarming events that has ever occurred in this city.

THE SACKING OF THE STORES

Mr. G. A. Purks: Rumors were prevalent several days before it came off that a riot would take place, and that a woman huckster in the Second market would lead the women in a break for bread. She being well-to-do herself, sought to benefit herself by espousing the cause of the less fortunate and also to add to her own stores.

The first I knew of the actual mob was on Cary street between Twelfth and Thirteenth streets. Here an immense crowd had gathered. The first house broken into was Pollard & Walker's, the next - Tyler's - both grocers; the next, was J. T. Hicks's, a shoe dealer; all of which were gutted in a short time, the goods put in wagons in waiting and carried off.

During this time the riot act was read and the crowd ordered to disperse, which they paid no attention to.

They then formed in line, two and two, and marched to Main street, corner Thirteenth, turned down Main until they got to a Mr. —- Knott's shoe store. Here, led on by some desperate men, they commenced breaking the windows, and putting some of the men inside they soon had the doors open and the work begun, the men inside throwing the shoes to the women on the sidewalk and the

The Richmond Bread Riot

citizens, of whom I was one, throwing them back as fast as they were thrown out.

While this was going on a citizen recognized a man as the leader and seized him and called for help. Several of us caught hold, and at that time a Confederate officer came up, drew his pistol, and we took the rioter to prison, and I think he was sent to the penitentiary.

Later in the morning Colonel Elliott's City battalion marched down Main street, and as he went warned the people to retire from the street.

Knott's shoe store was situated about where Mr. M. Millhiser's store now stands, between Thirteenth and Fourteenth streets on Main.

HOW PRESIDENT DAVIS QUELLED THE MOB

Mr. Polk Miller: In your Sunday's issue you give an account of the "bread riot" which occurred in this city in the spring of 1863. Major Daniel was not misquoted in saying that "Jeff. Davis" gave orders to Captain Gay. I was in three feet of Mr. Davis, and not only heard the grand speech made by him, but heard his order to Captain Gay. The first public officer who appeared upon the scene was Colonel Munford, who, mounted upon a furniture wagon at the corner of Twelfth and Cary streets, told the motley crew that he had come from the Governor's mansion and that the Governor said that he would see to it that there should be no suffering among the people in this city, but that it was his duty to see that the laws should be observed, and at all hazards he would put a stop to the proceedings if they commenced to pilfer. The crowd, composed mostly of women and half-grown boys, listened to his appeal for a few minutes, but the door of the Confederate commissary had by this time been forced open, and the various articles stored therein were being "toated off" in the direction of the river. Long lines of women and boys came pouring in from the direction of the Tredegar, and the turns of "fat middling" that some of the women carried on their shoulders would have done credit to the strongest man. Having emptied this store of its contents, and the mob by this time having become completely wild, they commenced to break into private stores on the south side

The Richmond Bread Riot

of Cary (near the Bank of Richmond) occupied by people who sold shoes and clothing which had come in through the blockade. The half-grown boys were pushed in through the windows, and on reaching the upper stories they would throw down the goods to the women. Many women would be freighted with shoes, blankets, and other articles of general merchandise. Here the Mayor (Mr. Mayo) came up and read the riot act to no purpose. The crowd then went down to one of the Government storehouses between the bridge and the market, and, joined by a caravan from lower Main street and Rocketts, the street was completely blocked. After sacking the most of the stores below Thirteenth street they started for Watkins & Ficklen's and Samuel M. Price & Co.'s. The friends of these houses had by this time rallied to their rescue, and although the large windows were smashed and the boys pushed through the apertures by the women from the outside, the defenders from the inside, composed of soldiers on leave and convalescents from the hospitals and citizens exempted from the service by reason of age or physical disability, fought them back and saved these establishments from utter ruin. The main body of the rioters were below Thirteenth street, and to that point the foiled "lovers of fine dry goods" retreated to rejoin their friends.

At this juncture the State Guard, under Captain Gay, appeared upon the scene, and, marching down Main street from Ninth, they halted at the corner of Thirteenth and stretched from Purcell, Ladd & Co.'s over to Putney & Watts's. At the same time Jefferson Davis, who had come down Governor street mounted a dry goods box at E.B. Spence's side door[169] and made not only "a grand speech" but a kind one. He told the people that he would see to it that their wants in the way of food and rations should be supplied, but it should be done in the proper way. He also told them that if they started out for bread it had wound up in a regular pilfering expedition. He ordered Captain Gay to fix his bayonets and load his guns, and, turning to the crowd, he said: "I will give you five minutes to disperse." Holding his watch in his hand he told them four minutes had passed. At this time the crowd had not shown the slightest disposition to move off, but as the military brought their guns from an order to carry arms

The Richmond Bread Riot

on the call of "time's up," the greatest stampede I ever saw took place. In ten minutes the streets were depopulated of the rioting element. I was in three feet of Mr. Davis when he gave Captain Gay the order to get ready. He was as cool as if on parade, and the great crowd of hard-looking women, armed with knives, hatchets, and spindles with "corn-cob" handles saw that he had the "old boy" in his eye and meant what he said. I very often see men on the streets here now who were (as boys then) engaged in the riot, and for years after the war I recognized many of the females. The first attack made was on a Confederate commissary, and for that reason I consider that Jefferson Davis was the proper man.

AN INTERESTING NARRATIVE

Dr. J. W. Anderson: The following account of the "bread riot" is taken from my war diary, and I can vouch for its accuracy so far as it goes. Like a soldier in battle, I saw only a small part of the "row." I saw nothing of President Davis nor of Governor Letcher on the ground, and certainly neither of them was present when Lieutenant Gay dispersed the mob at that point:

"April 2, 1863. This morning as I wended my way towards the office I was surprised to see a crowd of women assembled in the Square at the foot of Washington's equestrian statue. It soon became apparent that a "bread riot" was in contemplation, and I mingled with the throng to witness their proceedings. After a short consultation they marched in a body to the Governor's house, and told him he must give them bread or they would take it wherever they could find it. 'If you do,' said he, 'it will be over the point of the bayonet.' Not at all intimidated by this significant threat they rushed down the street, and dividing into companies attacked four or five stores at once. They were 'armed and equipped' in a most whimsical style. Some had rusty old horse-pistols, innocent of powder and ball, some had hatchets and axes, some clubs, some knives, and many carried bayonets in their belts, and specimens of those huge old home-made knives with which our soldiers were wont to load themselves down in the first part of the war.

The Richmond Bread Riot

About a thousand men followed these women, taking no part and seeming half amused, half indignant. I moved down to Cary street with one party, and mounting on a bag of potatoes standing beside a store door obtained a good view of the whole proceeding. They halted first in front of Pollard & Walker's store. A brief parley ensued, and I saw the owners attempt to close the doors. Instantly a shower of blows with fists, sticks, pistols, axes, and hatchets fell upon it. Glass flew in every direction. The doors gave way, and in a moment more the crowd rushed through with a fierce roar of triumph. Then began a scene of wild confusion and pillage. The women streamed out, carrying away bacon, flour, sugar, brooms, hats, and everything they could find. They seized upon - or, to use a military term, they 'impressed' - sundry carts and wagons that happened to be at hand and loaded them with provisions. Partly appeased but not satiated, they next broke into the adjoining building - a shoe store - and in ten minutes it was thoroughly eviscerated - not a single article left in it - and a large part of the crowd literally 'stood in the shoes' of the proprietor.

All this time similar scenes of violence were visible on Main and Broad streets. The rioters did not confine themselves to articles of food, but stole silks, ribbons, millinery, laces, hats, shoes, cigars, and everything they could lay their hands on. Doubtless some of those ragged women considered new bonnets and dresses as much "necessaries of life" as bread and meat. They did not, however, escape scot free in all cases. As long as the crowd held together they were safe, but the moment one of the female warriors separated with her booty she was gobbled up by the police and lodged in the station-house.

One of the policemen met an Amazon with a big piece of bacon on her head and a ham in each hand. "Madam," said he, suavely, "where did you get that meat?" "I got it from a store on Cary street." "Did you pay for it?" "Oh, no! We don't pay for bacon nowadays." "Indeed!" said the guardian of the outraged law. "In that case I must run you in. No sooner were the words uttered than, dropping one of the hams his prisoner drew a pistol, clapped it at his breast, and pulled the trigger. Luckily, it failed to fire, or that policeman had been then and there abolished. He held on, however, to his prey and lodged her, bacon and all, in the station-house.

An enterprising huckster-woman mounted a cart well laden with bacon, candles, &c., and setting gallantly on the top of the pile drove away in triumph. She had scarcely gone one hundred yards from the crowd and turned a corner when a policeman, emerging like a big spider from his ambush, pounced upon her and her commissary supplies and captured the whole concern without the firing of a gun. The cart and contents thus left standing without a proprietor soon attracted attention and a new-comer coolly took possession, but no sooner had she gathered up the reins for a start than forth came the inevitable policeman and she followed her predecessor to the cage.

After awhile the State Guard, under Lieutenant Gay, made its appearance, and forming across Cary street, made ready for action. 'I give you five minutes to disperse,' said the stern old man, as with a sharp rattle the bright bayonets were fixed. The hint was enough. In less than one minute not a single crinoline, nor anything in the likeness thereof, remained in sight.

The end of the affair was that the Young Men's Christian Association distributed a large quantity of provisions and promised further help. Thirty or forty of the rioters were arrested, and are now in jail awaiting trial and punishment."

A LETTER WRITTEN BY GOVERNOR LETCHER

Ex-Judge S. Bassett French, of Manchester, was Governor Letcher's aide-de-camp, and he furnishes the Dispatch with the following letter written to him:

"LEXINGTON, VA., APRIL 10, 1878

"Dear Colonel, - I enclose a paper published in St. Louis which contains an article from the New York Sun on the Richmond bread riot which occurred during the war. Mr. Davis is given great credit for quelling it and I am hardly known in the matter. You will recollect that it was I who gave the order from the cart, holding my watch in hand and allowing five minutes to elapse before the order was given to fire. The order to make ready was given and they stood waiting the word "fire," when the crowd dispersed.

"You will recall all the facts and I request that you will have the matter set right as soon as convenient and oblige.

'Your friend,
JOHN LETCHER."

Judge French says he well remembers that the incident related by Governor Letcher took place on Franklin street near the Old market.

Judge French thinks that upon the reception of this letter from Governor Letcher he made a publication of the facts in the Whig. He searched the files of that paper, and all he could find on the subject was the following:

[*Richmond Whig*, May 10, 1878.]

"We are in danger of a newspaper war about the bread riot in Richmond during the war. Major Daniel [quoted in the New York Sun] gave the glory of dispersing it to President Davis. Colonel French gives the post of honor to Governor Letcher. The Goodson Gazette ascribes the glory to Colonel John B. Baldwin. The Petersburg Index says there is a gentleman in that burg who was an eyewitness, and supports Major Daniel's version."

HOW THE QUESTION STANDS

Above are all the facts that the Dispatch has been able to obtain so far. They conflict very much. To reconcile them seems quite impossible; but that the President of the Confederate States, the Governor of Virginia, the Mayor of the city, and several State functionaries, aided by the military, took part in the suppression of the riot seems certain; and it may be assumed, therefore, that the affair was regarded as one of some consequence.

It remains for the historian or some one gifted in examining and weighing testimony to sift a clear and connected account out of the mass of contradictory evidence.

THE RICHMOND DISPATCH - SUNDAY, JANUARY 20, 1889, Page 8

BREAD RIOT, AGAIN
FURTHER REMINISCENCES OF THE SACKING OF STORES BY A MOB OF WOMEN IN 1863

A Memorable Event in the City's War History - Recollections of a Number of Well-Known Citizens

Recent publications in this paper of reminiscences of the "bread riot" of April 1[2], 1863, have awakened much interest and excited no little controversy, inasmuch as there is great conflict of statement. Some of those who fondly believed that they knew all of the facts find themselves confronted by testimony which cannot be contradicted, and yet differs materially from what they imagined to be the true history of that memorable day.

The chief matter of difference is as to whether or not President Davis had anything to do with dispersing the mob.

It is certain that on Franklin street at a point somewhere between the Old market and the Exchange Hotel Governor Letcher confronted the riotous and robbing crowd, and, taking out his watch, said in substance: "I give you five minutes to disperse, and if at the expiration of that time the street is not cleared I will order Lieutenant Gay to fire"; but there is an impression, evidence indeed, that at another locality in the city, where also the women were sacking the stores, President Davis also did what it is certain Governor Letcher did at the point just mentioned.

The difficulty in reconciling the statements of eye-witnesses seems to be that the mob gathered and was dispersed on several streets.

When in 1878 Governor Letcher wrote a letter on the subject to Judge S. Bassett French the Governor seems to have been under the impression that the dispersion of the mob was due to him alone, though he did not say so in terms; but it now appears, though the

The Richmond Bread Riot

Governor probably did not know it, that President Davis was at one of the scenes of disturbance.

The Public Guard was a company of State troops. It was, in fact, "Virginia's standing Army"; but its ordinary duties were to guard the armory (where its quarters were), the penitentiary, and the Capitol and Capitol Square. Its commandant was Captain Dimmock, but at this date he was acting as ordinance officer of the State, and the first lieutenant(afterward captain) Gay, was in command. The Guard was ordered from the armory by Governor Letcher, who sent his aide, Colonel S. Bassett French, to summon them to this special duty.

The contemporaneous records on this subject are very scant; it was not desirable to give the enemy any information concerning our internal troubles, and hence the affair was dismissed with bare and contemptuous notice; but that it was of much consequence may be judged from the fact that the military, the president of the Confederate States, the Governor of Virginia, the Mayor of the city, and numerous other functionaries were brought out, either to quell the rioting or to quiet the excited populace.

A fact not hitherto mentioned is that Bishop [John] McGill was sent for to assist the authorities in allaying the excitement.[170]

The riot act seems to have been read to the mob by divers persons at divers places, and, among others, by Mr. William Taylor, then a magistrate of Jefferson Ward. His store was on Main street in the neighborhood of the Old market, and Mr. James A. Scott, the president of the Council, came from the Mayor to Mr. Taylor asking the latter to read the act. Mr. Taylor caught up with the crowd at the corner of Franklin and Eighteenth streets, where, mounting a dry-goods box, he performed his duty, and soon afterwards the Public Guard fled into Franklin street from Main, and in a little while Governor Letcher made his decisive proclamation, enforced by the presence of bayonets.

An intelligent citizen says that while he does not claim to know what occurred down town, this he remembers, that after the unlawful demonstrations had ceased a crowd of people assembled on Main street in front of the post office (the granite building on Main street between Tenth and Eleventh) and were addressed by President Davis. While speaking a woman threw a loaf of bread at Mr. Davis, and Mr. Davis in the quietest manner possible and with signal eloquence used the incident to argue that bread could not possibly be so very scarce here, else it would not be parted with upon such small provocation.

The women who participated in the sacking of the stores in the main represented a rough element, but they did not belong to the most depraved class of their sex.

Those were grievous times. Bread was scarce and high. Meat was a luxury. Coffee and sugar had long since disappeared from the tables of the poor. Most of the able-bodied men were in the army, but the population was largely increased as the city was filled with refugee country people, many of whom left their homes in the night-time and empty-handed and fled to Richmond to escape the enemy's raiders and marauders. There was great suffering. With many, to this day, those times come across the memory like a black shadow. There was such privation as can only come to a beleaguered city. Withal, there were known to be here, in the midst of people unexcelled in patriotism and in ready self-sacrifice, some who availed themselves of the distresses of the community to grow rich by hoarding provisions and clothing and selling at high prices. In this conjuncture the bread riot came about. The mass of the community greatly regretted it. Many of the offenders were caught and punished, and nearly all of those who had participated in it grew ashamed of the parts they had taken.

In the letters following there is much readable information on the subject, and especially as to the parts taken by Governor Letcher and President Davis:

WHO ORDERED THE MOB TO DISPERSE?

Who gave the mob five minutes to disperse or be fired into? And whereabouts in the city did this occur?

I had heard in the early morning of the expected riot and was standing at the corner of the Old market on Main street when I saw the mob coming down Main and also turning into Main from Fifteenth street, at which point they commenced to break into and plun-

The Richmond Bread Riot

der every store on the south side of Main. I, in company with others, remained until the mob reached the Old market, at which point a stout, chunky man, without coat or hat, with axe over his shoulder, called out to the mob: "Now for Franklin street." The mob immediately turned into Seventeenth street to Franklin and started to pillage the stores near that point. Just as they turned into Franklin street a boy standing by me called out: "Here comes the Public Guard." On looking up Main street I saw the Public Guard coming down at a double quick. When they reached the Old market Captain Gay halted for a moment and called out to those present: "Which way have they gone?" The answer was, "Around to Franklin street." He immediately put his men in motion, and as he turned into Franklin street those present followed behind. When we reached Franklin street we saw men and women with arms full of goods scampering in all directions-up Seventeenth street, up Union street, up every alley, and anywhere to hide with their plunder. Those who were so unfortunate as not to get something were seen flying up Franklin street and mixing with the crowd who filled the streets between the Exchange Hotel and Governor street. Captain Gay halted his men about five minutes at Union and Franklin, by which time every rioter had left and everything was quiet. He then continued with his command (about twenty men) up Franklin street, I with others following. When we reached Governor street President Davis was addressing the crowd from Binford & Porter's corner. No order was given to fire on the mob; he only counselled them to go home.

That afternoon in conversation with my friend George A. Freeman (who I think was High Constable of Richmond at the time), who was present at the commencement at Twelfth and Cary streets, he informed me that Mayor Mayo addressed the crowd at that point; also that Governor Letcher addressed them at Spence's corner afterwards. I remember remarking to him that as the rioters were not there but lower down town, it reminded me of what we read in our histories in school-boy days of some officials "fiddling while Rome was burning."

From my own knowledge I am satisfied that all the credit of stopping the rioting and dispersing the rioters is due Captain Gay and the

Public Guard; that President Davis addressed the citizens and lookers-on with a large part of the mob, who fled before the Public Guard at Governor and Franklin streets; on authority of my friend George A. Freeman that Mayor Mayo addressed the citizens and lookers-on at Twelfth and Cary streets and read the riot act, and that Governor Letcher addressed about the same body at Spence's corner, Governor(13th) and Main.

From the time the mob started down Main street from the St. Charles Hotel there was not an officer, civil or military, who interfered or attempted to stay the progress of the mob, although they passed the First police-station. The only attempt was by the owners of the stores, which in most cases proved unavailing.
James Sinton

HONEST JOHN LETCHER'S DUES

Having read with much interest your papers on the bread riot, I wish to add my testimony, unless you think you have had enough. My recollection of the occurrence is very vivid, having been at the time almost in it. I resided in Richmond, being a member of the firm of Tardy & Williams, whose store, a large warehouse, with open windows on its frontage and side, was at the corner of Cary and Thirteenth streets. We conducted an auction business, and had weekly sales of such commodities as could then be had, and they [the sales] were frequently to large amounts and were largely attended. On the day of the riot we were to have had a large sale of tobacco and salt; also of other goods brought into the Confederacy by vessels from foreign ports that had successfully run the blockade. We were just about commencing to sell when the attention of our force was called to something going on up Cary street. I went to the door and found a crowd of women and boys coming down Twelfth from Main. It turned down Cary, and commenced breaking into the stores of Tyler and others, taking out everything they could lay their hands on. I just had time, with the help of Mr. Tardy, to close and bar the doors and windows before the mob was right in front of us. Our auctioneer (Gabriel Johnson, of Fredericksburg), a venerable and fine-looking

The Richmond Bread Riot

old gentleman with long white hair and beard, mounted a dray right in front of the store and earnestly addressed the mob, urging them to desist. After closing the store I was an interested spectator, and observed from my stand inside of one of the front windows the progress of the mob. Just then John Letcher came on the scene, accompanied by several gentlemen (Dr. John Mayo, I think, was one). He halted and addressed the crowd. I remember distinctly how grandly he looked. He was elevated above all other heads; his nerves as steady and his deportment as cool and determined as if such trials were of daily occurrence. In his remarks he stated that any one suffering for bread or anything else not only had his sympathy, but should be relieved as far as was practicable, but that he had no sympathy with mobs, and as long as he was Governor of Virginia they should not be allowed in Richmond, and he would use all the power under his control to suppress them. He then commanded the crowd to disperse, stating that he had sent for Captain Gay, and that he with his command was almost there. Drawing out his watch he gave them exactly five minutes in which to leave. If in this time they had not dispersed he would direct the officers to fire into the crowd. Still holding the watch he stood like a statue solemn and earnest. For a moment or so the crowd was still, and then it commenced breaking up on the edges. Three minutes passed. It had thinned out considerably, and in five minutes the last one had disappeared in different directions, the greater part going down Cary to Fourteenth. These people knew the man, and they fully believed that he would do what he promised, and so do I. There may have been other meetings of the mob (I think that quite likely) which were addressed and controlled by President Davis, but he was not on this scene. This mob was managed and well managed by honest John Letcher.

James T. Williams
Lynchburg, December 31, 1888

PRESIDENT DAVIS AND THE MOB

I had the pleasure recently of reading in the columns of your widely-circulated paper an interesting account of the bread riot of 1863 and it was the first mention that I have ever seen of it in the

The Richmond Bread Riot

public press. I saw the whole of it, from the sacking of the stores on Cary street until the mob dispersed on Franklin street, and if you will allow me space in your paper to briefly mention what I saw I may be able to throw a little light on that memorable event. I desire first to say that Mr. D.S. Doggett's statement, published with the numerous other conflicting statements, agrees with what came under my observation more nearly than any other. I was at the corner of Cary and Seventeenth streets when I first heard of the riot, and in company with a young friend soon ran to the scene, and found myself in the midst of at least 500 women who were wild with excitement. The sacking of the stores was in full play. I saw but few men engaged in plundering. I well remember one old soldier who took an active part in sacking Hicks's shoe store. I noticed six or seven pair of boots on his arm, and in answer to my inquiry as to what he was going to do with all those boots he gravely replied that he was getting them for his mess. At the sacking of these stores I do not recollect hearing the riot act read, nor seeing any soldiers. When the mob had finished its

work at this point it started in a wild rush for Main street, but on reaching the corner of Main and Fourteenth streets it divided, one portion going to Franklin and the other part proceeding to plunder stores on Main street. The leader of the mob, a Mrs.

J...., remained with the section on the latter street. She was a determined woman, to say the least of her. It was she who led the attack on Page's shoe store.[171] I saw her approach one of the large show-windows, and with one or two blows of her hatchet shiver the immense panes of glass, and followed by other women rush pell-mell through the opening into the store.

Whilst this scene was taking place on Main street the Public Guard came "double quicking" down the street, with arms at a right-shoulder shift, with Lieutenant Gay at their head. I ran along with them until they reached the corner of Seventeenth, when they wheeled to the left in the direction of Franklin. Here I was placed *hors du combat* by some one in the crowd. Why I was struck I have never been able to learn. However, soon recovering I followed on in the wake of the Guard, which was up Franklin to within a short dis-

The Richmond Bread Riot

tance east of the Exchange Hotel. Here the Guard formed in front of President Davis, who delivered an eloquent appeal to the mob to disperse, which had that effect. I was within three feet of Lieutenant Gay and heard him say to the mob, "You have seven minutes to disperse," and to his command, "Remember, men, your guns are loaded with ball cartridges," but his words seemed to have no effect on that wild, defiant mob. There were a number of soldiers from camp here and they told the Guard if they fired on those women they would return to camp and get men enough to "clean them out." Who gave the order to fire*I do not know, but it could not have been President Davis, for his words were of a most conciliatory character.

J. J. Gillenwater.
Washington, D.C.

"HONOR TO WHOM HONOR"

We have had numerous statements in regard to the bread riot (so called) in this city during the late civil war. I doubt not all the persons testifying are sincere in their impressions; but the question "Who struck Billy Patterson?" still remains undecided in the minds of some. To my mind it isn't difficult of solution. I take the simple statement of George I. Herring, Esq., an old resident, one who for years was in business here, and who consequently was well acquainted with the citizens and whose place of business was in the neighborhood of the difficulty and whose opportunity of knowing that about which he testifies was equal, if not superior, to most of those whose statements have appeared. He says: I saw the whole transaction; saw the Governor, heard him order the mob to disperse in five minutes, and saw the crowd disperse. Read, also, Major Baskerville's statement. He saw Governor Letcher, but failed to see the President. It is certain he wasn't present when the riot act was read, nor afterwards, as there was no occasion for his presence. But leaving out all other evidence, it seems to me Governor Letcher's letter to Colonel French should be conclusive to every unprejudiced mind. Those who knew the Governor need not be told that he wasn't the man to make an erroneous statement or to appropriate to himself the credit due to an-

The Richmond Bread Riot

other; that when he says, as he does in his letter to Colonel French, I gave them [i.e., the rioters] five minutes in which to disperse, he means that and nothing else. I have always understood that it was Governor Letcher who suppressed the riot and dispersed the mob. In corroboration allow me to say that my wife, not knowing anything unusual was occurring, called at the Executive Mansion and was there upon the return of the Governor after the riot had been suppressed. Upon Mrs. Letcher asking him about the affair he stated in their presence that he took out his watch and gave the crowd five minutes in which to leave, otherwise he would order the troops to fire, whereupon Mrs. Letcher exclaimed: "Oh, Mr. Letcher, you wouldn't have fired upon them, would you?" And he replied, "Indeed I would." And the noble old Roman would have been true to his word.*

P. T. Lieck

*There never was any order to fire given.—*Dispatch*

THE RICHMOND DISPATCH - Sunday, April 28, 1889, Page 7

HON. JEFF'N DAVIS
A Visit To Him At Beauvoir, Mississippi.
Talk with Him in Reference to the Bread Riot in Richmond.
(Special Correspondence of the Richmond Dispatch)

Beauvoir, Miss., April 19, 1889 - This place is certainly rightly named, for to those who are fond of water scenery no more beautiful view could be presented. Situated on the Mississippi sound, an arm of the Gulf, no land is visible over the broad expanse of blue waters except that occasionally on clear days the trees on Ship island, several miles distant, can be seen. It is an ideal southern home of the ante-bellum type and exactly such a place as would be at once conceded as specially suited for rest and leisure. To one who has been in harness for months with scarcely an opportunity to draw a long breath a visit here is like retiring to bed for a good, long, refreshing nap after a hard day's labor.

HOME LIFE AT BEAUVOIR

Home life at Beauvoir is delightfully simple and unpretentious, and it is that which here constitutes one of the great charms of existence. At present the household consists of Mr. and Mrs. Davis, Miss Winnie, 'the daughter of the Confederacy,' a title bestowed on her by Governor Gordon, of Georgia, and by which she is now universally known, and Miss Lizzie Waller, a niece of Mrs. Davis of almost the exact age of Miss Winnie. Up to a few days ago Mrs. J. Addison Hayes, now of Colorado Springs, Colorado, and her three children were also here on a visit. She is the oldest daughter of Mr. Davis, and is still remembered by many residents of Richmond as the "Little Maggie" of the days of the Confederacy.

DOMESTIC LIFE

During her stay he was surrounded by all the surviving members of his immediate family, and your correspondent, therefore, had an unusually fine opportunity to witness the domestic life of this distinguished gentleman in all its attractiveness. It was simply delightful to see the tender devotion manifested by him to his entire household, but more particularly to his young

grandchildren, all three of whom are remarkably bright, clever, and winsome.

The greatest charm of Beauvoir life, however-at least to your correspondent-consists of the many conversations which it is his privilege to enjoy with Mr. Davis. Though the ex-southern chieftain is in his eighty-first year his form is yet erect and his mind as bright as ever. With a wonderfully retentive memory, he has, in a life devoted largely to reading, study and thought, stored his mind with a remarkable fund of information, which he freely dispenses in the choicest language, while every topic of current, daily note is read and considered by him with as much care and interest as when he himself was an active contributor to his country's history. This and the varied career through which he has passed from the days of his early man-

RICHMOND BREAD RIOT

It was in the course of one of these conversations that Mr. Davis gave to your correspondent an account of his recollections of the famous bread riot in Richmond of which so much has recently been written. Thinking it might be of interest to your readers, I will endeavor to repeat his statement of that event as nearly literally as possible.

On the day of the riot (April 2, 1863) he said that he received word while in his office in Richmond that a serious disturbance, which the Mayor and Governor Letcher with the State forces under his command were entirely unable to repress, was in progress on the streets. He at once proceeded to the scene of trouble in the lower portion of the city, whither the venerable Mayor had preceded him. He found a large crowd on Main street, although the mass of the rioters were congregated on one of the side streets leading into that thoroughfare.

They were headed by a tall, daring, Amazonian-looking woman, who had a white feather standing erect from her hat, and who was evidently directing the movement of the plunderers. The main avenue was blocked by a dray from which the horses had been taken, and which had been hauled across the street, and it was particularly noticeable that though the mob claimed that they were starving and wanted bread, they had not confined their operations to food supplies, but had passed by, without any effort to attack, several provision stores and bakeries, while they had completely gutted one jewelry store, and had "looted" some millinery and clothing shops in the vicinity. The fact was conclusive to the President's mind that it was not bread they wanted, but that they were bent on nothing but plunder and wholesale robbery.

ARSENAL TROOPS

At the Confederate Armory in Richmond were engaged a number of armorers and artisans enrolled by General Gorgas, chief of ordi-

The Richmond Bread Riot

nance, to work especially for the Government. These men had been organized into a military company under the command of a captain, whose bearing was that of a trained, sturdy soldier accustomed to obey orders and ready to do his duty unflinchingly no matter what it might be. This company had been promptly ordered to the scene of riot and arrived shortly after the President.

THE PRESIDENT'S SPEECH-FIVE MINUTES TO DISPERSE

Mr. Davis mounted the dray above mentioned and made a brief address to the formidable crowd of both sexes, urging them to abstain from their lawless acts. He reminded them of how they had taken jewelry and finery instead of supplying themselves with the bread, for the lack of which they claimed they were suffering. He concluded by saying: "You say you are hungry and have no money. Here is all I have; it is not much, but take it." He then, emptying his pockets, threw all the money they contained among the mob, after which he took out his watch and said, "We do not desire to injure any one, but this lawlessness must stop. I will give you five minutes to disperse, otherwise you will be fired on." The order was given the company to prepare for firing, and the grim, resolute old Captain-who, Mr. Davis says, was an old resident of Richmond, but whose name he does not recall - gave his men the command: "Load!" The muskets were then loaded with buck and ball cartridges, with strict observance of military usage, and every one could see that when their stern commander received orders to fire he intended to shoot to kill. The mob evidently fully realized this fact, and at once began to disperse, and before the five minutes had expired the trouble was over, and the famous misnamed bread riot was at an end.

THE PRESIDENT'S PART

This is a succinct and truthful account of this trouble which created so much excitement at the time and of the part which ex-President Davis bore therein. The subject having been recently revived and extensively discussed, and quite a variety of statements having been made in connection therewith, this account of Mr. Davis will be read with great interest, and all who personally remember the scenes and incidents of that memorable occasion will no doubt fully substantiate its correctness. WGW

RICHMOND TIMES-DISPATCH **- Sunday, October 10, 1909, Page A-3**

THE RICHMOND BREAD RIOT
Facing Starvation, Women and Boys Sacked Warehouses and Stores

Shrouded in mystery and almost forgotten among the more stirring events of the war, the Richmond bread riot was a unique protest on the part of a famished people. Just before the Chancellorsville campaign began, and at a time when the Confederate authorities were exerting themselves to the utmost to supply the half-starved army in the field, discontent broke out in Richmond. The available supply of provisions, especially of flour and meat was largely in the hand of a number of dealers, whose lust for gold exceeded their patriotism. These men knew that more bread stuff could not be brought to Richmond in the course of the next few months, and consequently raised the prices beyond any that had been seen during the previous months of the war.

Misery was at once felt. Few were able to pay the prices exacted for flour. Defenseless women and children were on the verge of starvation. The President could do nothing to relieve the situation if, indeed, he half surmised its gravity.

Such were the conditions which precipitated the bread riot on Holy Thursday, April 2, 1863. One Mary Jackson, it appears, a huckster in the market, had harangued a gathering at the old African Church on the preceding evening, and, it appears, had called upon the poor people of the city to meet her in the Capitol Square the next morning. Their united efforts, she declared, could wring from the extortioners an ample supply of provisions, and their strength would be sufficient to demand bread, if it were not given them.

Her suggestion was promptly taken up. Early the next morning several hundred women and boys met in the Square and remained

The Richmond Bread Riot

there until the arrival of others made the mob number almost 1,000. There were few men in the crowd, and it was observed most of them were of foreign birth. After some brief discussion the women made their way down Ninth Street in front of the War Department and into Main Street with the avowed purpose of "getting bread." J. B. Jones, well known as the "Rebel War Clerk," watched them pass beneath his window and could but wish them success in their attempt to ward off starvation. The crowd went into Cary Street and at once entered the stores of grain merchants, pillaging at will and pilfering at random. They met with little opposition.

Emboldened by their success and urged on by a number of disreputable characters the mob then sacked the stores of other merchants-jewelers, dry goods merchants, dealers in fancy goods. In a word, almost all the merchants along Main and Cary Streets suffered at the hands of the mob.

Naturally enough this pillage in broad daylight aroused the authorities, who, nevertheless, realized the grievances of the people. The dire want in the city perhaps accounted for the leniency which was shown the women by the authorities.

Governor Letcher hurried to the scene, had the riot act read and threatened to fire on the mob, having meanwhile called out the city battalion. He gave the crowd five minutes' time in which to disperse, declaring he would have a volley fired if they did not go to their homes. All who knew Letcher will now agree that this was merely a threat on his part. The tender-hearted old Governor could not have ordered women and children mown down in the street, no matter how great their offense.

The crowd readily dispersed, and but few women were left in the street when President Davis arrived on the scene. Mr. Davis mounted on a wagon and made a fervent speech. He told the rioters that such conduct as theirs would really bring famine on the people, inasmuch as the farmers would not bring their supplies to the market. He declared with all sincerity that he would share his last loaf with the famished people and would do all in his power to alleviate their distress. His eloquent words had the desired effect. The few prople who remained in the vicinity of the robbed stores speedily went to their homes and before 3 o'clock had ended the trouble of the morning.

In view of the aggravated conditions which first led the mob to violence, neither the State nor the city authorities took any action against the women. The bread riot was overlooked and its details were suppressed for the time being. Richmond then, as ever, presented an unbroken front to the enemy.

RICHMOND TIMES-DISPATCH - Sunday, October 24, 1909, Page A-3

RICHMOND DURING BREAD RIOT DAYS
Mob of Women Appeared "Uptown"
and Demanded Provisions from Merchants

I was much interested in the classical description of the Richmond bread riot, given in The Times-Dispatch of the 10th instant. From that and from other writings, I am led to think that there were two divisions of rioters.

If such was true, I would like to recall some of the incidents in the rioting uptown. I was about eight or nine years of age, attending a primary private school on Marshall Street between Fourth and Fifth, and was vividly impressed. There was a little boy from the New Market attending the school, and he had asked the teacher, Mrs. Morse, if she was going to "turn out," adding that his mother would "turn out." She endeavored, but ineffectually, to learn from the child what he meant.

The explanation soon followed. Mrs. Morse had for a cook a gray-eyed feeble old negress. She sounded the alarm by frantically rushing into the school and crying, "Lord, Miss Morse, the day of judgment has come!" A loud noise was heard, and teacher and pupils ran to the front door. Coming up Marshall Street from Sixth Street was a mixed crowd of women, men and boys, women predominating.

They walked in the middle of the street, and had axe handles,

The Richmond Bread Riot

sticks and brooms for weapons. They were headed by two or three soldiers carrying muskets. It struck me as unusual that so much disorder should have been allowed by these soldiers, but the purpose of such escort was soon apparent. Flour was about $500 per barrel, and these soldiers were not to curb the rioters as long as their efforts were confined to obtaining food. Boylike, I followed the crowd, and in this instance at a safe distance, for it was an intimidating melange to me. The mob proceeded up Fifth Street, shouting and pushing, and turned up Broad Street.

When the Jewish merchants on the right hand side of Broad Street, going west, perceived the situation they rapidly closed their doors, and certain of them from the second-story windows threw down money and offered money to the rabble to prevent their doors from being knocked in. The Sublatts [Sublett], father and sons, had a hardware store on the south side of Broad between Fourth and Fifth Streets, and it was at this point that a quietus was placed upon the mob.[172] These women could not eat iron, and if they had been able to do so the Sublatts refused them admission, and stood in their doorway. Then the soldiers arrested Mrs. Jackson, "the general" and she was escorted to the Second Police Station.

Thus ended the bread riot there. The only consistent point of attack in the neighborhood of these women, after turning Fifth and Broad, was I.D. Briggs's bakery, between Fifth and Sixth Streets, but apparently they desired dry goods and iron. Although the city during the raids of the enemy was almost entirely free of men who could render service during interval trouble, this riot, and the looting of stores on Sunday night and early Monday morning after its evacuation, were the only two occasions of disorder during the war. Richmond was policed by only half-dozen or less men in civilian dress, called night watchmen.

General Butler, surnamed the Beast, urged that 3,000 or more troops be sent to him so that he could take Richmond easily. That he had about all of the defense of Richmond before him, which he said consisted of the police force, the clerks of the departments and a few others. That Duck-Legged Moore, the obese "Sergeant" Chalkley,

The Richmond Bread Riot

and the lank Mr. Seal, with a few others, armed with large, curved-handled canes, helped to so intimidate General Butler that the silverware of Richmond was saved. As on one occasion the cackling of geese saved Rome, so the other devoted city of the seven hills was perhaps saved by the night-watchman's whistle. As showing the extremity for men in defense, I may write that I overheard a fireman soundly berate my father for calling the fire department to the field, thereby exposing the city to destruction by fire.

According to my recollection there were not more than about seventy-five women in this raid for bread, and the excitement ended about 10 o'clock A.M.

The accurate contributor to The Times-Dispatch columns, who added several new incidents to this history, stated that the mob numbered almost 1,000, that there were few men in it, most of them of foreign birth, and before 3 o'clock the trouble had ended on Main or Cary Streets. It may have been that it was the relic of the rioters which had come uptown that so frightened old Aunt Litty in some way, causing her to think that the end of the world had come.

It is most probable that many of the women of that mob were intoxicated with liquor obtained in the purlieus of Pink Alley. As they marched certain of them tossed their dingy, long-eared bonnets into the air, and yelled in a treble key. They were the wives of fishmongers, costermongers and of the *canaille*.

While to many persons food was very scant in Richmond at that time, yet in the providence of God no one starved.

As illustrative of the scarcity of food, we children were allowanced at the table, and a piece of cheese about the size of a hickory nut was viewed with interest in the window of a German grocer as we went to and from school. That piece of cheese, denominated crawling cheese, gradually melted as it was said to move, and we saw no more cheese for over four years.

THOS. R. EVANS

ENDNOTES

Chapter 1: Rioting For Food

[1] Olwen Hufton, *The Prospect Before Her: A History of Women In Western Europe*. New York: Alfred A. Knopf, 1996, 463-477; George Rudé, *Ideology and Popular Protest*. London: Lawrence and Wishart, 1980, 42-43; E.P. Thompson, "The Moral Economy of the Crowd in the Eighteenth Century," *50 Past & Present* (Oxford Journals), 1971, 76-82.

[2] Rudé, *Ideology and Popular Protest,* 30.

[3] Numerous works consider Southern food shortages. The summary here relies primarily on Paul W. Gates, *Agriculture and the Civil War*. New York: Alfred A. Knopf, 1965, 3-126; Emory M. Thomas gives an excellent review of these causes in *The Confederate Nation, 1861-1865*. New York: Harper & Row, 1979, 199-201; Jerrold Northrop Moore, *Confederate Commissary General*. Shippensburg, Pa., White Mane Publishing Co., Inc., 1996; on Southern agriculture and railroads, see E. Merton Coulter, *A History of the South, Vol. VII The Confederate States of America 1861-1865*. Baton Rouge: Louisiana State Univ. Press, 1950, 239-254, 269-282.

[4] Gates, *Agriculture and the Civil War,* 10.

[5] Gates, *Agriculture and the Civil War*, 16-22.

[6] Coulter, *The Confederate States of America,* 246.

[7] For a detailed analysis of the plight of Southern rolling stock and railroad supplies, see David G. Surdam, *Northern Naval Superiority and the Economics of the Civil War*. Columbia: University of South Carolina Press, 2001, 75-80.

[8] *Id.*, 78.

[9] Mark Thornton and Robert B. Ekelund, Jr., *Tariffs, Blockades, and Inflation, The Economics of the Civil War*. Wilmington, Del.: SR

Books, 2004, 39-42; Mary Elizabeth Massey, *Ersatz in the Confederacy*. Columbia: University of South Carolina Press, 1952, 1993, 14.

[10]Quotation from J. Thomas Scharf, *History of the Confederacy States Navy.* The Fairfax Press, 1977, v; James M. McPherson, *Battle Cry of Freedom The Civil War Era*. New York: Oxford Univ. Press, 1988, 381; Thomas, *The Confederate Nation*, 206.

[11]Douglas B. Ball, *Financial Failure and Confederate Defeat*. Urbana and Chicago: University of Illinois Press, 1991, 231-232.

[12]Herman Hattaway and Richard E. Beringer, *Jefferson Davis, Confederate President,* Lawrence: University of Kansas Press, 2002, 203-210, 310-311; Gates, *Agriculture and the Civil War*, 46-52, 55-63; Edward Younger, ed., *Inside the Confederate Government The Diary of Robert Garlick Hill Kean*, New York: Oxford University Press, 1957, 41-53; Massey, *Ersatz in the Confederacy*, 33-53; Coulter, *The Confederate States of America*, 249-254. Similar issues were raised by the Confederacy's "tithing tax" or tax in kind on agricultural produced as levied by the revenue act of April 24, 1863. Gates, 63-65; Massey, 37-38; Michael Albert Powell, "Confederate Nationalism: A View From the Governors." (Dissertation, University of Maryland, 2004), 205-216.

[13]C. Vann Woodward, ed., *Mary Chestnut's Civil War*. New Haven and London: Yale University Press, 1981, 124.

[14]Jerrold Northrop Moore, *Confederate Commissary General Lucius Bellinger Northrop and the Subsistence Bureau of the Southern Army*. Shippensburg, Pa.: White Mane Publishing Company, Inc., 1996, 231.

[15]Hattaway and Beringer, *Jefferson Davis, Confederate President, 365-366.*

[16]Two excellent studies of the wartime plight of Southern women of all classes are George C. Rable, *Civil Wars Women and the Crisis of Southern Nationalism*. Urbana: Univ. Of Illinois Press, 1989, 91-111;

Drew Gilpin Faust, "Alters of Sacrifice: Confederate Women and the Narratives of War," Catherine Clinton and Nina Silber, eds., *Divided Houses Gender and the Civil War*. New York: Oxford Univ. Press, 1992, 171-199

[17]Jennifer Lynn Gross, "'And For the Widow and Orphan': Confederate Widows, Poverty, and Public Assistance," Emory M. Thomas, Lesley J. Gordon and John C. Inscoe, eds., *Inside the Confederate Nation Essays In Honor of Emory M. Thomas*. Baton Rouge: LSU Press, 2005, 213-220. Additional state aid would be provided following the food riots in the Spring of 1863, *Id.*, 216.

[18] Rable, *Civil Wars Women and the Crisis of Southern Nationalism*, 104-106; Gates, *Agriculture and the Civil War,* 87-89; for a comprehensive review of relief measures adopted in several Southern states, see E. Susan Barber, "'The Quiet Battles of the Home Front War'; Civil War Bread Riots and the Development of a Confederate Welfare System." (Masters Thesis, University of Maryland, 1986), 83-96.

[19]Reported in *Daily Progress* (Raleigh), Mar. 12, 1863.

[20]Mary Elizabeth Massey, *Women in the Civil War*. Lincoln: Univ. of Nebraska Press, 1966, 171; David Williams, *A People's History of the Civil War: Struggles For the Meaning of Freedom*. New York: The New Press, 2005, 171; Barber, "'The Quiet Battles of the Home Front War,'" 1-2.

[21]Williams, *A People's History of the Civil War*, 171-178; David Williams, Teresa Crisp Williams, David Carlson, *Plain Folk in a Rich Man's War: Class and Dissent in Confederate Georgia*. Gainsville: Univ. Press of Florida, 2002, 80-89; these two volumes provide the most complete published accounts of the many Southern food riots; a good summary and analysis of the riots is Barber, "'The Quiet Battles of the Home Front War,'" 12-18; Gates, *Agriculture And The Civil War*, 38; the 1862 incident in Tennessee, taken from the *Knoxville Register*, was reported in the *DRE*, Apr. 29, 1862.

The Richmond Bread Riot

²²Gates, *Agriculture And The Civil War*, 39; W. Buck Yearns and John G. Barrett, eds., *North Carolina Civil War Documentary*, 219; Victoria E. Bynum, *Unruly Women*. Chapel Hill: Univ. of North Carolina Press, 1992, 134.

²³*Southern Confederacy* (Atlanta, Ga.), Mar. 19, 20, 24, 1863; *North Carolina Standard* (Semi-weekly), Mar. 24, Apr. 18, 1863; E. Merton Coulter, *A History of the South, Vol. VII The Confederate States of America 1861-1865*, p. 423.

²⁴Yearns and Barrett, *North Carolina Civil War Documentary*, 219-220 (account from Salisbury Daily *Carolina Watchman*, Mar. 23, 1863); James Dabney McCabe, *The Greyjackets: And How They Lived, Fought And Died For Dixie. With Incidents and Sketches of Life in the Confederacy . . . By a Confederate*, Richmond, 1867 (Virginia Historical Society), 547-549; *North Carolina Standard*, Raleigh, N.C.(Semi-weekly), March 24, 1863 (undated account from Charlotte *Bulletin*); DRE, March 27, 1863; Paul D. Escott, *Many Excellent People Power and Privilege in North Carolina 1850 - 1900*, 65-67; Gates, *Agriculture and the Civil War*, 39.

²⁵Gates, *Agriculture And The Civil War*, 40.

²⁶(Raleigh) *Daily Progress*, Mar. 31, Apr. 6, 1863.

²⁷William D. Henderson, *Petersburg in the Civil War*, p. 60; William Kauffman Scarborough, ed., *The Diary of Edmund Ruffin*, Vol. II, p. 613; DRE, Apr. 4, 1863; *North Carolina Standard*, Apr. 7, 1863.

²⁸Yearns and Barrett, *North Carolina Civil War Documentary*, 220-221; *Savannah Republican*, Apr. 15, 1863; (Raleigh) *Daily Progress*, Apr. 22, 1863.

²⁹*Savannah Republican*, Apr. 15, 1863; (Raleigh) *Daily Progress*, April 4, 1863.

³⁰*Greensborough Patriot*, Apr. 13,1863; *Savannah Republican*, Apr. 13, 1863; *Southern Confederacy*, Apr. 4, 16, 1863; Williams, *A People's History of the Civil War*, 176.

The Richmond Bread Riot

³¹*Southern Confederacy*, Apr. 16, 1863; *Savannah Republican*, Apr. 13, 1863.

³²Undated account in Coulter, *The Confederate States of America*, 423.

³³Arthur W. Bergeron, Jr., *Confederate Mobile*, 101-102; Malcolm C. McMillan, *The Alabama Confederate Reader*, 335-337; Williams, *A People's History of the Civil War*, 175; Harriet E. Amos, "'All-Absorbing Topics': Food and Clothing In Confederate Mobile," *The Atlanta Historical Journal*, Fall-Winter 1978, Vol. XXII, Nos. 2-3, 22-23; Ms. Amos incorrectly places the incident early in 1863 and involving but 12 women; her account appears to derive in part from a description of a Mobile bread riot that supposedly took place on April 15, 1863, as described in an 1863 report on events in Alabama; in fact this particular report describes in its essence the bread riot in Atlanta, Georgia, on March 18, 1863. See *The American Annual Cyclopaedia and Register of Important Events of the Year 1863-75*, Vol. 1, 6.

³⁴Gates, *Agriculture And The Civil War*, 39-40.

³⁵Yearns and Barrett, *North Carolina Civil War Documentary*, 106; Escott, *Many Excellent People*, p. 67; *Official Records of the Union and Confederate Armies*, Ser. I, v. 53, 326-327.

³⁶*The Countryman*, Turnwold, Ga., May 3, 1864; E.B. Long with Barbara Long, *The Civil War Day By Day An Almanac 1861-1865*. Garden City, N.Y.: Doubleday & Co., 1971, 486.

³⁷Charles W. Hayes, *History Of The Island And The City of Galveston*, 617.

³⁸Escott, *Many Excellent People*, 67.

³⁹David Williams locates other incidents in the Georgia towns or counties of Forsyth, Calhoun, Marietta, Pickens and Thomasville in 1863 and Thomas, Stockton, Lowndes (Valdosta, Naylor), and Pierce in 1864; also in Floyd County and Abingdon, Virginia, in 1864. *A People's History of the Civil War*, 171-178; *Plain Folk In A Rich*

Man's War, 80-89. Still others took place in Waco, Texas, and Barnwell, S.C. Gates, *Agriculture and the Civil War*, 40. An excellent study of women riots and general unrest in rural North Carolina is Victoria E. Bynum, *Unruly Women*, Chapel Hill: Univ. Of North Carolina Press, 1992, 111-150; she locates riots in 1864 and 1865 in Granville, Orange and Montgomery Counties, *Id.*, 128, 129, 146.

[40] See Alfred J. Peacock, *Bread or Blood A Study of the Agrarian Riots in East Anglia in 1816.*

[41] Paul W. Gates reports two incidents of soldier food riots. In a Georgia brigade, 200 soldiers sacked a post commissary of large amounts of flour, bacon and other necessities. In Danville, Virginia, soldiers threatened to tear down a jail, "which brought appeals for quick aid." *Agriculture and the Civil War*, 40.

Chapter 2: Richmond's Woman Riot

[42] Coulter, *The Confederate States of America*, 423-424.

[43] W. Asbury Christian, *Richmond Her Past and Present*. Richmond: L.H. Jenkins, 1912, 240.

[44] A number of historians and diarists have described the circumstances of Richmond and the Confederacy at this time. Ernest B. Ferguson, *Ashes of Glory Richmond At War*. New York: Alfred A. Knopf, 1996, 179-193; Emory M. Thomas, *The Confederate Nation 1861-1865*, 199-202; Coulter, *The Confederate States of America*, 219-221, 251-253; John B. Jones, Earl Schenck Miers, ed., *A Rebel War Clerk's Diary*. New York: Sagamore Press, Inc., 1958, 144-185; Robert Garlick Hill Kean, Edward Younger, ed., *Inside the Confederate Government The Diary of Robert Garlick Hill Kean*. New York: Oxford Univ. Press, 1957, 40-48; *Richmond Dispatch* (editorial), Mar. 8; Mar. 19, 1863. Shelby Foote has provided a highly colorful account of Richmond in the spring of 1863. Shelby Foote, *The Civil War A Narrative Fredericksburg To Meridian*, Vol. 2. New York: Random House, 1963, 158-167. See also William J. Kimball, "War-

Time Richmond," *Virginia Cavalcade*, Vol. 11, No. 4 (Spring 1962), 33; Thomas C. DeLeon, *Four Years in Rebel Capitals An Inside View of Life in the Southern Confederacy from Birth to Death*. Mobile: Gossip Printing Co., 1890, chap. 27; Christian, *Richmond Her Past and Present*, 206-241.

Virginia's Governor John Letcher (1860-1863) felt that the Confederacy's impressment policy was the government's "greatest blunder of the war." F.N. Boney, *John Letcher of Virginia: The Story of Virginia's Civil War Governor*, Univ. Of Alabama Press, 1966, 213-214; Boney's is one of the better studies of conditions both in Richmond and in other areas of Virginia during the war. See also Robert L. Scribner, "Inflation In The Good Old Days," *Virginia Cavalcade*, Vol. 4 (Summer 1954), 14.

[45] Robert K. Krick, *Civil War Weather in Virginia*, Tuscaloosa: Univ. of Ala. Press, 2007, 89-90; Alfred Hoyt Bill, *The Beleaguered City Richmond, 1861-1865*. New York: Alfred A. Knopf, 1946, 155; Virginius Dabney, *Richmond The Story of A City*, 178; Jones, Miers, ed., *A Rebel War Clerk's Diary,* 152, 154, 162, 177-178; *DRE*, Jan. 23,26, Feb. 5, 23, Mar. 10, 11, Apr. 2, 1863.

[46] Michael B. Chesson, "Harlots or Heroines? A New Look at the Richmond Bread Riot." *The Virginia Magazine of History and Biography*, Vol. 92, April 1984,(hereafter, "Harlots or Heroines?"), 135; Chesson, *Richmond After the War 1865-1890*. Richmond: Virginia State Library, 1981, 76-77.

[47]*DRE*, Jan. 6, 10, 17, 19, 21, 24, 28, 30, Feb. 27, Mar. 14, 1863; *The Richmond Sentinel*, Mar. 14, 20, 23, 1863; David L. Burton, "Friday the 13th: Richmond's Great Home Front Disaster." *Civil War Times Illustrated* Vol. 21, No. 6 (Oct.1982), 36-41; Douglas Southall Freeman, *Lee's Lieutenants*, Vol. II. New York: Charles Scribner's Sons, 1943, 457-466.

[48] Jones, Miers, ed., *A Rebel War Clerk's Diary*, 180. My account of the Bread Riot draws heavily on the newspaper articles and other materials contained in this book; footnote citations are usually lim-

ited to sources not within the book, including the appendices. The author also draws from the following account: Douglas O. Tice, Jr., "'Bread or Blood!' The Richmond Bread Riot," *Civil War Times Illustrated*, Vol. XII, No. 10 (Feb. 1974), 12-19. The permission of the Editor of *Civil War Times Illustrated* to use this material is gratefully acknowledged.

[49] In addition to sources already cited, see Michael B. Chesson, *Richmond After The War 1865-1890*, 25-54; Dabney, *Richmond The Story of A City*, 159-183; Thomas, *The Confederate State of Richmond: A Biography of The Capital*, 117-122.

[50] Prices in Lexington, Virginia, were approximately one-half those in Richmond. Boney, *John Letcher of Virginia*, 290; Letter, S. Bassett French to James D. Davidson, Mar. 31, 1863, quoted in Bruce S. Greenawalt, "Life Behind Confederate Lines in Virginia," *Civil War History*, Vol.XVI, No. 3 (Sept. 1970), 221; Emory M. Thomas, "To Feed The Citizens: Welfare in Wartime Richmond, 1861-1865," *Virginia Cavalcade*, Vol. 22, No. 1 (Summer 1972), 22-29.

As mentioned in the text, S. Bassett French (1820-1898) was Governor Letcher's secretary or aide-de-camp. He was a lawyer and before the war had served as commonwealth attorney for Chesterfield County, Virginia, and as a clerk to the Virginia House of Delegates. As the governor's aide, French was appointed to a special position in which he served at times in the field with Generals Lee and Stonewall Jackson. After the war, he served as judge of Hustings Court in Manchester, then a separate township across the James River from Richmond and now part of Richmond. See Glenn C. Oldaker, ed., *Centennial Tales Memoirs of Colonel "Chester" S. Bassett French, Extra Aide-de-camp to Generals Lee and Jackson, The Army of Northern Virginia, 1861-1865*. New York: The Carlton Press, 1962.

[51] Coulter, *Confederate States of America*, 423. The *Richmond Examiner's* account of the Salisbury incident is in Appendix C.

[52] As reported in the *Richmond Examiner* accounts of Apr. 4 (Mary Woodward) and Apr. 6, 1863 (Lucy Jane Palmeter), some of the rioters would be arrested in wagons with captured booty.

[53] Josiah Gorgas, Frank E. Vandiver, ed., *The Civil War Diary of General Josiah Gorgas*. Tuscaloosa: Univ. of Ala. Press, 1947, 29; *DRE*, Apr. 2, 1863 (editorial).

[54] "Richmond's Flowering Second Market," *Virginia Cavalcade*, Vol. IV, No. 4 (Spring 1955), 8.

[55] Fiske Kimball, *The Capitol of Virginia A Landmark of American Architecture*, Richmond: Virginia State Library and Archives, 1989; Mary Wingfield Scott and Louise F. Catterall, *Virginia's Capitol Square Its Buildings and Monuments*, Richmond: The Valentine Museum, 1957.

[56] Boney, *John Letcher of Virginia*; W. Buck Yearns, ed., *The Confederate Governors*. Athens: Univ. Of Ga. Press, 1985, 216-231.

[57] *Philadelphia Weekly Times*, May 14, 1881, article by W.H. Wade. Thanks to Joseph Pierro for sending me a copy of this valuable article.

[58] Jones, Miers, ed., *A Rebel War Clerk's Dairy*, 183-184.

[59] The time is based on later testimony of Robert S. Pollard. *DRE*, Mar. 1, 1864.

[60] Manarin, *Richmond at War*. Richmond Civil War Centennial Committee. Chapel Hill: Univ. of N. C. Press, 1966 (hereafter, *Richmond At War*), 321.

[61] *Life of R.W. Powers*, unpublished manuscript, January 11, 1905, provided to the author by the late W. Roland Galvin. The *Richmond City Directory* for 1860 lists Robert W. Powers as a clerk for Purcell Ladd & Co., druggists at the corner of 13th and Main Streets. This location was in the path of the riot. *Second Annual Directory For The City Of Richmond To Which Is Added A Business Directory For 1860*, compiled and published by W. Eugene Ferslew, 1860 (hereafter, *1860 Richmond Directory*), 182, 184.

[62] For an analysis of the numbers involved, see "Harlots or Heroines?" 138-139.

[63] *DRE*, April 11, 1863.

[64] M. Ethel Kelley Kern, *The Trail of the Three Notched Road*. Richmond: The William Byrd Press, Inc., 1928, 102.

[65] Page's Shoe Store was not mentioned in the 1863 accounts. It is referred to in the account of J. J. Gillenwater in *Richmond Dispatch*, Jan. 20, 1888. (Appendix E) "Mr. Ezekial's store" is referred to in the case of rioter Anna Bell in *Daily Richmond Examiner*, April 11, 1863. Jacob Ezekial is listed for a dry goods business at 1813 E. Main Street in the 1866 *City of Richmond Business Directory and City Guide*, compiled and published by Mills & Starke (Richmond, 1866), 28.

[66] "Harlots or Heroines?", 171.

[67] *DRE*, April 6, 1863; *Richmond At War,* 313, 319.

[68] *Richmond Dispatch*, Dec. 30, 1888 (Appendix E, account of Polk Miller.)

[69] *Philadelphia Weekly Times*, May 14, 1881.

[70] Edward R. Crews. *The Richmond YMCA 1854-2004*. Richmond: YMCA of Greater Richmond, 2004, 39.

[71] The term, "reading the riot act," is derived from the English Riot Act of 1714. Under the 1860 Virginia statute in effect at the time, simple riot was a misdemeanor. The concept of the riot act was that a judge or justice was under a duty to attempt to suppress a riot by ordering (or reading the riot act to) unlawfully assembled persons to disperse; failure to disperse subjected those persons to arrest and trial. The statement read by Mayo may have been as follows:

"In the name of the law, I charge and command all persons here present riotously, tumultuously and unlawfully assembled, immediately and peaceably to disperse to their habitations, or to their lawful business, upon all pains and penalties of the law."

The Richmond Bread Riot

4 *Wharton's Criminal Law* (15th Ed., 1996), § 546, 208; 1860 Code of Virginia, Title 54, Ch. 195; Joseph Mayo, *A Guide To Magistrates: With Practical Forms For The Discharge Of Their Duties Out Of Court* (2d Ed., 1860), 574.

[72] The male rioter was Thomas Samanni, who was later convicted of felony for his actions at this location. Although Mary Johnson would also be charged with this attack, she was to be tried and convicted of felony in connection with her earlier activities at Pollard & Walker. See Chapter 6 and Appendix D.

[73] *Philadelphia Weekly Times*, May 14, 1881.

[74] Ernest Taylor Walthall, *Hidden Things Brought To Light*. Richmond: Dietz Printing Co., 1933, 24. The stated reason for Gay's nervousness cannot readily be verified although there are a few matches of surnames of women arrested with the 1863 public guard rosters. Of course, not all the rioters were arrested. According to Walthall, muskets were to be loaded with a ball and a buckshot, but Gay in his nervousness ordered the men to load two balls and a buckshot. *Id.*

[75] The names of other women leaders emerge from the accounts. However, Mary Jackson stands out as the main force behind the riot. See Chapter 9.

[76] For discussion of possible injuries, see Chapter 7.

Chapter 3: Reaction And Aftermath

[77] Copies of the messages are in *The War of the Rebellion: A Compilation of Official Reports of the Union and Confederate Armies*, Series I, Vol. XVIII, 958. The telegraph office was located in the riot area on the north side of Main Street between Eleventh and Twelfth Streets. Dr. William S. Morris was Confederate Chief of Military Telegraphs and President of the Southern Telegraph Company, which operated the telegraph lines in most Confederate states. Robert Luther Thompson, *Wiring A Continent The History of The Telegraph*

Industry in The United States 1833-1866. Princeton: Princeton Univ. Press, 1947, 374-375; editorial, *DRE*, Apr. 13, 1863.

[78] The minutes of City Council's meeting of April 2, 1863, are in Appendix B.

[79] *DRE*, Apr. 4, 1863. The mayor's remarks are in the same issue. See Appendix C.

[80] The full *Whig* editorial of April 6, 1863, is in Appendix C.

[81] The Richmond papers were the *Whig, Enquirer, Dispatch*, and *Examiner*, all of which were in publication prior to secession, and the *Sentinel*, an Alexandria paper, which began publishing in Richmond in March 1863. See J. Cutler Andrews, *The South Reports the Civil War*. Princeton: Princeton Univ. Press, 1970, 26-33.

[82] Id. 36-38; H. A. Trexler, "The Davis Administration and the Richmond Press," *Journal of Southern History*, Vol. XVI (May 1950), 177-195; Michael Houston, "Edward Alfred Pollard and The Richmond Examiner: A Study of Journalistic Opposition in Wartime," Masters Thesis, The American University, 1963 (Library of Virginia), 71. The *Richmond Examiner* and *Charleston Mercury* were the two leading newspaper critics of the Davis administration throughout the war.

[83] *Charleston Daily Courier*, Feb. 12, 1862; Andrews, *The South Reports the Civil War*, 29.

[84] *Id.*, 31.

[85] It appears that John M. Daniel and Edward A. Pollard wrote many of the *Examiner* editorials as did a number of other individuals. *Id.*, 30; Houston, 64.

[86] All five of Richmond's newspapers were located in this general area.

[87] *Richmond Sentinel*, Apr. 13, 1863.

[88] *DRE*, Apr. 6, 1863.

The Richmond Bread Riot

[89] *Daily Richmond Whig*, Dec. 1, 1865.

[90] Some of the participating judges and lawyers are described briefly in George L. Christian, "Reminiscences Of Some Of The Dead Of The Bench And Bar Of Richmond", *Virginia Law Register*, Vol. IV (1909)(hereafter *Virginia Law Register*). These include, Judge John A. Meredith, 663-64, Judge William H. Lyons, 665-66, John S. Caskie, 665, Thomas P. August, 743-44, John H. Gilmer, 745, Eaton Nance, 747, Robert R. Howison, 747, George Wythe Randolph, 751-52, Gustavus A. Myers, 821, A. Judson Crane, 821, Littleton Waller Tazewell, 833. For a biographical note on George Wythe Randolph, see *Richmond At War*, 631-32.

[91] The statutory provisions of the Mayor's Court are found in the 1852 Richmond City Charter as amended in 1861. These charters may be found in *Richmond At War*, Appendix A, Par. 50, p. 604, Pars. 91, 92, p. 620; *The City Of Richmond Business Directory And City Guide*, compiled and published by Mills & Starke (Richmond 1866), 121.

James K. Caskie (1812?-1868), a city alderman and friend of General Lee, was a tobacco merchant with the firm of Caskie and Harrison. He was active in Richmond civic affairs for many years. *Richmond At War*, 14, 150, 314, 462; Christian, *Richmond Her Past and Present*, 134, 136, 137, 140, 275, 399; *1860 Richmond Directory*, 69; S. Bassett French, Biographical Sketches, Library of Virginia Reel 333.

[92] *Richmond Daily Dispatch*, June 23, July 25, 1863.

[93] At the time of the fall of Richmond in April 1865, Mayor Mayo and Judges John A. Meredith and William H. Lyons were delegated by the city council to meet the approaching Federal military and surrender the city. S. Bassett French, Biographical Sketches, Library of Virginia Reel 333, 477; *Richmond Portraits for an Exhibition of Makers of Richmond 1737-1860*, The Valentine Museum, 1949, 128-129; Alexander Brown, *The Descendants In Virginia For Six Generations Of Major William Mayo* (1890), 10 (Brown erroneously states Joseph Mayo's year of birth as 1785, which has led to

confusion over the mayor's age during the Civil War.); *Richmond At War*, 627. Mayo was the author of *A Guide To Magistrates: With Practical Forms For The Discharge Of Their Duties Out Of Court* (2d Edition, 1860), commonly called *Mayo's Guide.* The nickname, "Old Joe", is taken from Emma Lyon Bryan, Reminiscences, New York Public Library Manuscript Division, Walter Fleming Collection (Box 5, Papers on Life of Jefferson Davis).

[94]*DRE*, Aug. 18, 1863; *Richmond Daily Dispatch,* May 1, 1862.

[95]*DRE*, May 13, 15, 1863.

[96]*DRE*, Apr. 4, 6, 1863.

[97]*DRE* Apr. 6, 8, May 8, 1863.

[98]John O. and Margaret T. Peters, *Courts of the Richmond Area A Primer*, Bar Association of the City of Richmond, 1969, 33.

[99]*1860 Richmond City Directory,* Appendix, 39-41; *The Stranger's Guide And Official Directory For The City Of Richmond* (Richmond 1863), 20-22 (reprint edition: *An Official Guide of the Confederate Government* (Richmond 190?), 19, 22); *The City Intelligencer: Or, Stranger's Guide* (Richmond 1862), 20-21 (reprint edition: *Illustrated Guide to Richmond, The Confederate Capital*, The Confederate Museum, The Valentine Museum, 1960).

William Henry Lyons was born in Richmond, May 29, 1831. He was a son of James Lyons, friend and counsel to Jefferson Davis. He was educated at the College of William & Mary and at the University of Virginia. Judge Lyons was the first judge of the Hustings Court for the City of Richmond, and it was said that he discharged his judicial duties with ability and distinction until replaced by a reconstruction judge. Judge Lyons died of typhoid fever on June 19, 1867. See S. Bassett French, Biographical Sketches, Library of Virginia Film No. 333, 387; *Virginia Law Register*, Vol. XIV (1909), 665-666.

John Alexander Meredith was born on March 4, 1814, in New Kent County, Virginia. He received a master of arts degree from the University of Virginia in 1833. Before becoming a circuit judge, he served as commonwealth attorney in Hanover County and in the Virginia Senate. He was elected the first judge of the Richmond circuit in 1852 after Henrico County and the City of Richmond were divided into two circuits under the Virginia Constitution of 1851. Judge Meredith was regarded as "able, upright and admirable," serving until he was replaced in 1869 by a military appointee, Col. Charles H. Bramhall. One Richmond lawyer stated in later years, that Judge Bramhall was "the most consummate ass that ever set on any kind of bench." Judge Meredith died on March 15, 1882. See S. Bassett French, Biographical Sketches, Library of Virginia Film No. 333, 551; *Virginia Law Register*, Vol. XIV (1909), 663-664; George L. Christian, *The Capitol Disaster*. Richmond: Richmond Press, Inc., 1915, 12-13; Christian, *Richmond, Her Past and Present*, 302-303.

[100]*Id.*, 33-35, 44; Code of Virginia (1860) Title 49, Chapters 157, 158, 660–661, 675-677; Charter of the City of Richmond, 1852, Amendments 1861, 1862 in *Richmond At War*, Appendix A, Par. 2, 597, Par. 3, 606, Par. 5, 607,Par. 17, 600, Par. 19, 609, Pars. 80-82, 85, 89, 618-620. The Hustings Court judge did not have absolute felony jurisdiction. Under the 1861 amendment to the Richmond City Charter, the court at the term held by the judge was given "original jurisdiction of all felonies committed within the territorial limits of its jurisdiction, except of felonies committed by slaves, and by free negroes, where the penalty is not death." Id., Par. 82, 618-619.

The justices of Hustings Court exercised the same criminal jurisdiction as did Virginia's county courts (as distinguished from the circuit courts). For wartime operations of the County Court for Henrico County, Virginia, which adjoined the City of Richmond on the north, east and west, see James H. Bailey, *Henrico Home Front 1861 1865*, Richmond: Henrico County Civil War Centennial Commission, 1963.

Richmond's mayor was also a justice of the Hustings Court, but his duty to hold mayor's court daily meant that he did not often sit with the hustings justices. The other justices of the court were 15 elected aldermen; throughout the Civil War, James K. Caskie served as recorder. The names of the other wartime aldermen may be found in *Richmond At War*, 314.

[101] As with most of Virginia's surviving court records, the original hustings minutes are held in the archives of the Library of Virginia.

[102] *Daily Richmond Examiner*, Apr. 13, May 2, 15, June 17, 1863; Feb. 11, Mar. 1, 1864; the lawyer's quote from *Exodus* (Ch. 22, v. 22) is found in the *Richmond Dispatch,* Mar. 1, 1864.

[103] *Daily Richmond Examiner*, June 24, 1863.

[104] J.T. Trowbridge, *The South: a Tour of its Battle-fields and Ruined Cities, a Journey Through the Desolated States, and Talks With the People.* Hartford, Conn.: L. Stebbins, 1866, 167.

[105] Judith W. McGuire, *Diary of a Southern Refugee During the War*, Richmond: J.W. Randolph & English, 1889, 202-203.

[106] Sallie A. Brock, *Richmond During the Confederacy: Four Years of Personal Observation by a Lady of Richmond*, Lincoln: Univ. Of Nebraska Press, 1996, 208-210. There are several editions of Brock's diary; the first, published in 1867, omitted her name as author

[107] E. Susan Barber, "Cartridge Makers and Myrmidon Viragos White Working-Class Women in Confederate Richmond," in Janet L. Coryell, Thomas H. Appleton, Jr., Anastatia Sims and Sandra Gioia Treadway, eds., *Negotiating Boundaries of Southern Womanhood.* Columbia: Univ. Of Missouri Press, 2000, 211.

[108] Michael Chesson wrote that "it was probably the leaders, the greedy, the unlucky, and the slow-of-foot who were apprehended." "Harlots or Heroines?" 138.

[109] *DRE*, Apr. 6, 1863.

[110] "Harlots or Heroines?", 131; Barber, "'The Quiet Battles of the Home Front War,'" 44-75; Edna Susan Barber, "'Sisters of the Capital': White Women in Richmond, Virginia, 1860-1880." Ph.D. Diss., University of Maryland, 1997, 263-278.

[111] Id. 270.

[112] *DRE*, April 20, 1863.

[113] The clemency petitions are located in the 1863 Virginia Governor's Papers for May (Anna Bell, Margaret Pomphrey), June (Minerva Meredith), and July (Mary Duke), Library of Virginia, Richmond.

[114] "Harlots or Heroines?" 171.

[115] *DRE,* Apr. 11, 1863.

[116] "Harlots or Heroines?" 135.

[117] Thomas Senior Berry, *Richmond Commodity Prices 1861-1865.* Richmond: Univ. of Richmond, The Bostwick Press, 1985, 17. The author of this valuable study concludes that shortages of goods was more likely the proximate cause of the riot than high prices.

[118] *Richmond At War*, 314-314, 320-321; Emory M. Thomas, "To Feed The Citizens Welfare in Wartime Richmond, 1861-1865," *Virginia Cavalcade*, Vol. XXII, No.1 (Summer 1972), 27-29.

[119] See discussion of bread in Chapter 7.

Chapter 4: The Bread Riot Joins The Lost Cause

[120] *Richmond Dispatch*, Dec. 30, 1888, 2.

[121] On May 17, 1878, the *Richmond Dispatch* published a brief follow-up note on the riot quoting (from the minutes of the meeting of April 2, 1863) the Richmond City Council's resolutions, which thanked only Governor Letcher, Mayor Mayo, John B. Baldwin, and Captain Gay and men of the Public Guard for their efforts. See Appendix B. The *Whig's* statement in its issue of May 10, 1878, is included in the *Dispatch* article of December 30, 1888. See Appendix E.

John Warwick Daniel(1842-1910) was a native of Lynchburg, Virginia. As a major in the Confederate Army, he served as adjutant of General Jubal A. Early's division; he suffered wounds in the Maryland campaign (1862) and at the Battle of the Wilderness (1864), from which he was crippled. Following the war he studied law and entered law practice in Lynchburg. A democrat, he later served in the Virginia legislature, the United States Congress and in 1887 was elected to the United States Senate. *Dictionary of American Biography*, Vol. V, 68—69; *The National Cyclopaedia of American Biography*, Vol. 1, 218; John Warwick Daniel, Edward M. Daniel, ed., *Speeches and Orations of John Warwick Daniel*. Lynchburg, Va.: J.P. Bell Co, Inc., 1911,

[122]The original Chesterman letter is included in the Jefferson Davis correspondence held in the Museum of the Confederacy and is actually dated January 1, 1888. However, the letter states that there is enclosed a copy of the *Dispatch* containing an article on the bread riot; because the only known *Dispatch* bread riot articles were the ones published by the paper in December 1888, including the issue of December 30, it is assumed that the writer of the letter made the common mistake of overlooking the passing of the old year 1888 to 1889.

William Dallas Chesterman(1845-1904), a native of Hanover County, Virginia, was a well-known Richmond journalist. During the Civil War he served as a private in the Richmond Light Infantry Blues; he participated in several campaigns and in 1864 received a disabling wound in the trenches of Petersburg. After the war he became associated with the *Richmond Examiner* and other publications, joining the *Richmond Dispatch* in 1874. See Clement A. Evans, ed., Jed Hotchkiss, *Confederate Military History*. Dayton, Ohio: Morningside Bookshop, 1975, Vol. 3, 802-03. Mr. Chesterman was the author of *Guide to Richmond and The Battlefields* (1881 and subsequent editions), *Richmond, Virginia: An Outline Of Its Attractions And Industries* (1888), and editor of the *James River Tourist*(1878 and subsequent editions).

[123]Earle Dunford, *Richmond Times-Dispatch The Story Of A Newspaper*. Richmond: Cadmus Publishing, 1995.

[124]William Griffin Waller (1843-1894) was a grandson of President John Tyler. He resigned from the U.S. Military Academy at West

The Richmond Bread Riot

Point in 1861 to enter the Confederate Army, and in 1864 he served as a captain on the staff of Brigadier General Beverly H. Robertson in the military district of Charleston, South Carolina. Waller married Mrs. Davis's sister, Jane Kempe Howell, on November 12, 1863. At least one account states this was the only wedding to take place in the White House of the Confederacy during the war. Jane Howell Waller died during the 1870s. Captain Waller, as he was known in Richmond, had served as managing editor of the *Savannah Morning News* before moving to Richmond where he worked for the *Richmond Daily Whig* and later the *Times*.

The War of the Rebellion: A Compilation of Official Reports of Union and Confederate Armies, Ser. I, Vol. XXXV, Pt. 1, 143; Lynda L. Crist, ed., *The Papers of Jefferson Davis*, Vol. 3 (1981), 121, note 10; *Richmond Dispatch*, July 25, 1894, 3. For information on Mr. Waller's Davis family connection, the author thanks Dr. Lynda L. Crist, editor of *The Papers of Jefferson Davis*. Thanks also to Mrs. Pat D. Fulks, former librarian at Beauvoir, for her efforts to verify whether Waller visited Beauvoir in early 1889.

Chapter 5: Jefferson Davis and The Bread Riot

[125] *Richmond Dispatch*, April 28, 1889, p.7.

[126] Felicity Allen, *Jefferson Davis Unconquerable Heart*. Columbia: Univ. of Missouri Press, 1999, 346; Clement Eaton, *Jefferson Davis*. New York: The Free Press, 1977, 271; Dabney, *Richmond The Story of A City*, 181; Thomas, *The Confederate Nation 1861-1865*, 203; Thomas, *The Confederate State of Richmond,* 119—120; Peter J. Parish, *The American Civil War*. New York: Holmes & Meier Publishers, 1975, 486; Frank E. Vandiver, *Their Tattered Flags The Epic of the Confederacy*. New York: Harper's Magazine Press, 1970, 236—237; Bruce Catton, *Never Call Retreat The Centennial History of the Civil War*, Vol. 3. Garden City, N.Y.: Doubleday & Co., 1965, 100—101; Foote, *The Civil War A Narrative Fredericksburg to Meridian*, Vol. 2, 163—164; Hudson Strode, *Jefferson Davis Con-*

federate President. New York: Harcourt, Brace and Co., 1959, 382—383. Cf. Long, *The Civil War Day by Day, An Almanac, 1861—1865*, 334.

A much more balanced and accurate account is Chesson, *Richmond After the War 1865—1890*, 40—43. A complete account of the riot, including a definitive examination of individual rioters and storekeepers is Professor Chesson's article, "Harlots or Heroines? A New Look at the Richmond Bread Riot," *The Virginia Magazine of History and Biography*, Vol. 92, 131 (1984); William J. Cooper Jr., *Jefferson Davis, American*. New York: Alfred A. Knopf, 2000, 708 n. 78.

A good description is in Ernest B. Ferguson's Civil War history of Richmond, *Ashes of Glory Richmond At War*, 193-196. Even so, Ferguson credits Jefferson Davis's implausible suggestion that he interrupted a riot in progress to make his talk.

[127] Letter, French to Letcher, April 17, 1878, John Letcher Papers, George C. Marshall Research Library, Lexington, Virginia. It would have taken French at least 23 minutes to complete a walk from the Capitol to the barracks and back to the riot area. However, it seems probable that he went there on horseback.

[128] Heber Ker, a Lieutenant of the Public Guard, also writing to Governor Letcher in 1878, indicated the governor's statement that the mob was to be fired upon if it did not disperse in five minutes was actually made as an order to Captain Gay but in a voice loud enough to be heard by "nearly the entire crowd." Letter, Heber Ker to Letcher, May 18, 1878, John Letcher Papers, George C. Marshall Research Library, Lexington, Virginia. This letter and that of S. Bassett French, cited in the preceding footnote, are invaluable with respect to the events surrounding the participation of the Public Guard in ending the riot.

[129] However, one witness did place Mary Jackson at about 11 a.m. in the vicinity where President Davis spoke. *DRE*, Apr. 27, 1863.

[130] *DRE*, Apr. 24, 1863.

The Richmond Bread Riot

[131] Elisha Jackson may have been referring to the real estate described below which was that of his wife. The 1850 Henrico County Slave Census reveals that he owned a slave. 1850 Slave Census, Henrico County, Richmond City.

[132] *DRE*, Apr. 4, 1863.

[133] *DRE*, Apr. 6, 1863.

[134] The locating of Jackson near the Custom House at around 11 a.m. is an indication she may have been in the crowd addressed by President Davis.

[135] *DRE*, Apr. 24, 27, 1863.

[136] Charles W. Allen was married to Caturah J. Perdue in 1850. His wife, Caturah, may have been Mary Jackson's sister. The 1860 *Richmond City Directory* states that Charles W. Allen was a member of the building firm, Green & Allen. In 1871, Allen was appointed to a commission to oversee the construction of a new bridge connecting Richmond to Manchester (9th Street Bridge). Virginia Marriage Bonds Richmond City, Vol. 1, 107; U.S. Census 1850 Richmond City-Henrico County, Virginia, 80; *Richmond Daily Enquirer*, Jan. 18, 1872 (obituary of Alice Perdue); *1860 Richmond Directory*, 35 (Bus. Directory, 8). The marriage and census records cited are located in the Library of Virginia.

[137] *Richmond Enquirer*, April 2, 1862.

[138] *The Richmond City Directory 1866* (compiled by William J. Divine & Co.), 71.

[139] Virginia Marriage Bonds Richmond City, Vol. 1, 97; Benjamin B. Weisiger, III, ed., Marriage Bonds and Ministers Returns of Chesterfield County, Virginia, 117; Register of Marriages, Chesterfield County, Virginia, 418; U. S. Census 1850 Richmond City-Henrico County, Virginia, 204; Virginia Bureau of Vital Statistics, Henrico County Deaths, Library of Virginia Reel 14, line 35.

The Richmond Bread Riot

The 1866 death record states that Mary Jackson was 51, which would make 1815 as her year of birth. This age conflicts with the 1850 census which shows her age as 28, indicating a birth year of 1822. I accept the younger age stated in the census for several reasons. The writer of the *Examiner* courts article of April 4, 1863, stated that Jackson was 40; Jackson's mother Alice Goode Perdue was not married until 1818; Jackson died in child birth in 1866, and her cause of death suggests it more probable that her age was 44 rather than 51.

[140] The 1856 *Richmond City Directory*, lists the Jackson family living north of the Methodist church on Oregon Hill. This church was located on Church Street just down the street from the Baptist church where the women met prior to the bread riot. Mary Wingfield Scott, *Old Richmond Neighborhoods*. Richmond: William Byrd Press, Inc., 1950, 209. *The Richmond Directory And Business Advertiser For 1856*, compiled by M. Ellyson, 153.

[141] Henrico County Deed Book Vol.74, 666. Reel 46, Library of Virginia.

[142] Henrico County Deed Book Vol. 75, 187. Reel 46, Library of Virginia.

[143] *Richmond At War*, 299.

[144] Henrico County Circuit Court, File No. 16 (Chancery), Library of Virginia.

[145] Henrico County Deed Book Vol. 98, p. 479. By this time Mary Jackson's widower Elisha had remarried. He and his wife Ann joined in a deed dated December 9, 1876, of the same property, apparently to transfer any marital interest he may have had in the property. Henrico County Deed Book Vol. 98, p. 285.

[146] This conclusion is based upon the testimony of John B. Jones that Jackson had been attempting to have her son discharged and the fact that the Jackson household in 1850 included a Francis who would have been 19 in 1863. This son may not have survived the war since he was not listed as one of Mary Jackson's heirs upon her death in 1867 or 1868.

Chapter 7: Other Tales Of The Bread Riot

[147] Ferguson, *Ashes of Glory,* 193; Thomas, *The Confederate Nation,* 203.

[148] Robert S. Holzman, *Adapt Or Perish The Life of General Roger A. Pryor, C.S.A.* Hamden, Conn.: Archon Books, 1976; Daniel E. Sutherland, *The Confederate Carpetbaggers.* Baton Rouge: LSU Press, 1988. Sara Pryor, nee Rice, wrote several books, all under the name of Mrs. Roger A. Pryor. Her second volume of reminiscences was *My Day: Reminiscences of a Long Life.* New York: Macmillan, 1909.

[149] John C. Waugh, *Surviving The Confederacy — Rebellion, Ruin, and Recovery – Roger and Sara Pryor During The Civil War.* New York: Harcourt, Inc., 2002, 189.

[150] Pryor, *Reminiscences of a Long Life,* 116.

[151] For a critical review of Waugh's unquestioning reliance on *Reminiscences,* see *The Virginia Magazine of History and Biography,* Vol. 110, No.4 (2002), 505(review by Sarah E. Gardner).

[152] *DRE,* Apr. 4, 1863.

[153] *New York Herald,* Apr. 11, 1863, reprinted in *DRE,* Apr. 23, 1863.

[154] Robert W. Waitt, "Recollections of Thomas McNivan and his Activities in Richmond during the American Civil War." Library of Virginia. For an excellent analysis and summary illustrating the unreliability of McNivan's recollections, see Elizabeth R. Varon, *Southern Lady, Yankee Spy The True Story of Elizabeth Van Lew, A Union Agent in the Heart of the Confederacy.* New York: Oxford Univ. Press, 2003, 103-105.

[155] David D. Ryan, ed., *A Yankee Spy in Richmond The Civil War Diary of "Crazy Bet" Van Lew.* Mechanicsburg, Pa.: Stackpole Books, 1996, 49.

The Richmond Bread Riot

Appendix A: The Public Guard, "Virginia's Standing Army"

[156]"We have had a dreadful riot here on yesterday, & they are keeping it up today, but they are not near so bad today as they were yesterday. But I will begin at the first.

"Thursday morning I went to the office as usual. A few minutes after I got in, I heard a most tremendous cheering, went to the window to see what was going on, but could not tell what it was about & so we all went down into the street. When we arrived at the scene we found that a large number of women had broken into two or three large grocery establishments, & were helping themselves to hams, middlings, butter, and in fact every thing eatable they could find. Almost every one of them were armed. Some had a belt on with a pistol stuck in each side, others had a large knife, while some were only armed with a hatchet, axe or hammer. As fast as they got what they wanted they walked off with it.

"The men instead of trying to put a stop to this shameful proceeding cheered them on & assisted them all in their power. When they [the women] found that the guards were on Cary st. they turned around & went up to the Capitol, & Governor [John] Letcher made them a speech, but it was like pouring oil on fire. After that the Prest. [Jefferson Davis] made them a speech, and while they were engaged in their robbery the mayor of the city [Joseph Mayo] came down to make them another. But it did no good.

"I think there were fully 5000 persons on Cary st., if not more, besides that many more on Main & Broad. This morning they began again but they were told that if they did not disperse they would be fired on.

"One woman knocked out a pane of glass out of a shop window, of which the door was fastened, & put her arm in to steal something, but the shopman cut all four of her fingers off. I was right in the middle of the row all the time. It was the most horrible sight I ever saw....

"Have heard how the riot ended this morning. Gov. Letcher told them he gave them five minutes to disperse & if they did not disperse he would have them fired on by the city guards. They immediately began to leave the streets & and in a few minutes they were comparitively(sic) vacant. The stores have been closed for the last two days."

The Virginia Magazine of History and Biography, Vol. LXXI, 203 (1963), with note by Stephen E. Ambrose.

[157] Walthall, *Hidden Things Brought To Light*, 24. Tyler & Son, a commission house and store on Cary Street, was attacked by the rioters. Two individuals, John P. Tyler and S.N. Tyler gave testimony in rioter court cases. *DRE*, Apr. 4, 8, 1863; Richmond Hustings Court Minutes, Apr. 15, 1863.

[158] *New York Herald*, Apr. 11, 1863, reprinted in *DRE*, Apr. 23, 1863.

[159] The three incidents are discussed by Professor Chesson in "Harlots or Heroines?", 152. For an account of gunfire with blank cartridges by troops on Broad Street, see article in the *Washington Post* of Mar. 4, 1888, discussed in this chapter.

[160] Reminiscences of Emma Lyon Bryan, from Papers on Life of Jefferson Davis, Walter Fleming Collection, New York Public Library Manuscript Division, Box 5; Letter, Senator G. G. Vest to Judge S. H. Letcher, April 3, 1903, John Letcher Papers, George C. Marshall Research Library, Lexington, Virginia.

[161] *The Richmond Sentinel*, Apr. 7, 1863.

[162] *Daily Richmond Examiner*, Apr. 4, 7, May 2, 6, 7, 1863.

[163] Article in Appendix E.

[164] The author thanks Robert K. Krick for furnishing a copy of the typed manuscript of "Aunt Mag Loughborough." According to a note on the manuscript, which is undated, it came from a niece of Aunt Mag, Mrs. Monie Chase, Eaglebrook School, Deerfield, Massachusetts. As noted, the manuscript was published in the *Washington Post* on Mar. 4, 1888.

The Richmond Bread Riot

[165] Jeffrey C. Weaver and Lee A. Wallace, *Richmond Ambulance Co., Herbig's Infirmary Co. and The Virginia Public Guard and Armory Band*. Lynchburg, Va.: H.E. Howard, Inc., 1985, 56-77; Walthall, *Hidden Things Brought To Light*, 24; Lee A. Wallace, Jr., *A Guide To Virginia Military Organizations, 1861-1865*. Lynchburg, Va.: H.E. Howard, Inc., 1986, 259; John Sergeant Wise, *The End of an Era*. Boston: Houghton, Miffin and Co., 1899, 59; E.M. Sanchez-Saavedra, "Richmond's Old Bell House," *Virginia Cavalcade*, Vol. 19, No. 2 (Autumn 1969), 4-11; Eugene Michael Sanchez-Saavedra, "The Beau Ideal of A Soldier: Brigadier General Charles Dimmock," M.A. Thesis, University of Richmond, 1971 (Library of Virginia Archives Misc. Reel 474). The author expresses appreciation to Mr. Sanchez-Saavedra for valuable information on the public guard.

The location of the guard's 1863 quarters in the 300 block of South 4th Street is the present site of Ethyl Corporation. The Virginia State Capitol Police claim a heritage extending back to 1618 when Virginia's colonial governor appointed a guard of ten men to protect the government. Walter S. Griggs Jr., "The Capitol Police" (1967), unpublished manuscript in the Virginia Historical Society. My thanks to David Boylan of the capitol police for the information on Griggs's manuscript.

[166] *Richmond At War*, 311-313.

[167] This is incorrect. Only one woman, Mary Johnson, was convicted of a felony and sentenced to the penitentiary, and her sentence may have been suspended.

[168] Northeastern corner of Governor(13th) and Franklin Streets.

[169] On 13th Street at Main.

[170] John McGill was the war-time Catholic Bishop of Richmond. He has been described as a "stanch Rebel" who did all he could to promote the cause. Very little information has been found on his activities during the riot. One Richmond historian mentions that "Bishop McGill was also sent for to assist in quieting the crowd, but without

The Richmond Bread Riot

avail." T.C. DeLeon, *Belles Beaux and Brains of the 60's*, p. 374; W. Asbury Christian, *Richmond Her Past and Present,* p. 241.

[171] Page's shoe store is not mentioned in the 1863 newspaper accounts.

[172] The 1866 city directory lists this store as "Sublett & Bro. Jno. T. Sublett & Geo. W. Sublett, hardware, 409 e Broad." *The City of Richmond Business Directory and City Guide*, compiled and published by Mills & Stark (Richmond 1866), p. 67. This location is on the south side of East Broad Street and is some 11 or 12 blocks from where President Davis addressed the crowd near the Custom House.

Addendum

A more recent and important study of Confederate agriculture should be noted. It is R. Douglas Hurt, *Agriculture And The Confederacy,* Chapel Hill, The University of North Carolina Press, 2015.

About The Author

Douglas O. Tice Jr.

Douglas O. Tice Jr. has lived in the Richmond area for over fifty years. He received his undergraduate and law degrees from the University of North Carolina at Chapel Hill. After may years of work as a lawyer in private practice, in 1987 he was appointed a US Bankruptcy Judge for the Eastern District of Virginia, from which he retired on December 31, 2013.

Judge Tice is a long time member and former president of the Richmond Civil War Roundtable. His primary interests in the Civil War have been civilian government and the home front. The research for this book began in preparation for a talk on a relatively little known subject, and it soon became an obsession. His article on the Bread Riot was published in the *Civil War Times Illustrated* of February 1974.

Judge Tice is married to the former Martha Murdoch, and between them they have five children and six grandchildren.

www.ingramcontent.com/pod-product-compliance
Lightning Source LLC
Chambersburg PA
CBHW020419010526
44118CB00010B/324